LIFE IS SHORT
(No Pun Intended)

*Love, Laughter, and Learning to
Enjoy Every Moment*

Jennifer Arnold, MD, and Bill Klein

HOWARD BOOKS
An Imprint of Simon & Schuster, Inc.
New York   Nashville   London   Toronto   Sydney   New Delhi

Ħ

Howard Books
An Imprint of Simon & Schuster, Inc.
1230 Avenue of the Americas
New York, NY 10020

First Howard Books trade paperback edition February 2016

HOWARD and colophon are trademarks of Simon & Schuster, Inc.

For information about special discounts for bulk purchases,
please contact Simon & Schuster Special Sales at
1-866-506-1949 or business@simonandschuster.com.

The Simon & Schuster Speakers Bureau can bring authors
to your live event. For more information or to book an event,
contact the Simon & Schuster Speakers Bureau at
1-866-248-3049 or visit our website at www.simonspeakers.com.

Interior design by Davina Mock-Maniscalco

Manufactured in the United States of America

10 9 8 7 6 5 4 3

The Library of Congress has cataloged the hardcover edition as follows:
Little couple (Television program)
    Life is short (no pun intended) / Jennifer Arnold, MD, and Bill Klein. —First
Howard Books hardcover edition
        pages   cm
1. Arnold, Jennifer, 1974–   2. Klein, Bill, 1974–   3. Dwarfs—United States—
Biography.   4. Television personalities—United States—Biography.   I. Klein, Bill,
1974–   II. Title.
   CT9992.A76A3   2015
   791.4502'80922—dc23
   [B]   2015007628

ISBN 978-1-4767-9470-9
ISBN 978-1-4767-9477-8 (pbk)
ISBN 978-1-4767-9471-6 (ebook)

CONTENTS

LIFE IS SHORT

INTRODUCTION

Bill and Jen

W HEN WE FIRST ENTERTAINED the idea of writing a book, we
weren't entirely convinced that our lives would be of interest to
others outside the sphere of our family and friends, and perhaps some
colleagues. And maybe some viewers of our television show. And, okay,
a few people from the Little People community as well. And did we
mention our moms?

But in fact, the process of working on this book has been a truly
illuminating experience for us. It has enabled us to look back and
recognize incidents, coincidences, and intersections, uncovered gems
and discovered patterns, challenges faced and obstacles overcome.
We've discovered remarkable parallels in each other's lives that serve
to reinforce what a sacred treasure our life trajectories have been,
what a blessing it is that we have found each other (especially after
repeated near misses throughout our lives, as you'll see).

So yes, we have learned so very much in the process of working on this book, which makes sharing our stories—and our story (since you'll see we are two different people but we are also in many ways one)—more rewarding than we'd imagined possible. We may at first glance seem different, but maybe you'll find we're not as different as you might think. We realized that regardless of our stature, our journey has a lot in common with other stories of people who have overcome great obstacles or challenges—as well as other great romance stories of people whose love transcended the odds of their circumstances.

As parents, it has been so moving to revisit our own childhoods and talk to loved ones about those years. Yes, ours is a tale of two people born with a physical disability that could have defined us. But instead we thrived and flourished, mostly because of the love and support of our families. They had to conquer so many fears and make so many personal sacrifices to make sure our opportunities were boundless. They were the ones who made sure we understood that our physical limitations should never compromise our dreams, that we could achieve anything we set our minds to. Because they believed in us, we believed in ourselves, too. And as a result of those beliefs, we achieved even more than we ever dreamed of. And now, with our own children, we get to put those hard-earned beliefs into practice.

One really fun aspect of our story is just how parallel our lives had been. We were both born with the same type of dwarfism and we had both received treatment at the very same hospitals and from the very same doctors, sometimes even at the very same time. In fact, as you'll read later, we had even met as children.

That first encounter was followed by a string of near misses and close encounters over the ensuing years that in retrospect may seem too oddly coincidental to be true. But when we finally did meet, we recognized each other as soul mates, destined to be together. As we

got to know each other, we were amazed at the parallel emotional journeys we had taken as well—as you will see in these pages.

In short (no pun intended), this book has given us the rare opportunity to step back and look at how character and events weave our
lives together, and provide new insights into each other and ourselves.
We may continue to juggle crises—challenges growing our family,
Jen's recent cancer, Bill's more recent surgeries—but having found
and built a life with each other makes us feel equipped with super-
powers to battle anything that comes our way.

So, we are thankful—thankful that we have each other, and thankful for our kids, our family and friends, colleagues, and what feels like
a great extended family of viewers. And we are thankful for you, dear
reader.

CHAPTER ONE

Jen

MY ARRIVAL!

WHEN I WAS YOUNG, just beginning to be "me," I had a theory about why I was smaller than everybody else. In my theory, my mother had purposely put contact lenses in my eyes so that I would see the world from a different perspective, that of a Little Person. I believed that one day, my mother would remove the lenses, and when she did, I would actually be average sized. I thought it was actually some part of a bigger plan she had for me, almost as if she was doing it to teach me a lesson. Since then, I have come to find out that many persons with significant physical and/or mental challenges often rationalize their difference as the result of a greater plan for themselves or the world.

I wasn't unhappy being a Little Person. Being a Little Person has always been and will always be normal to me. Even at a young age, I was used to the challenge of being a Little Person in an average-size world. For me, it wasn't like an accident occurred where my physical or mental capabilities changed. I was used to step stools, and always having my clothes altered, used to being observed and pointed at by strangers, and I was used to trips to the doctor in the hospital that would make other people keel over in exhaustion. But I didn't have time to feel that way. My parents always reminded me to count my blessings and be grateful for the things that were good in my life and that it could always be worse. I was raised not to focus on the negative, but be thankful for the positive. My parents embraced me to the degree that I thought other people might even be jealous of me.

My birth, my big arrival, happened on March 12, 1974, at St. Anthony's Hospital in St. Petersburg, Florida, and was nothing short of harrowing. My mother was expecting a completely healthy baby, as she had had an uneventful pregnancy. My parents, David and Judy Arnold, were young, just twenty-one, and completely overjoyed to be having their first child. However, the difficulties started immediately in the delivery room. Not only did I come out feet first, which is very risky for a vaginal delivery, but my mother was in labor for more than twenty-four hours before that. By the time I finally emerged, she was hemorrhaging, I wasn't breathing, and both of us almost died.

At least I weighed seven pounds, eleven ounces, a good, healthy size. But my respiratory distress was definitely life threatening, and I had two large hematomas under my scalp, which, with my disproportionally large head, made the situation even more dire. Although doctors knew something was terribly wrong with me right away, nobody knew exactly what it was. My parents were told I had "water on the brain" or hydrocephalus, which had all sorts of terrifying neurological implications. Doctors went as far as to say it would likely cause me to be mentally challenged to some degree, if I lived at all. It turns out that it wasn't hydrocephalus at all, but rather hydrops. Hydrops is a condition in which fluid or edema accumulates in multiple body parts of a newborn. This is a rare condition, but a known complication for babies born with dwarfism.

I was only at St. Anthony's Hospital long enough for an intensive care neonatal transport vehicle to race there, sirens blaring, snatch me out of the delivery room, and rush me to All Children's Hospital several miles away. Here was the best neonatal intensive care unit (NICU) in St. Petersburg—in fact, one of the best NICUs in all of southwest Florida. My mother didn't even have a chance to lay eyes on me before they took me away. She was still so out of it from all the anesthesia and pain medications they had given her that she didn't even know what was happening. She had lost so much blood that she needed two transfusions and a week in the hospital to recover. I recall my mom telling me that although she didn't get to see me for some time, her parents, my grandmother and Papa, had seen me and kept telling her not to listen to the doctors. They were certain that I was perfectly perfect and was going to be fine.

I was seven days old when she finally got to come to the NICU to meet me. Before she got there, she had heard so many terrifying terms to describe my condition, she had no idea what to expect. No matter how many issues the doctors enumerated and described, she didn't fear bonding with me. She totally loved me and only loved me that much more when she finally saw me.

My mom had a strong faith that God would take care of her small family, as He had never presented her with an impossible situation or guided her wrong before. In fact, to this day, she credits her faith with getting her through my birth, which undercut the happiest day of her life with extraordinary, terrifying unknowns. Her motherly instincts kicked in with a vengeance, and she instantly became my protector, advocate, and supporter with everything she had.

My mother was not shy about expressing that at first glance she and my father were not the ideal parents for me. They were young, practically broke, and very naïve. But, they got through it all with strength and perseverance.

I had two traumatic weeks in the NICU. Even after my respiratory distress became less life-threatening, I still had many problems. The doctors were throwing out all kinds of diagnoses, but, through no fault of their own, they didn't hit on skeletal dysplasia. It was not a well-known diagnosis and often it can be difficult to see the physical features of skeletal dysplasia soon after birth. For the moment, the doctors and my parents were just happy I no longer needed assistance breathing. The neonatologists were still concerned about the hydrops, though they hoped it would resolve on its own.

MY PARENTS HAD been married for about a year when I was born. They had met at a Winn-Dixie supermarket in St. Petersburg, where my mother was a part-time cashier and my father was a manager. My father had a crush on my mother from the moment he saw her, but the feeling wasn't, at least at first, mutual. When he learned she loved horses enough to save all her paychecks to buy one, he capitalized on their common interest. He loved horses, too, having been raised around them. When he heard about my mother's purchase, he knew the perfect gift—a bridle. She was so impressed that he had tuned in to her interest that the romance budded immediately.

When my mother became pregnant, my parents moved into a little apartment in my maternal grandparents' house in St. Petersburg. My grandfather, aka Papa, had converted the two-car garage of the house into a cozy apartment for them. My grandparents wanted my mother nearby, and with the baby coming, there was the added benefit of a houseful of people who could help them out—besides my grandmother, my mother's two younger sisters, my aunts Barbara and Chrissy, still lived at home. Barbara was sixteen, five years younger than Mom, and Chrissy was eleven. I grew up very close to both my aunts. My uncle Wayne, who was just finishing high school at the time, also lived there.

My mother set up a beautiful nursery for me in the corner of the apartment, with the nicest crib she could buy and a wardrobe full of pink onesies and bonnets. She was half terrified, then thrilled when I was finally released from the NICU. She did her absolute best not to be too consumed with the state of my future health.

My trips to the pediatrician were far more frequent than those of newborns without issues. As the months went by and my pediatrician kept tracking my height, weight, and head circumference, I kept slipping further and further off the chart for height and weight, even as I climbed the chart in head circumference. Very concerned with my body mass, the pediatricians diagnosed me as "failing to thrive." They thought maybe it was a nutrition issue, plain and simple—that my mom wasn't feeding me enough, which is not unusual for a first-time mother. That possibility terrified my mom, who thought that if I had malnutrition, child services might come to intervene and take me away. She tried so hard to make me eat more, she was beside herself! I mean, how much baby food and formula can a baby tolerate? Because no one had diagnosed me with a form of dwarfism, they didn't realize that nutrition and food quantity was never an issue. My condition was rare, and the pediatricians were only going through a process of elimination, but they had my mother frantic.

Then came the next stressor. Right before my first birthday, we moved to a small rental apartment in Orlando, a hundred miles from St. Petersburg, after my father accepted a job from my mother's uncle. He was going to be managing a string of gas stations in the boomtown. My aunt Barbara, with her parents' permission, moved with us and stayed a year.

The Walt Disney World Resort had just opened, although it was so small and new that there were only three operating hotels on its whole forty square miles. However, because of the resort, the city was already the hottest, hippest town in Florida. My mother got a part-time job waitressing at the Fort Wilderness area inside the park. Fort Wilderness was a vacation spot within Disney World with rustic cabins and campsites featuring a Wild West theme. My mom had to dress the part of a cowgirl, but she didn't mind. She made many friends working there that she might not have met otherwise.

The first thing my parents did after the move was find a new pediatrician. Without knowing anyone with kids to give them references, they took a chance with Pediatrics Associates of Orlando, a group practice not too far from our neighborhood. By the purest stroke of luck, the doctor in the group who saw me first was Dr. Colin Condron, who turned out to be the link to determining my diagnosis. He had done his pediatric training at Johns Hopkins Hospital in Baltimore, Maryland, which was the finest pediatric orthopedic unit in the country, with specialized clinics for genetic-based issues, including dwarfism. He told my mother he wanted her to take me to the Moore Clinic, a genetics clinic, as he thought they could confirm my diagnosis. He also arranged to have all our travel expenses paid for by the hospital by enrolling me as a participant in a study currently underway. Back then it wasn't unusual for academic hospitals to admit a patient with a rare or unusual diagnosis for evaluation.

I spent two weeks at the Moore Clinic, undergoing every medical workup possible. What good fortune to have on my case Dr. Victor A. McKusick, a professor of medicine and medical genetics at Johns

Hopkins Hospital with a reputation around the world for his expertise in unusual hereditary diseases! He is often referred to as the father of clinical genetics and was the original author of *Mendelian Inheritance in Man*, the most extensive database of all inheritable diseases. He was the first person to diagnose me with spondyloepiphyseal dysplasia (SED), type Strudwick, the specific type of dwarfism I had been born with. I believe he did this with a physical examination and a few X-rays.

SED is a type of skeletal dysplasia that involves significant skeletal abnormalities affecting the spine, long bones, and joints. What the diagnosis meant for me was a childhood filled with orthopedic surgeries just to maintain mobility. SED is characterized by anomalies of the growth plates, joints, and spine, resulting in debilitating deformities such a scoliosis, knock knee, early osteoarthritis and joint degradation in your twenties, and other major joint problems. SED is rare, occurring in only about one in one hundred thousand births. Although it can be passed down from an abnormal gene from one parent, the majority of cases result from spontaneous mutations. Unfortunately, it turned out my case was quite severe, and Dr. McKusick said I'd need many surgeries.

The fact that Dr. Condron had had such great training and expertise to identify that I likely had a skeletal dysplasia and sent me to the specialists at Johns Hopkins Hospital early was a miracle. Of course, once Dr. Condron got me to the Moore Clinic, my parents also got to meet someone who would forever change our lives, Steven E. Kopits, MD. Dr. Kopits would become my orthopedic surgeon and my lifesaver. At the time we met him, Dr. Kopits was the chief resident of pediatric orthopedics at Johns Hopkins Hospital, a position he cherished. He was from a long line of orthopedic physicians, as both his father and grandfather were orthopedic surgeons in Hungary, his native country. After World War II, the Kopits family left Hungary and settled in Argentina, where *my* Dr. Kopits got his medical degree at the Universidad de Buenos Aires. He then came to the United States, doing his internship at Union Memorial Hospital in Baltimore and his residency at Johns Hopkins Hospital. It was then and there that his interest in patients with skeletal dysplasias was born. Not only was he a talented and dedicated physician and surgeon, but he also invented procedures no one had ever tried before that often led to lifesaving treatments for children with skeletal dysplasias. He was somehow able to see a patient's deformity and tailor a surgical procedure to make what was not functional before work. There were times when Dr. Kopits would come out of the operating room and tell a patient's parents that he used a technique he had never used before during the operation, but ta-da, it worked, and he expected outstanding results!

Dr. Kopits hadn't always been a specialist in dwarfism. However, because Johns Hopkins had such a large patient population with genetic illnesses, he found himself working with many genetic-based orthopedic problems, and his passion soon became the skeletal deformities of dwarfism. He had told me that it was evident to him that this was a unique patient population with unique issues, which no one had yet taken an interest in caring for.

Dr. Kopits was certifiably a hero, a miracle maker, to each and every Little Person who had the pleasure of being his patient. In fact, to those whom I know who were blessed enough to see him, he was infinitely more than a physician. We all considered him a beloved friend and a true member of our families.

According to my mother, that first trip to Johns Hopkins Hospital and the Moore Clinic was much more traumatic for her than for me. She had absolutely no idea what to expect, and two weeks seemed like forever, so she was in a whirlwind of fear. On the one hand, she was relieved to have gotten a diagnosis for me, but she was equally overwhelmed by that diagnosis. One of the genetic specialists gave her an informational pamphlet about the size of a comic book that was filled with black-and-white photos of different people with my condition. The picture pages showed the severe orthopedic complications and deformities of children and adults. It was enough to scare her to death.

Dr. Kopits, a miracle worker to parents as well as patients, assured my mother that I would be well taken care of and that my prognosis was fairly good, but the list of surgeries he thought I would need throughout my life was something no parent wanted to hear. It was clear it wasn't going to be easy.

My first surgery was about a year later, when I was two. It was probably the biggest surgery I'd ever have, a cervical spine fusion on account of the instability in my spine. I had to have my top two vertebrae, C1 and C2, fused together. These two are the highest on the spine, right behind the skull, and when they are as unstable as mine were, any significant fall or jolt to one's head or back could cause paralysis, or worse. The fusion essentially turned those two vertebrae into a solid piece. However, it also meant I would have limited mobility in turning my head from side to side and flexing up and down.

The fusion was difficult, and I was under the knife for at least nine hours while my parents anxiously paced back and forth in the designated waiting area outside the operating room. The surgery involved taking bone from my hip to use as the "glue" for the fusion itself. Then, my spine was carefully manipulated and aligned to Dr. Kopits's satisfaction. Next, he secured my head and neck by placing me in a halo. A halo is a contraption that holds your neck stable after surgery while you heal. It involved four metal screws bolted into the four corners of my skull affixed with a circular metal ring around my head—where the name halo comes from—with bars that went down from the halo and attached to a belt-like fixture anchored at my waist.

I guess I looked pretty beaten up when I came out of the operating room. I was in the halo and was admitted to the Pediatric Critical Care Unit. Even though all this had been explained to my mother beforehand, and she thought she knew what to expect, she still fainted when she first got sight of me in the recovery room. This would turn out to be a recurrent thing for my mom, so much so that Dr. Kopits started carrying smelling salts every time he met my mom in the recovery room.

My mom had to take me home in the halo to heal for about twelve weeks, which wasn't easy for her first experience of surgery for me. She made the best of it. She said carrying me around was easy because the halo device functioned like an oversized handle, and I was so light. She could grab me by the bar anchored to the belt at my waist.

After I was discharged from the hospital, my mother and I flew home to Orlando where my aunt Barbara would help me recover. However, I have come to realize that things don't always go smoothly, or as you hope, in these situations. I had come down with some sort of bad cold, which in itself wasn't the problem. The crisis began when my mom was at work, and my dad and Papa, who was visiting from St. Petersburg, were at home with me and Dad tried to give me a dose of cold medicine. This was when giving children over-the-counter cold medicines was recommended by pediatricians, and I got so upset about the taste of it that I started thrashing my legs around and kicked so hard I literally forced out the front two screws in my skull that held the halo in place.

My mother got a desperate call from my dad to get home immediately, if not faster. When she busted through the front door and into the living room, she found my dad and Papa standing rock-stiff on either side of me, looking terrified, not daring to move a muscle as they held my head in place.

"What the heck is holding her head going to do? We need to secure her head!" my mom yelled as she ran to grab towels to stabilize my head within the halo and then to the phone to call 911.

My first memory ever is of riding in the back of the ambulance that came for me. The lights were flashing, and my parents were tucking towels around my head, trying to make sure I was secured for the trip to the hospital. Only one of them could go with me, so my dad offered to go, and my mom followed in her car. Once the back door closed and the ambulance started to move, I remember my dad singing me rhyming songs he made up on the spot to distract me while holding a tiny stuffed lion he brought with us. I still remember the words—*"the flying lion stops the crying."* He sang it all the way to the hospital in an effort to calm me down.

My dad was always the creative one, with a great imagination, whether or not there was an emergency. He loved creating stories and tales to make me feel better, and his plan usually worked. The "flying lion," made famous in the ambulance, became so special that my dad would later use him as a character in stories that became a full series. To this day, I still remember the plot lines.

My mom was always the tough one, always getting the job done. Their roles were complementary and equally important. My mom was already anxiously pacing the emergency room of Orlando Regional Medical Center when the paramedics raced me in on the stretcher. An adult orthopedic surgeon, Dr. Johnson, met us there. At that time, he had never seen this type of halo before, let alone a head halo that was displaced and semidangling. He and his staff began trying to communicate with Dr. Kopits's office at Johns Hopkins Hospital. When they were told he was in South America and not reachable (this was the era before cell phones), the situation became increasingly intense. I was admitted to the hospital while my entire family, the office in Baltimore, and Dr. Johnson tried to reach Dr. Kopits to get instructions on how to replace the halo. Dr. Johnson didn't want to just react without speaking to Dr. Kopits. However, because of the time passing and concern for injury to my spinal cord if I moved, he offered to attempt to replace the halo.

However, my parents really wanted to wait for Dr. Kopits, confident somebody would reach him. The last thing they wanted was for someone not familiar with the halo to mess things up and paralyze me forever. They had been warned that this was a possibility. They figured as long as I was in the hospital, secured, and monitored closely, I was safe.

Four days after I was admitted, there was still no word from Dr. Kopits. Dr. Johnson announced he and his team were going to have to take me into surgery to try to reset the halo. As terrified as my parents were, they agreed to go ahead.

Just as the surgical team was prepping me for the OR, into the waiting area walked Dr. Kopits! My mother and father practically fainted at the sight of him, breaking down in tears and thanking God for a miracle.

According to Dr. Kopits, intuition told him he needed to call his office, and when he followed his instinct and checked in with the office in Baltimore, he heard what was going on with me in Florida. He went straight to the airport, caught the next flight to Miami, and then drove the three hours to Orlando at ninety miles an hour in a rental car. What made the story even more exceptional was that he was in South America to receive an honor for his orthopedic work back where he had trained, and he left right in the middle of the dinner to take care of me before he could even receive his award.

After he arrived at the hospital, Dr. Kopits spoke briefly with Dr. Johnson, and soon he was scrubbed and ready to accompany him into the OR. The whole thing made my mom a firm believer in Dr. Kopits's dedication to his patients. With Dr. Kopits's direction, the halo was resecured. As he left, Dr. Kopits hugged both my parents and said to my mom, "Little mother, I am going to teach you how to care for the screws so this doesn't happen again." Dr. Kopits taught my mom how to tighten the screws in my halo, which had to be done every couple of days, and we never had another "halo emergency" again. Soon, I was back at home for the rest of my recovery.

The most unbelievable part of that whole story is that Dr. Kopits never charged my parents for any of it. I later heard of other stories about Dr. Kopits traveling across the country to care for one of his patients, and always without charge.

The spinal fusion was just the first of many surgeries I would have. It would be followed by numerous osteotomies on my hips, knees, and ankles. These osteotomies were corrective surgical procedures in which bones were broken in order to realign my deformities. Without these surgeries, my bones would likely become so deformed that I would be wheelchair-bound. My first osteotomy was on my hip when I was three years old. My primary nurse at this surgery was named Donna, and she became one of our closest friends. At each yearly checkup in Baltimore with Dr. Kopits, he would tell me if this would be a year for one surgery or two, as he would often do two at once. Of most concern to him were my knock knees and the fact that my femurs were growing at different rates, causing severe deformities that, if not corrected, might not be fixable down the line and would make me unable to walk. My knock-knee legs made it extremely difficult for me to keep up. Walking long distances was difficult, so I'd have to use a stroller, wheelchair, or when I was old enough, a scooter for distance. At school I had the aid of some device for distance for as long as I can remember. At Disney World, I may have gotten to jump the line in a wheelchair, but of course would have preferred to walk with everybody else.

CHAPTER TWO

Bill

IT'S A BOY!

MY MOTHER AND FATHER, William Walter Klein, Sr., and Barbara Jane Diecidue, were both from Long Island, New York. They grew up only a few miles from each other, as my father was from Levittown, a five-minute drive from Mom's hometown of North Massapequa. They met for the first time when my mother was in her senior year of high school, and my father, three years older, was home on leave from the army. He had been stationed at a base in Alaska.

They started their relationship as pen pals. A friend of my mother's was "pen palling" with my father, which was a common thing to do with soldiers back then, and she thought my mother would enjoy it, too. Mom didn't know it, but this friend, a former girlfriend of Dad's, suspected the two might be a good match.

My parents' first in-person date was actually when my father was home on Long Island for a twenty-one-day leave before being shipped to Southeast Asia for a tour of duty in Vietnam. By then, he and my mother had already been "dating by mail" for one year. The story goes that when Dad came to Mom's house to take her out, Mom's younger sister, Lori, answered the door. According to Mom, Dad probably thought that Lori was his date and was surprised when his real date, the little preppy schoolgirl named Barbara (my mother), popped up behind her.

Dad volunteered to serve in Vietnam, and in 1970 he was deployed to serve one tour of duty. Shortly after arriving, he volunteered to serve as a door gunner on a UH-1H helicopter and was immediately assigned to an aviation detachment stationed in Phu Bai. Afterward, his unit was relocated to an airbase in Da Nang. When not flying, Dad and other members of his unit visited orphanages in hopes of helping some of the kids displaced by the war. I think that is what my father is most proud of. It speaks to both his character and the character of the other servicemen who served with him in Vietnam. Like most veterans, my dad never really speaks about Vietnam or the war. I know he was (and still is) proud to have served our country.

I was born on October 13, 1974, at Mid Island Hospital (now St. Joseph's) in Bethpage, Long Island. The doctors knew immediately that something was wrong.

To begin with, I was cyanotic, a blue baby, which meant that I had some sort of heart malformation that prevented my blood from being fully oxygenated. I was in respiratory distress and had to be provided with oxygen in order to breathe. But there was also something really wrong with my proportions. I was seventeen inches long, fairly normal, but the concern was I was all head and torso, with very short appendages, so there was definitely something not right.

My parents were actually taller than average. My father was exactly six feet, when the average height for men at that time was five-eight. In fact, my mother was five-eight, four inches taller than the average woman. There was tall stature in the genetic pools of both their families as well. My mother's brother is six-four, and an uncle on Dad's side is six-two.

It has been speculated that my father's exposure to Agent Orange while serving in Vietnam was a contributing factor to my short stature. The exposure, which can result in flu-like symptoms among other things, is now known to denature the sperm's DNA, causing random mutations. But they don't know for sure if what happened was a mutation associated with exposure to Agent Orange or if it was a true random genetic mutation.

The delivery took a long time. At one point the doctor sent my father home and promised to call when I was closer to making my debut. Just as my father was arriving at my maternal grandparents' house, the phone rang. A nurse from the hospital said the doctor wanted my father to know I had been born, but that something was terribly wrong. He added to "not rush." *Not rush?!* My father drove at breakneck speed from North Massapequa back to Bethpage in less than five minutes, a ride that normally took double that. The doctor who had delivered me had already disappeared. According to my father, he was so seemingly nervous or unable to negotiate the terms of my novel condition that he never returned, ever. None of us ever saw him again.

Dad demanded to see me as soon as he got to the hospital. The baby nurse in the nursery held me up so he could see me through the glass window. He was in shock when he realized the severity of my condition. As the day progressed, the doctors and nurses were at a loss for words. But wanting to help in some way, they moved my mom to a private room, something that was unheard of then. With Mom not yet knowing exactly what was going on with me,

Dad made the decision to decline the private room, fearing it would cause her undue stress. He also knew that this decision would dictate how my life would be, and he didn't want me to be segregated because of other people's prejudices, even if their intentions were good.

Nobody knew how my mother would handle the news, so for a couple of days, the medical team taking care of me avoided bringing me to her. Because of the difficult delivery, she was heavily medicated, and they told her I was still getting treatment. Finally, three days after I was born, my mother absolutely demanded to see me, so a nurse on the unit got up enough nerve to carry me in, hand me over, and run out of the room.

My mother's sister was a nurse in the hospital, but even she didn't know exactly what was going on. She knew the buzz that it was bad and everybody was upset, but other than that, my condition was still a mystery. I was baptized many times over just in case I didn't make it.

I can't fathom the fear my mother must have had. Her first baby, her little bundle of pride and joy, had arrived, and everyone on the medical staff was scratching his or her head, bewildered. You can almost imagine my mom, in her room agonizing, scared, wondering, and waiting, the door closed to the conversation of the doctors going on in the hall. The secrecy made it even more difficult, as the doctors seemed to be mumbling things to each other, but not to her. My parents only had each other.

At one point, the pediatrician came in to talk to my mother. She told Mom she didn't know what was wrong with me; as far as she could tell, I only presented as "short."

"He's a dwarf, isn't he?" my mother blurted out, which caused the pediatrician to almost fall over in disbelief. Mom knew of somebody

whose child had growth issues, and doctors were considering dwarfism. Otherwise, she probably never would have come up with this
idea, but the pediatrician was in no way ready to agree.

My breathing issues continued for at least four days, so finally the
decision was made to send me to the NICU at Nassau County Medical Center in East Meadow, now called Nassau University Medical
Center. The neonatologist from that unit who had been assigned to
my case came with the NICU transport to collect me. I was lying in
the isolette that I would be transferred in, and he wheeled me over
to my mother and told her she could say good-bye to me now, if she
wanted.

"No, I am not saying good-bye to him," she responded with defi-
ance. "This is 'hello,' and I will see him later." She said that after she
gave the specialist this correction, she and I made complete eye contact, which is very unusual for a newborn. With my big blue eyes,
I told her, "I am not going anywhere, Mom. I'll see you soon."

Not long after my departure in the ambulance, Mom was also
discharged and my parents were by the side of my isolette within
an hour. They kept vigil in the NICU for hours every single day for
the next three weeks. There was one doctor on the unit who said he
thought I had a form of dwarfism called achondroplasia, because
of my very large head and very short arms and legs. This was the
most common form of dwarfism, characterized by short limbs and a
large head with a prominent forehead. Apparently, if you stretched
out my arms and lifted them up, they didn't reach the middle of my
head.

Having a baby in critical care without a diagnosis was extremely
hard on my parents. They had two or three relatives and five or six
friends who were having babies at the same time they were, and those
babies were all healthy and thriving. In time, they learned there was a

better shot at getting hit by lightning three times over than being born with my condition, but at the moment, they only had questions without answers. It was almost a miracle that I made it.

A month later, I was finally well enough to get out of the NICU. Most of our family and friends avoided us, because nobody knew the best way to deal with a situation like ours. The ones who did come around were awkwardly delighted to meet me. All this was causing my mother unbelievable stress and isolation, which was breaking her heart. But never for an instant did my parents falter in their love for me.

My parents worried about how I would be accepted, and I still had many very critical health issues they needed to deal with. My breathing often sounded like a wheezing squeak of an underoiled see-saw. Sometimes, these episodes were so critical, I had to be hospitalized. This happened six or seven times my first year of life. When I was nine months old, I almost died. I had just been released from the hospital after another breathing episode, and had been given penicillin to take at home. To this day, Mom is still suspicious that it was a bad batch, recalling its horrible smell. Whatever the reason, the penicillin or not, within days of getting home I became so dangerously dehydrated that I had to be rushed back to the hospital, where I spent a solid month in guarded condition. Meanwhile, my parents were still dealing with a tangle of diagnoses and treatments.

My mother followed the doctor's direction diligently and sought out every bit of wisdom she could find. My father, too, was unbelievably accepting of my condition. Many times, according to psychologists who understand the stress that a less than "perfect" baby places on a marriage, it is the man who really struggles with the idea of a long-term disability. Before I was born, they had decided to name me

William Junior, after my father. Mom offered to let Dad choose another name, particularly the name that would eventually be given to my youngest brother, Joseph Scott, if he didn't want me to be his namesake. My father would have none of it. "He is William Junior," he announced with sincere pride.

My father was a graduate of the Nassau County Police Academy and a police officer on Long Island. He was perfect for the job—tall, athletic, a people person, and a hard worker. My mother was a loving stay-at-home mom. She worked as a bank teller before I was born, but once I arrived, she always intended to stay home with me. She just didn't realize her new role was going to require navigating this much stress.

When I was still an infant, my mother actually had a nervous breakdown. Obviously, I was too young to remember it, but she was hospitalized for a full week and a half and was put on tranquilizers. It must have been terrifying for her, so young, scared, naïve, and in desperate need of answers, which nobody had.

Mom dealt with the situation as best she could, but she found it difficult to express how she felt about having a child with such pervasive health problems. People could say such nasty things when she took me out for even simple things, like to run errands. Their comments were devastating to Mom: "Look at the midget, look at the dwarf!" or "Look how funny looking he is!" One time somebody actually said I should have died in childbirth, and that both Mom and I would have been better off.

Dad was just the opposite. While the negative comments about me hurt him, he would shrug them off. His main concern was my health and finding out exactly what my condition was so we could deal with it. Dad always said that people handle things differently and that his way of dealing with adversity was to work the problem, something I emulated as I got older. I used my dad's approach of "working the problem" to handle a lot of the obstacles in my path.

People all too often made inconsiderate comments or asked ignorant questions, to the point where my mother became afraid to leave the house.

One story I love involves an event that took place in the supermarket when I was about four. Mom and I had gotten into a bit of a disagreement. Most likely, I was just being obnoxious and stubborn. But a woman overheard us from the other side of the store. She ran toward us, and when she reached me in the cart, she declared to my mother in a stern voice, "How dare you yell at that infant!" Before Mom could respond, I said something that, well, let's just say it wasn't Mom's proudest moment. The stranger was as stunned as Mom was embarrassed and quietly slunk away.

I wasn't always that bad. But I was a tough son of a gun to take shopping. I had a way of letting myself out of the stroller by sliding down and slipping out of the harness. I might have been the size for the baby stroller, but I wasn't a slobbering infant. I was like a very young Houdini. If Mom was preoccupied looking at clothes, I could escape and disappear on her. I was fast, too, and could walk under anything without clunking my head. Sometimes, the only way Mom could find me was when she heard a stranger saying, "Oh, my gosh, look at the size of him!" and then she'd give me that look and scoop me up. She had captured her little rascal, but I knew I could escape again soon.

There were strategies Mom devised to buffer me—and herself—from these awkward situations. Whenever she could, she tried to go to the store with friends. There was strength in numbers. She figured that way people would be less willing to make comments. There would still be the rude person who would point and say something inappropriate, but now she had support. Her friends would tell the gawkers to leave us both alone, that we are just out shopping, just like them.

I WAS DEFINITELY a bit of a medical nightmare and enigma at the same time, but I was at least making progress in some categories. As for physical milestones, I was behind, but cognitively I was ahead on the charts. For example, I was six months delayed in walking, partly because my head was so big. I would have to drag it around when I crawled, which consequently made it harder to hold up when I finally walked. However, my verbal skills were light-years ahead of the average range. I started talking at ten months. By fourteen months, I could speak in full sentences, my favorite being, "Mommy, please get me some milk because I am hungry." I looked like an infant but had the vocabulary of a fifth grader, like a Benjamin Button without the wrinkles. What you lack in one area, you tend to compensate for in others, which might explain why I was such a talker.

My parents tried to be as well-connected and informed as they possibly could be, but it wasn't easy. Mom kept calling different organizations that might have knowledge or information about dwarfism. By the time I was six months old, she had found out about the Moore Clinic at Johns Hopkins Hospital. The geneticist working there was Victor McKusick, the top physician in growth issues and dwarfism. Mom made an appointment for me, and Mom, Dad, and I headed to Baltimore.

Dr. McKusick was an extremely tall man. He had a portrait in his office of him sitting in a chair with a patient, an Amish Little Person, perched on his lap. The first thing he told my mother was that the doctors at Nassau County Medical Center were right about the dwarfism, but were wrong in thinking that it was achondroplasia. He wasn't ready to commit to exactly what type affected me after only one visit, but he was going to put together a profile of my presenting conditions and send it to all of the doctors he knew around the world who were working with growth issues. If I ended up being in a unique category all by myself, Dr. McKusick said he would name it "Klein Syndrome," after me. His charm and bedside manner finally had my mother feeling a little more at ease.

I was fourteen months old when I finally met Dr. Steven Kopits, who was also Jen's doctor at Johns Hopkins. He agreed with Dr. McKusick that my dwarfism wasn't achondroplasia. I had spondyloepiphyseal dysplasia (SED), which manifested itself differently. People with SED are characterized by more proportionate arms and legs; hip, knee, and ankle instability and deformities; and increasing curvature of the spine, including kyphosis lordosis and scoliosis. Unfortunately, SED is also characterized by many requisite surgeries to correct the irregular growth of the lower limbs.

First memories are always a bit suspect, because there is always a possibility that the memory is just created from overhearing someone else's story. But this was not the case with my first memory. I was three years old, and I woke up in the operating room. I remember the lighting, the smells, the sounds, and the movements of the scene. I remember the bright, absolute white lights, the way I was lying on the operating table, and the crowd of people around me, even though their eyes weren't really focused on me. There was that distinct smell that still haunts me, that postanesthesia stench that sticks inside your lungs and your nasal cavity for a long, long time. I could hear that all-too-familiar Hungarian accent of Dr. Kopits speaking in a sharp tone. I remember a nurse saying something to me, although I can't remember the details.

EVER SINCE I can remember, Mom was always at my side. She supported me through my toughest times and encouraged me to be better. When I was very young, she would stay in my room through the night just to watch over me. When I started school, she would greet me with a smile when I came home and ask about my day. Hugs weren't in short supply, either. We were a close family, and my mother always embraced us with a warm hug—to congratulate, to heal, to say I love you. My father, too, was very supportive and always there for me. He refused to let other people's doubts dictate the way my parents raised me.

My mother was beautiful. Her hairstyle went through different phases, from shorter bobs to the longer wavy style when that was in fashion. When she was happy, she smiled with her eyes. When she was unhappy, I could see it in the way she looked at me. She could also express surprise, disappointment, anger, fear, and joy by the way she looked at me.

Mom was very stylish, even when money was tight. She had her two seasons of outfits, shorts and short-sleeve shirts or sundresses in the summer, and blouses, pants or jeans, sweaters, and heavy coats in the winter. She was particularly fond of her coats.

My father was in great physical shape in his younger years. He worked hard and kept up his appearance. His hair changed with the fashion of the times, and I followed his lead with things like how to part mine. However, when he went with the then-stylish perm, I elected to abstain even if it meant I was "uncool."

Both my parents raised the kids, but my father was the authoritative one, and I admired him. His size and demeanor commanded attention. As a police officer, he was a respected figure, and everyone who had an association with our family saw him that way. Dad wore a uniform well. He looked like a cop, for sure. He wore his hat down a bit to the brow, shoulders out, back straight, no slouching. His holstered sidearm was a revolver when I was young, but he graduated to a nine-millimeter later on. I was proud that my father was a cop. He had power that not many other dads had, and I thought, foolishly, that his power therefore extended to me. To mess with me was to mess with a cop, and I could kick some serious butt like he did. When Dad looked at me, I knew it. When he smiled, he laughed along with it. When he was angry or disappointed, he looked through me. I felt it without the need for words. I wasn't a big troublemaker, but I got my fair share of both looks.

I am the oldest of my parents' three sons. My brother, Tom, was born two years and ten months after me, and Joe came along four years and two months after that. They did not have my condition, but they saw me go through many of my procedures and recoveries. Even with my physical limitations, being the oldest meant being responsible for my siblings. It was my duty to keep them in line, despite the fact that they quickly surpassed me in height at young ages. Tom eventually stopped growing when he was six-foot-four, and Joe reached a height of six feet. The two would always help me out when I was home and bedridden after a surgery. I often felt bad that I dominated my parents' time. But they never held it against me. In fact, they both looked up to me as their big brother.

I was built like a Mack truck, and I always fought my battles aggressively. The age difference between my brothers and me was big enough that they were a pain when we weren't getting along. Feats of strength were often needed to reinforce my place atop the sibling hierarchy. From traditional punches and chokeholds to the occasional throwing of a little brother clear across a room, I did what needed to be done to continue to command the respect an older brother needs to possess. That was kind of the way it went. My brothers were younger than me, and even though they were taller as well, they were not stronger. I managed to successfully establish myself as the oldest, and I was strong for a person short in stature, so, physically, I always won.

CHAPTER THREE

Jen

DRAGONS AND FAIRIES

BY THE TIME I started kindergarten, my family had moved from our first apartment in downtown Orlando to a nice ranch house on a hill in one of the many planned communities that were popping up all over the greater Orlando area. My father's new job as a route salesman for Orange News Company paid better and meant we could afford to buy something bigger, and my mother loved the idea of living in this type of neighborhood. The communities were self-contained, family-friendly, and offered lots of recreation and social events. They also had catchy names. Ours, called Rosemont, was on the shore of Lake Orlando and only about a twenty-minute drive from Disney World and downtown.

Barbara came with us when we first moved, but then, after my grandparents divorced, my grandmother and aunt Chrissy came to live with us, too. My mother didn't mind her mother and sisters living with us. In fact, she enjoyed it, as they were a big help. I grew up very close to Chrissy and Barbara. They were not only great as babysitters and playmates, but they would also let me accompany them on their dates with boyfriends or to their high school outings. This was a sign of just how much they loved me.

Soon after my grandmother and aunt Chrissy moved in, my aunt Barbara moved back to St. Petersburg to be with her high school sweetheart, Jack, who would later become her husband and my favorite uncle.

No matter where we lived, my mom always enjoyed making sure our home felt lived-in and comfortable. She was a fantastic decorator, and to this day, I wonder if she missed her calling as an interior designer. Her flair for detail and organization meant every room was dressed to the nines.

My bedroom was no exception. My wallpaper had delicate flowers that climbed the walls from the floor to the ceiling, making it seem like I lived in a garden. Today, I might not find that floral look so attractive, but it was the rage in the early eighties. Need I say more? I had a four-poster bed decked out with a white eyelet ruffled bedspread and crowned with a matching canopy. The nightstand and dresser completed the bedroom furniture set. My favorite stuffed animals and dolls were usually lined up along the built-in shelves, as my mom was a bit of a neat freak and liked me to keep them orderly. To accommodate my short stature, my dad put a lower rod in my closet, not only making it easy for me to get to my clothes, but also doubling the space.

There were definitely enough adults around that my parents didn't need to hire many babysitters. Because my father worked during the day, my mother chose to work at Walt Disney World at night, thereby assuring one or the other would be at home with me. If my dad worked late, my grandmother would take care of me. It was nice to have her in Orlando with us. We became very close, and she became a true confidante to me as I grew up. Chrissy always helped, too. She and I were only eleven years apart, so she was more like a big sister than an aunt. Although she went to high school during the day, she went out of her way to spend lots of time with me after school and on weekends. She loved photography and writing and wanted to become a journalist. We would dress up in all sorts of crazy outfits and take silly Polaroid pictures for hours. I have pictures of us dressed up as cowboys and Indians, Elvis and other entertainers, tennis players, you name it—we did it. We even set up a photo shoot with me hidden in the middle of all my stuffed animals, kind of like *Where's Waldo?* Chrissy had great taste in music. She taught me how to sing the Beatles, Rod Stewart's "Hot Legs," and Elvis songs. We even made voice recordings of me impersonating famous artists as I sang some of their popular tunes. As we were both growing up together, my aunt Chrissy and I became best friends.

My grandmother had always been a stay-at-home mom. But now that she was divorced, she really wanted to get into the workforce and make some money. She found a job at Disney World as a telephone operator for Buena Vista Communications. I used to love calling her on Disney's main phone line and requesting "Lorraine Shipman, please." I admired how she had gone back to work after dedicating all her time to raising her kids. I also admired how much pride she had in her job and how seriously she took it. Like my parents, she worked full-time, but her hours were regular enough that she would be home in time to make dinner when my mother was doing her night shift.

My grandmother was someone I went to for advice and just pure comfort, especially if I had gotten into an argument with my mother and father. She somehow always knew the right thing to say, and if all else failed, she would rub my back with "tickles" to make me feel better. She might have spoiled me just a *little*, but I loved her for that.

When my mom worked, she often came home after midnight. My dad was incredibly thoughtful, and not only would he wait up for her, he would often make her favorite meal, breakfast for dinner with bacon and eggs. My favorite nights were when he would let me wait up with him. I'd keep him company in the kitchen while he set the table, prepared his pans, and tidied the kitchen.

Mostly, though, I was to be in bed with lights out long before my mother got home. This was my parents' one chance to be alone and decompress together. Our home was always neat as a pin and filled with love, but this was not an easy, pressure-free household. There was stress, both financial and emotional, on many fronts. There was the juggling of job schedules, surgeries, and travel for me, and like every family, dynamics to manage. However, somehow, my family always made sure I came first.

I DIDN'T REALIZE I was a Little Person until I was six or seven years old. It didn't really matter much to me, however, and I did all the things most kids at that age did. I went to birthday parties of kids in the neighborhood, played outside, and sped around the block on whatever bike I was currently riding, with my dad or Aunt Chrissy following closely behind. Like most kids, I loved pretending, and dragons and fairies were my favorite characters. It was not unusual for all the neighborhood kids to gather on our lawn while Aunt Chrissy, Dad, and I started a game of "dungeons and dragons."

My school, Rolling Hills Elementary, was directly behind our house, but in another subdivision called Pine Hills. It was too far for me to walk, but too close for busing, so my mom or Grandma would drive me there and back, which wasn't horribly inconvenient for them. To get around the hallways, I had my Chubby Chopper, a tiny plastic yellow tricycle that fit me perfectly and moved like a speedboat. My best friend was a girl named Cara, who lived so far at the outskirts of town that her property was like a farm, with tons of farm animals. I always looked forward to playdates at her house for fun with her family's horses, cows, and goats.

When I was seven, my brother was born. My parents later told me that they had held off having a second baby until they had genetic counseling to determine the odds of having another child with dwarfism. Since neither of them was a Little Person, and my type of dwarfism is a dominant trait, the likelihood of the same genetic mutation was nominal. As much as my parents adored me, my mom didn't think she was capable of raising another child who needed so much medical attention. I think she still feared for my own happiness and long-term potential, and didn't want another child to have to go through the same struggles she saw me having to endure. It was very emotionally taxing for her and had taken a serious toll on her coping skills.

The morning my mother went into labor, I went to school, knowing that I was soon going to have a baby brother. My parents named him David Eugene, and even though he had my dad's first name, he wasn't officially a junior. His middle name was chosen in honor of my grandfather Issac Eugene Shipman. My grandfather, whom I called Papa, had four children—one son, my uncle Wayne, who was the eldest, and after that, three girls. He had always wanted another boy, whom he wanted to name David Eugene. My papa had a heart attack days before my brother was born, so when my mom delivered my brother, they were both in the hospital. After the delivery, my mom called Papa, and the first thing he said was "How is my David Eugene doing?" That was how my brother got his name.

A year later, my papa had a second heart attack, and this one took his life. Even after my grandparents' divorce years before, I had stayed very close with my grandfather. He meant so much to me that some years after his death, I had a dream that I went up to heaven to visit him. I sat on his bed where he was watching football, which he loved to do, and we had the most amazing conversation. He told me about the afterlife and that he was watching over us and that most important, he was all right.

My brother was a full-term, average-statured newborn without any presenting medical issues after birth. He was home with us in twenty-four hours. My parents were thrilled to have a second child, especially a boy, join the family. I don't recall being particularly excited or upset about having a baby brother, but I did know that I loved him from the moment he came home. He was a very cute newborn, and I liked holding him, but once he started walking and running around like a typical toddler, slowly morphing into a menace who liked to make a mess of my room and crash my slumber parties, it was a different story. Turns out brothers and sisters can be very different, not always compatible, but always lovable.

I think some of the bantering David and I had growing up likely related to our age difference and the fact that he was a boy, which in my mind meant we didn't have much in common. It also might have been because of all the medical attention I needed. With medical attention came other types of attention from family and friends. I cannot imagine how hard that was for him. Because he wasn't having surgeries all the time, I was also confused. I actually asked my mom one day, "So when does David have his first operation?" Similarly, he even once asked my parents when he was going to have his surgeries, possibly because he saw me getting presents and lots of attention before, during, and after all of mine. The strain of having a child in the family with complex medical needs can be a challenge for both younger and older siblings.

Early childhood was at times good and at times bad. Yes, the house was more chaotic, and I had to share my family with my brother. But I was also at an age when kids really began to notice differences between one another. My kindergarten graduation was the first time I noticed that I was truly shorter than everybody else. I remember an incident in the first grade when we were playing tag in the field, and another boy yelled at me, "Why do you have such a big head?" I didn't acknowledge him at the time, but when I came home and reported this event to my dad, his response was, "Next time, tell him it's because you have more brains!" That was my dad, always quick with funny retorts!

In second grade, the movie *Annie* came out, and I adored it. My good friend Kristie, who was a budding theater buff, and I were bonded by our love for *Annie*. We would sing all the songs out loud together and watch the VHS over and over every time we had a playdate. These "girl times" were extraordinary, but when Kristie tried out for the part of Annie at one of our local theaters and landed it, I was a little jealous for the first time. I wasn't envious in that mean way, as I knew Kristie made a great Annie, and I even got to see her in one of her shows. But I, too, loved the character of Annie so much, and I had even dressed as her the previous Halloween, orange wig and all. I knew deep down that I could be a good Annie. I wondered—if I had tried out, would I have gotten it? Or would they have dismissed me because I was a Little Person? I would never know, because I never tried out. That was a lesson I would learn from this experience. I knew I had limitations due to my stature, but you can never succeed at something if you don't try.

As a young child with dwarfism, I missed some typical opportunities for fun. My parents wouldn't allow me to go to water parks, even though all my friends were going, because despite swim lessons, I couldn't swim, tread, or float in the water due to my skeletal dysplasia. I couldn't ride certain rides with height restrictions at Disney World. Despite the fact that I really wanted to play the violin, my mom couldn't find an instrument small enough to fit me.

Things like this were very upsetting, but ultimately I learned I had to deal with these challenges and overcome them in order to be happy. If I was upset, my mother would always remind me that these were minor defeats and there was so much more I could do. She would tell me not to wallow in self-pity, as it wouldn't do me any good. She told me how much I had to be thankful for. My aunt Chrissy would also advise me that no person or situation made us happy or sad. Our emotions were our choice. As I grew older, I came to realize that if I wanted to be happy in life, I had to make myself happy, or at least not let obstacles or disappointments overpower me. This was the life I had been given, and I needed, more important, *wanted* to make the most of it.

Of course growing up I had many positive experiences, too. Sports activities were not exactly in the cards for me, but I found other ways to participate in competitions. With my mom's encouragement, I entered my very first dog, a miniature collie named April, in a special dog race for family pets at the Sanford-Orlando Kennel Club in Longwood. To my delight, she won honorable mention, and we both went home with smiles and a ribbon.

Dogs, judgment-free and unconditionally loving, were a mainstay of my childhood. April was even more important, because she was *my* dog, given *just to me* by my parents. Her previous owner was one of my mom's colleagues at Disney World, and she came to me when she was just out of her puppyhood. I nicknamed her Boo Boo (mostly because I was not a fan of her given name, April) and personally taught her many of her winning tricks. I was so proud when she won the special "Race Your Pet" event at the greyhound racetrack. The best part was that the local newspaper ran a story featuring us. I might not have been Annie, but Boo Boo and I were stars.

CHAPTER FOUR

Bill

KINDERGARTEN, HERE I COME!

I GREW UP IN PORT Jefferson Station, a typical suburban town on the North Shore of Long Island about sixty miles east of New York City. The area was then called Terryville, a small hamlet in the town of Brookhaven. It was a typical suburban landscape, with newly built homes in three or four different styles of ranches, split levels, and colonials.

My parents picked a house to buy in a location that would best serve my needs. They understood that I was a Little Person who might have a problem with walking to and from school or climbing the steep three steps of a school bus, so they chose a house that bordered the schoolyard. My school days were still a couple of years off, but my parents were planning ahead, especially as "mainstreaming" children with mental, emotional, and physical disabilities into the student population was just beginning to become policy. My mother had heard from different people who had children who were "little" that it wasn't easy. These parents were having a hard time getting their children into the schools. The school districts didn't want to deal with issues or accommodations; they didn't want to do anything different for the kids, really. Even though the Education for All Handicapped Children Act of 1975 was now in place and schools had to provide for children who were different, my mother was still afraid there would be a glitch, and I would end up being steered toward a "special" school that could accommodate me.

By taking my need for busing out of the equation, my mother had one less thing to worry about. A house next to the school was perfect. Just a few hundred feet between our house and the back door to the school meant no bus, minibus, or special bus after kindergarten. Just my Keds and backpack.

I started at the Boyle Road Elementary School when I was five years old. I took the bus at first along with all the kids going to school for the first time, and it wasn't the easiest task to climb up the steps, but I did it. And once I got to school, I could see my house from the classroom, and on occasion, I would look toward the backyard to see if there was any activity. Sometimes, I would see Mom doing something back there, but I didn't necessarily know what. I was happy and reassured that I could see her from school.

Mom had already taken a very active role in the school, which helped her feel a little in control of our situation. Our neighbor, who was one of her best friends, had signed her up for the PTA before she could even think about it. She came over one day and told Mom, "You are coming to the next meeting, you are already a member, and you will love being involved." It was perfect, because my mother was on the shy side and not very outspoken. However, with that small push, she quickly made herself known to the entire elementary school staff, teachers and administrators alike. She understood that when you have a child with special needs, you need to be outspoken. For example, following the doctor's advice, Mom made sure that all my health forms stated that in the event of a fire or fire drill, I was to be carried out of the building so that I wouldn't be lost or trampled. In fact, somebody was required to double-check that the teacher had me. Later on, my father, a volunteer in the Terryville Fire Department and eventually a captain there, created a training program that was piloted at Boyle Road Elementary, in my classroom, to help ensure all students learned about fire prevention and how to evacuate a home or school.

By the time kindergarten orientation for parents rolled around, Mom and Dad were my advocates almost to a fault. The staff had heard so much about me and was so well prepared that one of the kindergarten teachers came up to Mom at the meeting and said she had just finished a course on teaching children with special needs and was looking forward to having me.

"One question," my mom said, "are you a pushover or are you a tough, strict teacher?"

At the response that the teacher did not consider herself strict, my mom announced her decision. "I am very sorry," she replied, "but you can't have Bill in your class. He is a charmer and can melt down the strictest of the bunch, so he will certainly take advantage of you. I need someone who is able to see past his charm." My mother felt bad, because she knew the teacher had gone out of her way, but Mom knew me all too well!

Still, it didn't take long for me to notice children around me treating me differently because of my size. My friendships were not the same as the friendships between other kindergartners. Some people would bully me and others would pick me up and tell me how cute I was. I heard the word "midget" being thrown around, too.

My mom always knew the situations in school between my classmates and me, even if she didn't hear something from me. She was that well-connected. One time, Mrs. Muller, the teacher Mom had handpicked for me, called her up.

"We have a problem here, Mrs. Klein," she told her.

"What is the problem?" my mom inquired.

"Billy's got a fat lip."

"What?"

"Yeah, one of the kids here just keeps picking on him and I have no idea how to stop it."

My mother knew how to stop it. "Do me a favor," she said to Mrs. Muller. "Call up the mom of the child and ask her to call me. I want to invite her and her son over to my house for lunch, and I want him to see that Billy is just like him. I want him to see Billy has a bedroom, a play yard, all kinds of toys and books, and a really nice family, just like him."

It all worked just as Mom planned. The kid and I remained friends throughout elementary school, junior high, and high school. Mom knew that was the best way to treat bullies—invite them in rather than shun them or fight back. Everybody had to get involved, the families, the kids, and the parents. Mom said that sometimes we couldn't know what was going on in the other household, and maybe that child was having some other problem, and that I was just an easy target. Mom really was a remarkable mother who tried to work with understanding rather than anger.

My father was also there in my defense if it was ever needed. From consulting with me on how to handle a situation to showing me how to defend myself, my dad made sure I had the tools to take care of myself in the event I didn't have anyone to back me up.

Still, things happened. One time in class, the kindergarten built a papier-mâché volcano several feet high. It was so big it covered the entire top of a round table in the classroom. As the vinegar, baking soda, and red dye number five concoction, which was the lava, bubbled over the mouth of the volcano, I was surprised to see one of my classmates motioning for two other boys to pick me up. Sure enough, they lifted me up and held me over the active volcano, although they never did actually put me in it. I knew they were picking on me because of my size.

For the most part, my early childhood was not compromised by my stature. In my mind, it just couldn't be. I was not in the least bit "sickly." In fact, I was robustly active and always on the go, unless it was bedtime. Even then, my parents couldn't count on me to turn in. There was almost nothing that anyone else my age was doing that I thought I couldn't do as well, if not better.

Like most of the boys in my neighborhood, if I wasn't in school, I was busy with activities. I was a Cub Scout in Pack 603, played Little League baseball and flag football, playacted soldiers and army with my friends, and rode my bicycle around the neighborhood. But I didn't have to be with other kids to create fun. If I was on my own, I played in the fields and the woods around my house, swam with supervision in our pool in the summer, occupied the clubhouse that my father built for me with his own hands, and rode my Big Wheels and bicycle—nothing like a boy and his bike.

With so many boys, my parents needed a lot of rules in the house. They didn't coddle me, though. They just let me be a boy, the same way they treated my brothers. We had routines and chores Mom wanted us to do—cleaning, meals, homework, and so on—but she also trusted that we could take care of ourselves while giving her enough respect to do what was needed. We were responsible for our evening baths and showers, or lack thereof. We honored her bedtime for us, but once we got into bed, we could stay up and watch television if we wanted. Mom wouldn't say much about it to us, except "Good luck waking up tomorrow morning." She knew we'd have to learn to regulate our sleep time on our own when we saw how tired we were in the morning.

As I got older, I really loved Robin Williams as Mork in *Mork and Mindy*. Everybody I knew tuned in for Robin Williams's extraordinary physical comedy and his brilliantly absurd characterization of Mork from Ork, but beyond enjoying it, I related to it. Mork reminded me of me. Through no fault of his own, he found himself witnessing human behavior and social norms as an adorable outsider. If things got sticky, he extricated himself with humor. He was on the border of being a regular guy, but if it ever bothered him that he wasn't like everybody else, he managed it and emerged the better at the end of every show.

The Princess Bride was my favorite movie, which still holds true today. Again, you had this trio of completely lovable outlaw misfits— the incredibly short (though not a Little Person) criminal mastermind, Vizzini, played by Wally Shawn; Inigo Montoya, the absurd Spanish swashbuckler hell-bent on revenge, played by Mandy Patinkin; and my antithesis, Fezzik, a giant Turkish wrester—*truly* a giant! Fezzik is played by André the Giant, a Frenchman who in real life was seven-foot-four, so tall that by age twelve he could no longer ride on a school bus. These three characters didn't fit in any normal sense. They were too odd, too weirdly clever, but charming, though you couldn't put your finger on why. They all far surpassed in humanity what you would guess by their looks. And they were funny, which happens to be the characteristic of being human I like best.

Besides TV and movies, my pets kept me entertained. We always had a lot of them. There was Lassie, a cat, not a collie, who brought eight more cats in when she had kittens. We also had a schnauzer named Rascal, a mutt named Coffee, a Maltese named Teddy Bear, and the niece of Teddy Bear, Midnight, nicknamed Middy. Middy was affectionate and loyal. She was my sanity during many of my post-op stints at home, when I was in casts and barely mobile. I remember the times when everyone else in the house would go upstairs to their bedrooms, and I would be left in my temporary quarters, the living room with the rented hospital bed. With everyone fast asleep, I would lay there in extreme discomfort, alone, helpless, and in the pitch-black dark. But Middy would always stay with me. She would often go to sleep on the cast itself, not caring if that was her least comfortable option.

We had smaller pets, too, beyond the cats and dogs. We had hamsters, which ate each other and their offspring, and a couple of parakeets, Tweety One and Tweety Two, that found life too challenging and met their demise by falling from their perch and breaking their necks. I once had a turtle, until Mom accidentally boiled him. She had put him outside, thinking he would like warming up in the sun, but maybe because of the lack of shade, he got sunstroke. I didn't know anything about it until after the fact. Mom tried to save him by throwing him in the little wading pool in the yard, but he did the dead man's float.

CHAPTER FIVE

Jen

SCOOTERING AROUND

I N THE MONTHS BEFORE fifth grade, my mother and father started getting back into religion. They hadn't been going to church much since our move to Orlando, even though my mom had been raised Catholic, which had a mandatory church attendance precept. Now, with two children, she missed the sense of community and comfort that comes with Sunday mass.

My dad had never been a Catholic, but he was willing to take classes and convert. He had been raised as a Southern Baptist, but had not practiced since he was a kid. After he was baptized into the Catholic faith, he and my mother renewed their vows in a Catholic ceremony, and David and I did our sacraments—David was baptized, and I had my First Communion.

When the fifth-grade school year began, my mother moved me from public school to parochial school. Not only did she want me to have an education with religious study, but she also thought

St. Charles Borromeo Catholic, the Catholic school I would be attending, might be a safer and more supportive school environment for me. The class sizes at Rolling Hill Elementary were getting ridiculously large, as the Rosemont/Pine Hills neighborhood where we lived was expanding rapidly. She liked the idea of my brother and me going to a Catholic school like she had, where Catholic religion, faith, respectfulness, and kindness were part of the education. I was perfectly happy to leave Rolling Hills. My friendships were changing. Kristie and I had drifted apart when she began becoming part of the popular crowd, and although I would miss my friend Cara, we were still going to have play dates on weekends.

When I started at St. Charles in the fifth grade, my brother started preschool there. I also retired my Chubby Chopper and got my first motorized scooter, called the "Pony." It was a battery-powered, three-wheeled scooter designed for kids. It had a sailboat-like tiller for steering, an adjustable seat with lumbar support, and three speeds— slow forward, faster forward, and slow reverse. It even had a little wire basket on the back where I could put my books. At first, I was a little afraid to ride it, since I was the new kid and was worried I would feel embarrassed in front of my classmates. But soon everyone wanted to take a ride on it. Sometimes, in good fun, my friends would write me "speeding" or "parking" tickets and leave them on my seat for me to find when I came out of class. During festive times at school, like the week before Christmas, we would dress it up with garlands and ornaments.

There was only one class per grade, with thirty students in each class, and I really appreciated how everyone knew each other and for the most part were friends. Despite all the ways the school tried to promote diversity and the idea that everybody is special, I *still* had nagging moments of feeling like an outsider. There was no question that I was liked, and that my friendships were sincere, but even now, it is hard to describe how I viewed myself in the bigger community. I worried, not obsessively, that my friendships weren't the same as those between other children. I mean, I had lots of friends and I was well known even in the other grades, to the point that pretty much *everybody* in the school knew who I was. However, there were moments, usually during social and extracurricular activities, when I felt like a bit of an outsider, as if I was accepted, but it was conditional and could change at any time. I wasn't confident in the stability of my friendships. I had been dealing with so many health issues and surgeries that I came into middle school having a very different childhood experience than most kids.

The fact that I looked different, too, and had to ride a scooter in the halls, often made me question how others perceived me. It was tough, but I learned to persevere, trying to keep the focus on all the good people my childhood afforded me, and all the good times. I tried to enjoy friendships and social events and not focus on moments when I felt left out, but there was always a certain amount of social stress.

In the long run, I was very thankful my parents transferred me to St. Charles. It was a good fit for me. It turned out I did pretty well in a strict Catholic school environment. To this day this seems odd to me, but I had, and to a certain extent still have, a people-pleaser personality and liked to do the right thing. In Catholic school, there was little doubt about what was right and wrong. That worked well for me.

Additionally, Little People tend to grow up fast because of our life experiences. I had a tendency to relate more to and enjoy the company of adults over other kids. Relationships with adults seemed more solid and less tenuous. From as early an age as six, I loved late nights of staying up and "catching up" with the grown-ups around the kitchen table after my mom got home from work. I could sit for hours and talk about *their* gossip. I always liked to be "in the know."

My weekends and school breaks were often spent at the beach in St. Petersburg with my aunt Barbara and uncle Jack. Their home was located within a few blocks of the Gulf of Mexico, and it became a tradition for me to visit with them on weekends and every spring break and summer vacation that I wasn't having surgery. My aunt Barbara was my ultimate beach buddy, and she still is today!

My mom would drive me down after school on Friday and we'd usually be there by dinnertime. Sometimes she'd stay the whole weekend, but more often than not, Aunt Barbara and Uncle Jack would take care of me for the three days. They were like surrogate parents. When my aunt Chrissy was a little older, she would drive me down. I liked this best of all, because it would turn into a girls' weekend.

My time in St. Pete Beach was centered on die-hard days at the beach, rain or shine. Then we would go back to Barbara's house, shower, and head out to a fun seafood dinner. Usually one night we would stay in, order pizza, and "hang with Jack," and he would school me on classic rock and TV. The entire weekend would be so filled with activities, especially at the beach, that it seemed as if I had just arrived when Sunday came. We could be at the beach for hours (and I mean hours) if the weather was good. Unbelievably, I didn't burn, and even if I did get a little red, it would fade into a tan in no time. I think my grandfather on my father's side being a quarter Cherokee Nation had a lot to do with my tolerance for the sun. We used sunscreen some of the time, but back then it wasn't really as common. (Now, my parents can't believe how much of a stickler I am for lathering my kids up every time we are outside.) I would spend hours sitting right at the water's edge, the best place to collect shells. I didn't need to worry about getting knocked down by the waves. The Gulf Coast didn't really get waves unless there was a hurricane.

I loved walking into the water, even though I was not really a good swimmer. Because of my body structure and orthopedic issues, I had trouble keeping my head above water. I am like a marble and just sink to the bottom of any body of water. Because of the shape of my rib cage, I also have a restrictive lung disease, meaning no matter how fully I inflate my lungs, I still won't be able to do the dead man's float like most people, but rather, I sink like a stone, lungs fully inflated. However, with a snorkel, I could swim forever . . . well, almost.

Aunt Barbara and Uncle Jack have always been big animal lovers. My aunt worked in a veterinary clinic and loved taking in rescues, to the delight of Uncle Jack. They always had tons of cats and a few dogs. Inevitably, some of our beach time would include taking the dogs to a dog-friendly beach. My aunt actually gave me my first kitten. There are many pictures of me sleeping on the couch in St. Pete with anywhere from four to five cats surrounding me. I became a big animal lover, too. I always had pets—dogs, cats, fish, turtles, guinea pigs, and birds. Not all at once, of course.

BEGINNING IN THE sixth grade, I became part of a best friends' threesome—Kimberly, Anna, and me. Kimberly was very pretty with lots of freckles and shoulder-length brown hair. Because she lived only a few streets from me, we could ride bikes to each other's houses, which was really nice. Anna had thick wavy dark hair and a bubbly personality. She lived farther from Kimberly and me, but so close to St. Charles that her property actually shared a backyard fence with the school. This meant her house was extremely easy to get to for after-school fun and homework.

Being in an official girlfriend group thrilled me beyond my wildest dreams. The three of us spent most of our after-school hours and weekends with each other, indulging in sleepovers, going to the movies, and doing girlie things. We'd spend hours doing each other's hair and making friendship pins out of beads, which we wore to signify our unity. As we got further into sixth grade, the practical jokes began. We'd freeze the bra of the first person to fall asleep or smear toothpaste all over her face. One of the get-togethers I remember the most was the weekend we spent at a beach condo rented by Anna's family. Her mom invited Kimberly and me to join them, which was incredibly generous. For sixth graders, there was nothing more fun than being together on an exotic adventure. We spent three days hanging out by the pool, boy-watching on the beach, and messing around in the surf. This was one of those weekends when I truly felt like one of the girls!

Then, after an uneventful seventh grade with my girl gang, things changed. One day early into our eighth-grade year, I suddenly stopped being invited to things. Kimberly and Anna were still hanging out at Kimberly's house, but without me. They'd go to the movies, do homework together, and seek each other out, but without me. They didn't invite anyone else to replace me, per se, but they turned into a twosome while I was left out entirely. It was unbelievably painful, as my self-esteem with these guys as my friends was at its best *ever*. The thought that maybe I wasn't cool enough to hang out with them anymore plagued me. I confronted them about dropping me, and they confirmed they had been doing things together. They weren't even particularly mean to me, but they were steadfast that they were fine with the new "twosome" arrangement, and I was out.

It was too hard to think about why things had changed. I had many theories, but none that eased the pain. My leading theory was that because they were starting to get interested in boys, I must not have been a boy magnet and therefore not cool enough to hang out with anymore. No specific event seemed to precipitate this change, as there had never been a fight or even an argument. What was so hard was the fact that this change happened without any warning or even an explanation.

For the first time in my life, I felt rejected because of who I was, a Little Person. This was one of those moments when I learned the value of putting a protective barrier between others and myself. It wasn't that I didn't want to continue to create and develop close friendships, but I knew I had to be cautious, because I didn't want to feel that pain again.

CHAPTER SIX

Bill

DOWN DAYS AND TOUGH TIMES

AT AGE EIGHT, MY height and my skeletal problems really started to put me at a disadvantage on the athletic field, and I hated it. This was the age when competitive sports were becoming the be-all and end-all—not only participating in them, but winning.

More than anything I dreaded Field Day, which was nothing but a hot, humid Indian-summer day filled with the spirit of bloody combat. The chance of my winning anything in the individual competitions was nonexistent. For the battles of the two sides, my particular contribution was irrelevant. If I was on the red team, and we happened to win, it had nothing to do with me. From strategy to execution, my involvement was strictly related to attendance.

It wasn't just during Field Day that things were changing, and it wasn't just because of sports. I couldn't deny it—kids in school were really beginning to pull away. I didn't really have a great school friend who was my age who wanted to hang out with me after school.

I would see people at school and everybody was always friendly, but they didn't want to do anything with me out of school.

For a while, I had Jason Pasternak, a schoolmate who was almost forced to be in my company. He became my best friend in a circuitous fashion. It was fourth grade, and he was the smartest kid in the class. Mrs. Sorley, our teacher, was teaching us how to convert improper and mixed fractions, and I was having a problem with it. For whatever reason, I wasn't getting it. In frustration, I threw a pencil in her direction, which got her very upset with me. As punishment, she appointed Jason as my in-school tutor to help me. I resisted, since we weren't really friends, but I started studying with him when I was told I had no choice.

By fifth grade, we were best friends. The summer before, I had undergone a surgery and was in a wheelchair when school started, and Jason would enthusiastically push me around from the classroom to the lunch room or library, to the gymnasium or the enriched science class. We were almost inseparable. We'd go to lunch before the rest of the classes and celebrate our unfettered access with a chocolate milk and French bread pizza, and get our pick of any seat in the house. Afterward, recess was often spent playing together or sitting on the curb in the parking lot. Boy how things have changed.

For winter vacation, Jason went to Florida with his family and he never came back. From what I remember, he had an allergic reaction to something so severe that it sent him into anaphylactic shock, and he couldn't be saved. He was only ten years old.

My two best friends, Andria and David, were from my neighborhood, but they were older and not in my grade. Dave was four years older than I, and Andria was a year older. Our social time took place after school. I didn't even realize how most cliques of this age didn't cross gender lines. But we three made up the coolest clique there was. Our three houses were fairly close together, with me on the corner, and Andria and David two and four houses down respectively. These were my most favored friends of all time. To this day, I speak with both of them. Of course, the subject matter has changed, though I can't say it's any more mature in content.

Dave used to get a little guff for hanging out with a younger kid. But I was mature for my age, probably because of my circumstances. I am fairly certain that people who have a medical issue or other serious challenges in their childhood tend to mature ahead of their peers. We grow up quicker and lose a little bit of our childhood. When I reached a certain age, I had to sign a release before every surgery in which I acknowledged that I understood there was a chance I might die on the operating table. That was an adult situation that I was presented with on a rather regular basis. I grew up realizing that kids older than me were easier to get along with, more relatable.

Dave's, Andria's, and my parents were all friends, too. However, when Andria's parents split up, the dynamics of the group changed. It wasn't a couples' thing anymore, so the group didn't hang out like it used to.

Not long after, my parents also separated. I have no doubt all my surgeries and needs put an enormous strain on my parents' marriage. They had heard from the very first meetings and symposiums at Johns Hopkins that parents of children with disabilities divorce almost twice as often as couples without that kind of stress.

I still felt guilty that I needed so much attention, which had denied my brothers their fair share of my parents' time, largely to their detriment. While I was sure there was some resentment on their part, I also believe they let it go quickly, knowing it was not intentional, and that I didn't want the attention anyway. I loved and still love my brothers as much as any brother has in history.

I found out that my parents were getting divorced by accident. There wasn't one of those joint parent "we love you three boys, just not each other" conversations. Instead, one night, I woke up to discover my mother crying into her hands at the kitchen table, alone, angry, and abandoned. I didn't even know what to do or how to respond. I stayed with Mom a few minutes, but she wanted me to go back to bed, and I did.

As a person with a disability, I was used to dealing with grown-up situations, as I had been dealing with them for a long time. But when my parents split, I went from being the oldest of Mom's three sons to being her best friend, man of the house, primary helper, and concerned older, mature brother to Tom and Joe. The pressure was enormous. The situation was difficult for everybody.

After my parents' divorce, my dad married Debbie, who became my stepmother. Her two sons, Jonathan and James, who were just two months younger than Tom and me, became our stepbrothers. Dad and Debbie bought a house in our town so Dad could be involved in our schooling. The four of us, Jonathan, James, Tom, and I, attended the same junior and senior high schools. My brother Joe was much younger, so he didn't have a sibling, blood or step, to go through school with. For the most part, the five boys got along very well. All things considered, the relationships we had as siblings, blood or step, helped provide the stability necessary to get through such a challenging time in our lives.

At my mom's house, I was suddenly the man of the house after my parents' separation, and I tried to look out for everybody. My mother was simply overwhelmed. She was thrust into being a single mom with a mortgage to pay and three kids to feed. She had minimal work experience, so she returned to school to work toward her degree. My dad worked three jobs to support two households, and, as anyone who comes from a divorced family can attest to, money got stretched really fast. Ultimately, public assistance and welfare were Mom's only option.

Mom entered the workforce willing to give anything a try. And once Joe started school, she started working as a sales rep for various food distributors. She'd go to the supermarkets within her territory to check for expired or almost-expired products and remove them from the shelves, alerting the restocker about the change in inventory. She would perform store resets and document the work with photos. Even though the work didn't pay that well, she was able to get a lot of food free that way, which was the unexpected perk that benefited us the most. With three boys at home, food was a big part of the home expenses. After traveling long miles between supermarkets in the mornings and afternoons, Mom usually got home after Joe, Tom, and I got home from school.

She would often run out of money no matter how much she stretched her dollar. The food stamps helped, but I wanted to help, too. I developed an uncanny ability to fix things or work for pay. I learned to repair anything I could to help out, maybe even to prove I could be the man of the house. I'd mow lawns in the neighborhood. Once, Mom got a super extra-large box of pretzels, and my brothers and I set up a stand similar to a lemonade stand and sold them for a dollar each. Another time, after the old dryer broke, Mom got a new one, but she was going to have to pay someone fifty dollars to rig it up for her. I told her I could figure it out, and soon I had put the whole thing together. I still laugh at how entrepreneurial I was. I had a motorized, two-seater go-cart rigged up with pedal extensions that my dad got me for my tenth birthday. It was the most awesome toy to tear up the fields behind Boyle Road Elementary, and I'd charge a dollar a ride for a quick trip around the neighborhood.

Meanwhile, there was life at Dad's. With his three children and my stepmother's two, there were five rambunctious boys quite close in age under one roof. To accommodate everybody, Dad and Debbie's house had four bedrooms. Two of the bedrooms were for the kids— one for James and Jonathan, of whom Debbie had full custody, and one for Tom, Joe, and me. Dad made sure the house was in the same school district to help make life easier for all of us when it came to school and continuity.

Nobody was given preferential treatment, even though Jonathan and James lived with my father and Debbie full-time. The kids' bedrooms had bunk beds and/or a twin in each one, and everybody had the run of the house beyond that. Dad and Debbie didn't have children with each other, so I never had half-siblings, even though I would have liked a baby sister.

My dad had joint custody of us, and he would have us Tuesdays, Thursdays, and every other weekend. If it were a school night, we would go from school, hang out with James and Jonathan through dinner, and get driven back to the house by nine o'clock. Dad was extremely reliable and missed a designated day only if there was absolutely no way around it, such as if he had to work unexpectedly for any of his three jobs.

My brothers and I lived pretty much the same lives at both houses, but we did have a list of pros and cons for each. At Dad's, we had our stepbrothers. They had some newer toys, a computer, more games for the Nintendo, and so on. But the rules were a bit stricter. Our chores were more regular and playtime was predicated on our willingness to do our chores.

At Mom's, we had our long-time neighborhood friends, David and Andria for me; a neighbor by the name of Andrew for Tommy; and a boy named Michael for Joey. We also had a Nintendo, a TV, and many toys. Mom's house was a bit more comfortable, meaning that because she was too busy to police our chores, things were a bit more relaxed. She relied on me to help wrangle my brothers and their games, clutter, and clothes. I didn't mind. Strangely, I liked vacuuming and dusting the house. Frankly, I didn't want to have friends over if the house wasn't in tip-top shape.

Besides the strain of living in two houses, I still had the unbelievable stress of those trips to the hospital for surgery. These were the worst, and I was always scared! I made a number of trips to Baltimore over the years. Before my parents' divorce, they would both make the trip and would normally leave my brothers in my grandmother's care. After the divorce, this, too, became a bit more complicated. Now, normally one parent would make the trip with me, and the other would stay in New York with my brothers. Other times, they would make the trip in two cars. And on rare occasions, my brothers would come and we would make it a family affair. My lengths of stay would depend on the procedure I was getting done, but because this was the skeletal system, I would often have to be in Baltimore for a period of weeks.

Pre-op routines varied by circumstance, but they always involved me starving myself before the physical so I would be lighter and easier to manage. Blood work and X-rays were also part of the deal. After we checked in, we would get the lab stuff out of the way, and then the radiology, where the hospital gowns were always too big in the front and too cold in the back. Then we'd have to sit around until the doctor was ready to see me. Mom would struggle with nerves, and Dad would fall asleep in the waiting room chairs while we killed time. I wish I could say I took naps, too, but I was too nervous. I would normally pace around the waiting rooms, unable to sit still and going through the possible scenarios of what we would hear from Dr. Kopits.

These were always difficult trips. We never knew what the doctor would say in terms of how much surgery he was going to do, and
we always anticipated there would be some bad news in there somewhere. The upside was that as time went on, we would see the same
patients over and over, and we became friendly. Soon, the anxiety of
those surgeries was tempered by anticipation of seeing old friends at
the hospital.

Johns Hopkins Hospital was huge and intimidating, with
color-coded stripes on the floors and pipes to follow to lead you to
your destination. St. Joseph's in Towson, Maryland, where Dr. Kopits
eventually moved his practice, was a much smaller facility, newer-
looking and very accessible. There, he was able to have an entire ward
appropriated for his patients. Two North, the floor we were on, was
great. The lounges were nothing special, but the playroom was fantastic, and we had access to an arcade game almost 24/7. Movies were
accessed via a separate AV cart and a wait list. Everything in the physical therapy department was customized for Little People, so the tables were very low, the equipment was designed for short-stature
individuals, and a custom pool went from two feet to four feet deep.
The water was kept at a balmy ninety degrees. For those getting cut
out of their casts, there were also appropriate-sized whirlpool tubs.

The rooms I stayed in usually had two patients, with a shared
TV and bathroom. The room was pretty plain, and maybe twelve by
twenty-five feet. Most of the time, I had a roommate. Some of them
I liked, some I didn't, and some I conned for candy machine money
because the hospital food wasn't that good. It wasn't that bad either,
just hospital food. For the most part, I ate a lot of BLTs and drank
a lot of iced tea. For dessert, the best they had was the lemon me-
ringue pie.

Since most of us were not "first-timers," we already knew the staff, nurses, nurse practitioners, physical therapists, lab techs, and each other. I liked the primary nursing staff. There was Mary Beth, Katie, Janine, and Bill. They were all great, but my buddy Bill was the best. I think he was the best in most people's minds. Janine was pretty awesome, too.

Mom would normally stay in the hospital or at the Pierre House, a home on the grounds of St. Joseph's Hospital that was afforded to the families of those undergoing procedures who needed a place to stay. If Mom and Dad were there, Mom would stay at my bedside, and Dad would stay at the Pierre House. If the Pierre House wasn't available, the Quality Inn was the go-to hotel with reasonable rates.

The surgeries were like works of art executed by a fine sculptor. For something like an osteotomy to correct a curved femur, a surgery I had more than once, the surgeons would cut you open, then cut your femur in half, take out a triangular wedge, and reconnect the two bones together with a plate, a couple of screws, and some surgical wire. Then they'd reconnect all of the muscles and tendons and sew you back up.

I would be out of school for two to three weeks for the surgery, then up to three months to heal in the cast at home, and then six to eight more weeks for inpatient physical therapy at the hospital. To avoid falling behind in school, tutoring was imperative. During my recovery in the spica casts, many of my regular teachers would tutor me at home in addition to their school schedule. This made for a consistent learning experience and helped me perform well in school. When I relocated to Baltimore for six to eight weeks of inpatient physical therapy, I had tutors there, arranged through the hospital, and they would receive instructions, lesson plans, homework assignments, and exams for me to take from my school. Normally, my parents would come down for the initial cast removal and first few days of physical therapy. Afterward, they would travel back to New York and return to my brothers, stepbrothers, and their jobs.

As far as my spirits were concerned, I definitely had my moments, lying in a hospital bed with a cast up to my rib cage, asking, "Why me?" There was a part of me that was angry that I had to deal with this stuff, and I was old enough to have those feelings, but I was also old enough to know there was nothing I could do about it, so why complain?

For a while, my family and I were involved in Long Island's chapter of Little People of America, the Islanders. It was the local branch of the national nonprofit organization for people of short stature. The group convened for occasional get-togethers to discuss experiences, discovery of innovations, or solutions to problems common in the world of people with dwarfism. Sometimes, field trips to the movies, amusement parks, or tourist attractions in New York City would punctuate our regular meetings. Unfortunately, many of the people in our chapter of LPA were older than I was, and many of the children were much younger than I was. Because of that age gap, I didn't participate very regularly.

I did have one Little Person acquaintance, Frank, who was a couple of years older than me and lived a few towns away. We would hang out once in a while, but for the most part, I was busy navigating what was happening to me in school. I was beginning to get picked on by the bullies in earnest. In my sixth-grade class, I was once poked in the eye with a paperclip. Another time, my pants and underwear were raked down in front of everyone. My teacher, however, turned a blind eye. He really made me feel powerless by not seeming to care. I suddenly feared that once people figured out my vulnerability, I would have even less recourse than I already had. Now, every situation had the potential to turn into something threatening, or become a chance for me to be excluded or ignored or negated, as if I didn't matter.

Mom was still an incredible advocate for me. She wanted the kid who was the instigator of the pants-pulling incident suspended, but the school principal wouldn't do it. So my mother talked to the other boy's mother instead. She addressed the issue with the boy's parents, as she had done a few times before with other kids' parents. At least nobody ever pulled my pants down again, but I can't say all the teasing stopped.

There was the embarrassing gym class situation, in which kids were taking my clothes and throwing them above the locker. We addressed this problem by asking the gym teacher to allow me to change before everyone else, both before class when we were getting into gym clothes, and after class, when we were changing back, so that no one could bother me. The teacher agreed, and with that, another problem was solved.

Not everything ended badly. I remember uplifting things from my childhood, too. When I was in the third grade, I had a surgery at Children's Hospital in Silver Springs, Maryland. It was there that I met someone who changed my life. Her name was Lori and she was a patient there.

Dr. Kopits had temporarily moved his practice to Children's Hospital while the new unit dedicated solely to skeletal dysplasia was being built for him at St. Joseph's Hospital in Towson. As I was cruising down the hallway of the hospital wing where I would be staying for my inpatient physical therapy, I came upon a room that said ISOLATION—DO NOT ENTER. There was plastic over the door and a doorbell outside the room on the wall. I didn't see anyone in there, so I kept going. On my way back, I saw a person sitting in a wheelchair inside the room. After I got her attention, she came to the door, exuberant, cheerful, and welcoming.

At the sight of her, I was more upset than frightened. She looked like a burn victim who had a slim chance of surviving the night. Her skin, taut and blotchy, was so tight that it pulled on her face. She had no eyelids, and her eyeballs protruded from her skull. She had no hair, barely any lips, teeth that were crowded behind each other due to a malformed jaw, no legs below the knee, and not much of a nose. Her arms were so thin that she wore a finger watch around her wrist. She looked as if she had a severe skin disorder or leprosy.

While the initial sight of her was shocking, we soon became great friends. Lori was quite a bit older than me, somewhere in her early twenties. She had been abandoned by her family when she was very young and had been a resident of that room and others like it for twenty years. But, despite that, she was the most upbeat, positive, inspiring person I have ever met.

Lori was a "lifer," someone who would stay in this kind of setting forever. Louis was another "lifer" on that wing, afflicted with cerebral palsy. For some reason, my most fond memory of Louis was that for Halloween, he dressed up as a Ghostbuster. He had the logo on the back of his power chair and was riding around the halls, squirting everyone with an IV bag of solution, with tubing and a cannula, which made for a perfect stream. The lifers were on the pediatric floor even though they were no longer adolescents, mostly because the care typically provided on pediatric floors and in pediatric hospitals is much more compassionate than that of an adult hospital. (And no, Jen didn't make me say that.)

Lori had a weakened immune system, which was why she had the plastic sheet over her door. It hung from the ceiling to the floor and created a positive pressure environment so air wouldn't go into the room, but only blow out. She had a very rare skin condition that lent itself to other complications, which was how she'd lost her legs just above the knees. I remember the freshly changed gauze wrapped around the amputation sites.

Besides the bell, Lori's door had a sign that described what you needed to do in order to enter the room. There were enormous precautions involved, from wearing a surgical mask to covering everything with fully sterilized gear. I would visit her multiple times a day.

Lori's room was set up with everything she needed. She had a microwave and a fridge. I, on the other hand, was on the quintessential hospital food diet, a scoop of green Jell-O with lima beans, green beans, or string beans bouncing around in the middle. How could you do that to patients, when everybody in here was already hurting and miserable?

Lori didn't seem to mind the hospital food as much as I did. She didn't worry about things like that. She smiled all the time, and she never complained. She was always upbeat, and she was always happy when she saw me. I could never understand how she could muster up such a positive attitude when she had so many things she could be miserable about. I have never met anybody like her.

I am proud to say I had a friendship with someone as incredible as Lori. I was so glad I didn't turn away from her because of what she looked like. Her attitude, the way she carried herself, and her personality far outweighed any physical detractions. That was the key to that relationship and why it was so influential in my life. I realized that personality and heart go a heck of a lot further than physical beauty. You have to wrap your brain around the idea that it takes time and openness to get past the physical barrier. Even now, when I might start to feel sorry for myself, I think of Lori and the wonderful courage she displayed. I know she didn't live much longer after I saw her for the final time, but meeting her was one of the greatest things that ever happened to me.

After I left the hospital, I had to heal at home for a few weeks. It was during this time that one of the kids in my third-grade class wrote a story about me and my positive impact on him and my other class-mates. The story was about a salamander, me personified via the sal-amander, and how the salamander had gone away and the things that had happened to him while he was gone. Through perseverance, the salamander was able to make it back home, to the great pleasure of his community. It was such a cool story. The kid who wrote it was a really good artist, too, so he even illustrated it. When I did come back to school, my schoolmates were super thrilled, maybe in part because of the salamander fable.

It was the first time I realized that I might have something spe-cial to offer because of the things I had been experiencing, and that my influence was greater than I had given myself credit for. With this in mind, I tried hard not to feel sorry for myself. Besides, I wasn't that type of person.

CHAPTER SEVEN

Jen

SUMMERS IN BALTIMORE

MOST SCHOOL-AGE KIDS REALLY look forward to summer vacation and those crazy lazy fun-filled days of July and August, but I often feared and dreaded the last day of the school year. That was because most of my surgeries were scheduled for the summer. As my classmates were gearing up for days at the shore or a week or two at summer camp, I was en route from Orlando to Maryland for orthopedic procedures and six to twelve weeks in either a leg or full-body cast, and then a return trip to Baltimore for more weeks of physical therapy. It wasn't uncommon for me to undergo several consecutive orthopedic corrective surgeries in one summer, because often so much reconstruction was needed that it would have been impossible or dangerous to attempt it in one surgery. My surgeries could last anywhere from six to twelve hours at a time.

My dysplasia was more complicated than most cases, so I had many more surgeries than many kids with other skeletal dysplasias.

By the time I was eighteen, I had had twenty-two surgeries, including one for the placement of thoracic scoliosis spinal rods in my back when I was fourteen and many osteotomies on my knees, hips, and ankles. My last "reconstructive" surgery was in college, and then I had a relatively calm period until I was twenty-eight and had hip replacements while I was doing my pediatric residency.

A huge chunk of my childhood was spent anticipating, undergoing, and recovering from surgery. We would make the decision to have surgery as early as five or six months before I would actually have it. I would see Dr. Kopits in January, and we would schedule a procedure for the summer. I can't recall how explicit Dr. Kopits was when he described what I could expect, but he knew not to tell me too much, for fear of making me more anxious than I already was. He had a warm, positive bedside manner that made everyone in the family feel comfortable that everything was going to go off without a hitch. As I got older, I just knew what was coming. It was kind of a no-brainer. My main concern was how many surgeries I would have, whether I was going to be in a body cast or a leg cast after surgery, and whether I would miss any school. I had my preference. "Please, just make it a leg cast," I'd plead, always pushing for the option that would at least keep me from being fully prone and plastered from head to toe for six to eight weeks.

The type of cast I got depended on the surgery. If Dr. Kopits was operating on my hips, I would end up in a full-body cast, known as a spica cast. I was more likely to have a leg cast when he operated on my knees and below, but even then he might put me in a body cast. I think he was worried that little kids liked to move around too much and we could inhibit the healing and potentially mess things up. Each surgery would involve breaking many bones, so stability and alignment during healing was critical. Dr. Kopits was a little old school and believed that the hip spica cast was more stable and better in the long run.

Being confined to a hip spica was not much fun. It was a plaster cast that went from right around my belly button all the way to my toes. My toes would be peeking out, and my legs would be spread apart with a bar, like a two-by-four, wrapped in plaster of Paris. It was a great tool for my parents to lift me, because it was actually plastered right into the cast and was very secure. There would be an oval cutout around my bum that was open from the front to the back so I could pass urine and have bowel movements.

When I was really young and in and out of body casts all the time, Donna, my primary nurse, loved to joke around with me about the "taping of the buns." This was a "ritual" a few days after surgery. She'd come into my hospital room after my surgery, hold up a roll of pink tape, and announce the inevitable. The pink tape was a waterproof tape that the nurses would have to mold around the opening in the cast to protect it from getting wet. Things weren't as high-tech back then, so "waterproofing" was literally putting one strip of pink tape at a time all the way around the entire border of the cast's "bathroom" cutout. This way, if you soiled, it wouldn't actually soak into the plaster of Paris and smell and stink and stay wet for the next six to eight weeks. The tape could even be changed, if necessary, without having to do anything to the cast.

Donna was my super-heroine, my super-nurse. All the primary nurses had huge roles in a patient's post-op and recovery regimen. They worked closely with Dr. Kopits in terms of care plans, from medication issues to meals to morning baths and hygiene. Even though they were charged with more than one patient on the floor at a time, they were as close to a private nurse as you could get. Donna, my second mother, seemed to be with me every waking hour.

Surgery in general was rough for me. I was always scared, but I would try not to think about it too much. Each spring when I had a surgery planned for the summer, I would begin my ritual of counting down the weeks before the big trip to Baltimore: "Oh, my surgery is only twelve weeks away. . . . Oh, it is only three weeks away." I knew it was coming, but by counting I felt I was in more control than if I completely ignored it.

My mom was a straight-shooter, a no-nonsense person. "Everything is going to be okay, and we've got to do it," she'd say to me without an abundance of emotion. Of course, I knew it had to be hard for her watching me being rolled toward the operating room surrounded by a surgical team on a gurney. She tried to hide her fear, especially from me. But, during my eight- to ten-hour surgeries, she would pace in the waiting area, desperate for word on my status. Sometimes my dad was with her, other times one of my aunts. Probably too many times, she was alone during these summers of surgery. My parents knew that skipping these surgeries and opting for a more conservative treatment approach was not an option. They had met children who had not had any orthopedic care, and most of them had debilitating complications from their skeletal dysplasias, sometimes resulting in shortening their life span. For example, their scoliosis might be so bad they would be unable to walk, eat, or even breathe on their own because their distorted skeletons put too much pressure on their lungs and diaphragms. My parents knew they were incredibly lucky to have found Dr. Kopits and his team. Before every surgery, right before anesthesia, he would try to comfort my mom and at the same time distract me with silly jokes. As I became older, I came to notice how on the morning of surgery, he was not only the compassionate and dedicated surgeon I had grown to know, but also a serious surgeon with his "game face" on.

As I got older, even Dr. Kopits's reassurances could not stop me from panicking. Starting around middle school, I could become paralyzed with fear at what might happen. "Oh, my goodness," I'd say to myself, "this might be the end. This might be the time I don't make it. How many surgeries can one person have and still come out okay every time?" I would be lying on the operating table as they were giving me anesthesia, desperately trying to be positive. *Okay, just try to imagine yourself* . . . and I would think of milestones in my life I wanted to achieve, then even bigger milestones. *Can I imagine myself graduating from high school? Can I imagine myself graduating from college? Can I imagine myself getting married? Can I imagine myself being a mom?* When I couldn't imagine, really visualize any of my fantasies, I would think, *Well, that is because I am going to die, because I am never going to experience it.* It sounds very morbid now, but that was what would consume me as I lay on the operating table, looking up at all the eyes above the surgical masks. Whenever I had trouble visualizing my future, that was my sign that this surgery was going to be my last. I couldn't tell my mom, though, because I was even more afraid that if I said it out loud, it really would happen. I knew she would say, "Don't be ridiculous," just to make me feel better, and that was not what I wanted to hear.

I still do this visualization routine even to this day, when something scary or big is happening. For example, when Bill had his first surgery after we got married, I felt almost too lucky to have found this love of my life. When he had surgery, I would force myself to visualize: *Okay, he is going to come out, he is going to be fine.* I would have to tell myself that over and over. I have gotten better about it as I have gotten older. Actually, I do this when I am on a plane and there is bad weather, because I hate to fly. I think to myself, *Okay, can I visualize myself landing and just calling Bill and saying I landed safe?* And sometimes I can and sometimes I can't. It's when I can't that I start to hyperventilate.

My parents, especially my mom, always tried to build me up right around the times of my surgeries. She would always try to plan something fun for me to look forward to either before we left for Baltimore or after we arrived. It could be a week at the beach with my aunt Barbara and uncle Jack in St. Petersburg, which I loved, or a big party for my school friends and me.

One year, she threw an amazing luau party, a full-on genuine luau in our backyard! My mom had started waitressing at the Polynesian Village Resort at Disney, and she knew all the staff, so she got everybody to come over and do a real Polynesian performance at my party. Basically we had a live Walt Disney World–quality luau show in my backyard. We had kids who weren't technically invited hanging off the fences trying to see the fire dancers, and I mean climbing up anything they could climb to get a view. There was a DJ running the music, and my mom brought in a huge grill to prepare the food. One of her girlfriends even made me an official luau skirt.

In the photos of me, my one leg is completely bent. That pre-op leg looks horrible to me now, but I was so thrilled showing off my luau skirt that I wasn't self-conscious. I see the pictures now and recall the greatest presurgery party any girl could wish for, thanks to my mother.

WHEN I WAS an only child, often both my parents accompanied me to Baltimore for surgery when they could, but after my brother David was born, typically just my mom and I made the trip, while my dad, Aunt Chrissy, and Grandma stayed home with him. My mother did not like to fly, especially after one particularly scary flight that had us flying through heavy turbulence in a thunderstorm. That was a flight to Baltimore after my cervical spinal fusion with my aunt Barbara. Aunt Barbara didn't get on another plane for over thirty years due to the trauma from that flight. Fortunately, I was too young to remember. Back in the 1970s, plane crashes were not as uncommon as they are today. Given her fear of flying, my mom and I would often drive to the Amtrak auto-train station in Sanford, Florida, not far from Orlando, where we'd check in the car and board the overnight train to Lorton, Virginia, right outside Washington, D.C. From there, we'd drive the couple of hours to Baltimore.

Once in Baltimore, my mother and I would try to have our traditional presurgery dinner with Dr. Kopits, which always made me feel as if I was as special as it got. It was almost as if there weren't anything inauspicious looming in my future. I was a person, not a patient. I think because I was one of Dr. Kopits's first patients with skeletal dysplasias, he and my mom became very close. We'd also try to get to a Maryland crab restaurant with Donna, my primary care nurse. Sometimes, Diane, Dr. Kopits's nurse practitioner, would join us for fun, too, and we'd spend hours laughing and catching up. Diane had also become a very close family friend. She was Dr. Kopits's right-hand woman, always keeping up with all his patients and helping us with the medical and social challenges we faced. To this day, I feel extraordinarily lucky to have had Diane, Donna, and Dr. Kopits as such close friends—basically family—in our lives.

Mom and I would stay a couple of nights in a hotel near the hospital. After my surgery, my mom always stayed with me on a cot in my hospital room, no matter how long my stay was. If my dad was with us, he typically stayed in a hotel somewhere nearby. There was a Ronald McDonald house nearby, which was available for the parents or families of patients, but my dad liked the hotel idea better, for both privacy and amenities. For one of my early surgeries, my dad stayed in Reed Hall, a dormitory on the Johns Hopkins Hospital campus, where I would later live my first year of medical school.

Post-op was probably the most miserable time, especially the first couple of days. I was so nauseated and sick due to the pain meds (opioids), which did not agree with me, that I would be vomiting for two to three days straight. They didn't even really take the pain away, they just took the edge off and sedated me some. My bones had just been surgically hacked apart, and every nerve in my skeletal system was complaining. Even post-op, I was at huge risk for blood clots, infection, or nerve damage, and some of those were life-threatening. More than fear of complications, though, I just hated the nausea and vomiting and never got used to it. I'd usually be in the hospital two to three weeks before I was able to be discharged home safely.

My mom and I got to know lots of other kids being treated for skeletal dysplasia by Dr. Kopits who were on this same kind of summer surgical schedule. We were all about the same age, and our skeletal problems usually manifested at the same time. There was Jenny, exactly my age and with the same first name. Jenny was from Idaho, had blond hair, and had SED like me. We both had a fracture that wouldn't heal in our humerus bones in the exact same spot. Dr. Kopits called us twins. Besides "growing up" with Jenny, I remember Martha, Mark, David, and Vincent by name, too. And then there was Benji, who was a little younger. He ended up being my first kiss many, many years later when I was in medical school. We all knew each other because we crossed paths and shared surgical journeys. The fun part after check-in for surgery was figuring out who else was going to be on the unit at the same time and how long they were going to stay. It was a two- or four-week summer session at Camp Why-Do-We-Have-to-Be-Here.

My post-op hospital stays varied in length and depended on what procedures I was undergoing. My mom was always pushing for me to be discharged ASAP, as she was missing work, my dad, and my brother. I have to admit that I was always relieved to be on my way home as well, even if I was still struggling with pain. Some of my buds would be gone already, some in the middle of their stay, and some just checking in, but I would see them soon enough, and I had paid my dues.

My mother and I would typically not take the auto train home. Instead, she would drive the seventeen hours back to Orlando on a route she had memorized, so that she knew exactly how long it was going to take us door-to-door. If I was in the body cast, I wouldn't be able to sit up, so I would have to lie down for the entire trip. My mom was a pro at positioning me in the back of the SUV, supine and safe. One year, she even agreed to transport our friend Donna's Weimaraner from Baltimore back to Florida with us, so I had to share my space with a seventy-five-pound hunting dog. Donna is an avid Weimaraner owner and breeder. My mom would stop at roadside rests to put me on the bedpan, and when she was done with me, she'd walk and water the dog. Crazy times!

Recovery time at home meant long periods of frustration and pain. I wouldn't be strong enough to turn or flip myself for several weeks, so I would just scream for someone to come and help me. I would cry out at least five times a night, because I would just be so uncomfortable and in so much pain, completely unable to help myself. Even if I wanted to go to the bathroom, I had to wake somebody up. The feeling of not being able to control your own destiny on a day-to-day basis was very trying as I got older.

When I was really young, I would sleep in my parents' room during these periods. They would put a mattress on the floor and cover it with padding, blankets, and pillows, and they could get to me right away. They were incredibly patient. They'd work around me and prop pillows in weird ways, and say, "Okay, let's try it on your back." The cast had my legs sticking straight up in the air, and I couldn't turn my neck because of the surgical fusion. I couldn't lie flat on my belly and turn my head, so I became very good at leaning, half turning my torso and trying to find a comfortable stretch for my neck. It was pretty hideous. There was basically not much my parents could do, but they tried. And fortunately, most nights they were patient. I know I am not always an easy patient to take care of.

When I was older and recovering in my own room, I had a TV to keep me from being bored out of my mind. It didn't always work. I'd be stir-crazy to get out of the house. "Take me to the movies, take me to the grocery store. Just get me out of the house!" I'd beg. Even if my request wasn't practical, I could not stand all those hours of being cooped up at home and found it incredibly depressing.

My parents tried to take me on outings occasionally, but it was a huge undertaking, with many complicated details, especially if I was in a body cast. The more restrictive the cast, the harder it was. I remember going to the movies a couple of times, and my dad setting up the wheelchair on an angle in the aisle, so I could be on my back and still be able to see the film. Sometimes, I'd go with them to Home Depot or Costco if I were in just a leg cast. These days, I am not fond of going to Home Depot, but during those times, it might have been the highlight of my week.

Basically, I was pretty isolated during recovery time. I didn't get a lot of visits from my friends, but my mom's or Aunt Chrissy's friends would come by the house to say hi. They'd try to do things for me to make me feel "normal," to keep me feeling like I mattered. That I was in a body cast didn't mean I couldn't have a haircut or perm if

I wanted. Back then, perms were pretty popular, so my mom's friends would help my mother cut and perm my hair on the kitchen table and sink.

Sometimes, I would still be home recovering when school started again in the fall. My teachers would send get-well notes and cards, and my mother would always figure out a way for me to see my classmates, whether she took me to school for a visit or she invited all the kids to come to me, and I would have everybody sign my cast. Then I'd look at the signatures over the next few weeks and be very grateful I had friends, which I'd lose sight of in some of the longer periods of isolation. My schoolwork and assignments were sent home for me to complete and return, and tutors came to the house to provide home instruction.

When I was older and more stressed from the workload of school, I started to like these "down times" more than I had previously. I still had schoolwork, homework assignments, and people visiting, but now I almost liked my time to check out from the world. I could watch TV whenever I wanted. I'd stay up late, and sleep in. I don't want to make it sound as if it was a walk in the park or fun, because I was still completely dependent on others, unable to get comfortable because my legs were in a cast in a hot and humid Florida summer, and I was in a constant state of sweat, pain, and itchiness. But I was finally learning to appreciate my time to not have to stress about anything. I had no choice but to chill, and I tried to like it and accept it in a positive way.

My recoveries at home became more complicated when my parents got divorced. I was thirteen and David was six when we first learned that they were separating. My mom told us it had nothing to do with us kids. They had married young, had had kids right away, and now they were thinking their time together had run its course. But it was rough on all of us.

My parents agreed on joint custody, which had David and me going back and forth on weekends. My father insisted we stick to the schedule even when I was home and recovering from surgery. Having to change houses in that condition was difficult and upsetting. To complicate matters, not long after the divorce, my father got remarried to his longtime secretary, so I had to stay with them and all of her cats! Life was crazy during the divorce years.

Things at home had been changing, too, and although I was aware of what was going on, I felt more distant from these changes. More than ever, I immersed myself, both academically and socially, in college life. No sooner had I settled myself somewhere else than my parents announced that they were getting back together after years of separation and divorce. Both of my parents had moved on and had been seeing other people. My father had been with a new wife, Susy, and Mom had been engaged to one of her high school boyfriends from the distant past, Matt. I had gotten to know both Susy and Matt well over the years and had accepted their relationships with my parents. In fact, for the most part I was just happy if they were happy. No more fighting was welcomed in my world. However, my father had recently been diagnosed with bladder cancer, which had caused them both to have an "epiphany moment." They had come to the realization that they had made a mistake in divorcing.

As I was immersed in my academics, I am not clear on all the details of their reunion. As I remember it, I came home for summer vacation and they announced they were getting back together. My parents were trying to make it work.

For my younger brother, who was still in high school during all this, this was a dream come true. He had been so young during the divorce that it had been very hard for him. However, I don't think he remembered as well as I did the tough times that we all had gone through. When I heard the news that my parents were getting back together, I was concerned that they would still not be happy. The years surrounding the divorce were very tough, with quite a bit of drama. I didn't want that to happen again. Of course, if my parents were going to be happy together again, then great, so be it! All I wanted to do was keep focused on school and hope for the best for them. Amazingly, my parents have been back together ever since.

The surgeries and recoveries were long and lingering, but getting my cast off was the best thing that could happen to a girl. There was the seventeen-hour drive back to Baltimore, as I still wasn't auto train material, but this time I would look forward to the haul. I'd have to spend another three to four weeks in the hospital for intensive physical therapy, but that was doable after what I had just been through. First, I'd have to get a fresh pair of sneakers, something Dr. Kopits required, and something I looked forward to. A new pair of sneakers meant a day pass to leave the hospital to shop after my cast was removed so I could try on shoes! Day passes were the best, and my mother always made the time away from the hospital fun. Sometimes, she would even sign out another kid my age to join us for lunch and a few hours of people-watching down by Baltimore's inner harbor.

Dr. Kopits's rule that we have fresh sneakers to begin our recovery made sense. By habit, people walk with a gait without really giving it much thought, so if you are someone who drags your feet or walks more on the inside of your feet, you would wear out the backs of your shoes more quickly, whereas others might wear out the toe or outside edge. An old pair of sneakers would already carry the mark of a potential bad habit, which could adversely affect the gait going forward. Any excuse to buy a new pair of shoes was welcomed by me!

Essentially, after each surgery during physical therapy, I would have to learn how to walk again. Having been immobilized and in a cast for so long, I was always stiff, and even the slightest movement was difficult and often excruciating. If I had been in a full-body cast, it could take a week of physical therapy just to get to the point where I could sit up completely. The first day, I would just be starting to sit up, just getting cut out and propped at an angle in the whirlpool tub to get rid of as much dead skin debris as possible. The first thing I did after getting my cast removed was go directly to the whirlpool. It was heaven! Not only had I not had a real bath in six to twelve weeks or more, but my skin was so sensitive from lack of contact that just touching my legs felt like a full-body massage. The second day, I would be in the whirlpool again, maybe this time with a little bit of bending of the knee. Everyone was required to do physical therapy twice a day, morning and afternoon, every day of the week. The goal was to regain my range of motion and build up all my muscles, which had atrophied to the point that I lost most of my strength while I was in my cast.

I would start off doing the harder part of physical therapy right from my hospital bed, the first-level leg exercises to build my abductors, quads, hamstrings, and calf muscles. After a few days, I would graduate to the designated physical therapy unit on the first floor, which had two evaluation rooms, a line of fully cushioned therapy tables, and exercise equipment—everything from exercise steps, to parallel bars, to stationary bicycles, to a wall of resistance stretch bands and weights. There were also several whirlpool tubs for warming up our tense muscles before we started. As you progressed, you would get to start afternoon pool time—walking for the first time in the water, where you were weightless.

I preferred my afternoon sessions to my morning sessions, because the afternoon included time in the shallow, heated, glass-enclosed pool. In the pool, I was weightless, and even though I was working out against my own body weight, I could move around much more freely and without the pain I experienced when exercising on land.

Dr. Kopits wouldn't discharge me until I could walk confidently on crutches, go up and down a flight of steps with crutches, and master typical daily living activities such as putting on my socks and shoes, taking a shower, going to the bathroom, and tending to my personal hygiene.

Eventually, he would give me clearance to return to my normal life. Typically, I would go back home using my crutches for about two to four more weeks until I had forced or willed my way off them.

Whether or not school had already started, after we returned from Baltimore my mom and I would hit the malls, trying to find clothes for the new school year. It was a challenge to find clothes that would fit me that were stylish and not juvenile or babyish. We could be at several malls all day and still come up empty, but we would head out the next day to keep our mission going. My mom was an absolute hero on these expeditions. She knew how frustrating this was for me, trying to be fashionable with my unusual body, and she never tried to hurry me along or talk me into getting something that wasn't a really good choice. I loved how generous she was with her time with me during our shop-till-you-drop outings. We'd find a nice place to have lunch halfway through the day, discuss items I needed to fill my wardrobe, and figure out a way to efficiently travel to the stores where I usually had the most success. It was almost like a true treasure hunt to find exactly what I wanted and needed.

Finding Gap Kids sometime around the age of thirteen changed my world! All my classmates shopped at the Gap, but their clothing was too big for me. Gap Kids had the same styles, only in smaller sizes. On my first visit there, I got a pair of white khaki pants, a white button-down shirt, and a yellow sweater. At thirteen, I had just become the clothes connoisseur I still am today. When we found something that worked, my mother would learn to buy it for me in every color. Button-down shirts were the kicker, especially once I got a chest. Sadly, there is still not a Gap Kids shirt out there that can accommodate a pair of boobs!

Who knows if it was the many trips for new sneakers after surgery or just an innate love of fashion, but I am probably most fond of shopping for footwear. Shoes, of course, have also been the most difficult part of my wardrobe to fit. For much of my childhood, I had to wear lifts in my shoes to keep my legs equal in length and maintain proper alignment of my hips and spine. If I bought a new pair of shoes, I couldn't wear them right away, because I had to have the lifts put in. I also had to wear heel cups, because my ankles were so flat, and they curved out where they should have curved in. Over the years, Dr. Kopits had tried experimental surgeries on my feet, and I now have an arch on one side. Sadly, we never got to the other foot. But all that was okay. After all I had just been through, I didn't mind a little lift in my shoes and a kick in my step!

CHAPTER EIGHT

Bill

I WILL MARRY HER SOMEDAY

WHEN I WAS TEN, I met Jen for the first time. I had had a single leg osteotomy a couple of months before and I was in a partial hip spica cast, which meant that on the leg that was operated on, the cast went all the way down to my toes, and on the other leg the cast went down to my knee to aid in immobilization. The cast still went up to my rib cage, with a space cut out for bathroom purposes. I had to be immobile and lying down for three months, but unlike many of my prior surgeries, this time I had one knee that I could move around a bit more and scratch without the aid of a hanger.

The hip spica cast was incredibly uncomfortable, and I was incessantly itchy and miserable. It was hard to sleep, but I'd try to be on my side, with one leg up against the wall, and then on my stomach, and eventually on my back once more.

I went back to Baltimore to be liberated from the cast. That was an experience in itself, riding in the back of the dark metallic blue '78

Oldsmobile Cutlass Supreme in a full-body cast. We had a couple of station wagons when I was growing up. I'd lie down in the back on a crib mattress because I had to be flat. The mattress, which had a bed sheet and a fuzzy blanket, was placed on top of the rear seats, which folded flat.

There I'd be, lying on a crib mattress in the rear of the station wagon with no seat belt, a forty-pound kid in a fifty-pound lump of plaster going seventy-five miles an hour down the turnpike for the five-hour drive. I'd have my bologna and American cheese sandwich, a ginger ale, and my portable urinal in case I needed relief.

I wasn't always on my back in the car. I'd rotate between my back and stomach, like a small chicken on a rotisserie, but it was something I had to do to avoid pressure sores. The roof of the car wasn't very high, so once in a while I would whack my cast during my rotation. In a hip spica cast, your legs are spread out as far as they can go, and then you have a piece of two-by-four wood that is plastered into the cast that keeps you locked in a big triangle, like a big Y. It provided structure to the cast and also served as a way to help lift me when needed. To rotate, what you normally did was some sort of slick "slide" maneuver, kind of like flipping an egg over easy when you didn't want to break the yolk, a really quick "flip." The further out from surgery I was, the easier moving around on my own became. After a while almost anything was possible, from flipping over to getting in and out of the fully reclined wheelchair to get around the house.

Trips to Baltimore to get the casts off were infinitely better than going in for surgeries. Getting out of the cast wasn't that complicated. The doctor uses a cast saw, which looks like something in a carpenter's toolbox, a small circular saw with a vacuum attachment to catch the plaster dust. Although it makes an enormous amount of noise and can be very frightening, the blade works by vibration, not rotation. When it is put against the hard plaster surface of the cast, it vibrates through the material. However, it can't cut the soft tissue underneath, because even if it does touch the skin, it stops vibrating because there isn't enough resistance. The worst it can do is give you a minor burn.

There is one particular cast removal story I am fond of. I had gone to the hospital after a long stint being in the cast at home to finally have the cast removed and begin rehab. The cast removal room was basically an exam room with a table and a cast saw mounted to the wall and a very large trash receptacle for the cast material. I was wheeled into the room and put on the table, disrobed, and the doctor had begun cutting when a girl about my age suddenly (and without an invitation) entered the room. Her name was Wanda. I had met Wanda a couple of times before, so we had a level of familiarity and comfort with each other. She had been in the hospital for a few weeks for rehab. She was a huge fan of Kenny Rogers and had a major crush on Dr. Kopits. She barged into the room to serenade him with her karaoke-style rendition of a Kenny Rogers song—and didn't care that I was in the room or what clothes I might or might not have been wearing! I quickly covered my privates with my folded gym shorts and turned a few shades of red.

Wanda's impromptu concerts aside, it was always great being cut out of the cast. It was cold at first. My legs would be hairier than ever, thanks to the humid and still environment inside a cast. They would be stinky and pale in color, skinny and itchy. Almost immediately after being cut from my shell, I would get placed in a whirlpool bath set at a balmy one hundred plus degrees. There, I'd watch my dry skin flakes float around on top of the water and do my best to begin moving again. It was relief, grossness, and progress all at once.

I knew the best way for me to handle these surgeries was to try to make parts of it fun. If I didn't know all the patients on the unit already, after a couple of days I certainly would. And as I grew up, my interest in the opposite sex grew as well. Two North was a great place to be if you were a Little Person with a growing interest in flirting with members of the opposite sex, too. In fact, it was one of the only places on the planet that teenagers who were short in stature would be congregating in the same place and dealing with similar circumstances. One of my first teenage crushes was on a girl named Nicky. She was the same age as me, hailed from the West Coast, was cute and funny, and laughed at all of my jokes.

But Nicky wasn't the only girl in Two North. There was also a girl named Jen I was about to meet. She had just had a surgery—for what exactly, I didn't know. Dr. Kopits was so amazing that each of his patients received a uniquely tailored operation designed specifically for him or her. He had personally trained all of his staff—his nursing staff, nurse practitioners, anesthesiologists, everybody who worked with him—on how to work with his patients. The level of complexity and sheer necessary trauma to our bodies was so extensive that it demanded everyone's best efforts every day they came to work.

Anyway, Jen was in a private room in the haze of post-op medication. I, on the other hand, was feeling great. I was out of my shell, sitting up and riding around in my wheelchair, humming along with tunes I was playing on my Sony Walkman and feeling the freedom. The wheelchairs on Two North served patients that were in hip spica casts as well as those who were in the hospital for rehab and able to sit up. The wheelchairs had no arms and could shift from upright to nearly flat with just a couple of twists.

When you are finally free from a spica cast, you feel great. You want to talk to everyone, flirt with everyone, laugh, and play. When I rolled into Jen's room, I didn't realize she was in such pain. It was totally customary to pull into other people's rooms and say, "Hey," but Jennifer was miserable. She angrily grumbled something, and I can only presume that her mom or one of the nurses told me to leave. So, I did an about-face and went into the next room to the next victim of my joy. I don't remember seeing Jen again during that trip.

FAST-FORWARD TO THE eighth grade, where girls were on my radar. I wasn't sure they liked boys on crutches, and I certainly didn't like being on crutches either. However, the year before I had had surgery that had not gone exactly as planned. Surgeries were always risky, but I was always willing to try. After the surgery, I went to intense out-patient physical therapy two or three times a week. I was supposed to wean myself off the crutches. My physical therapist encouraged me to go at my own pace, but I often depended on my parents to encourage me and stay on top of my rehabilitation, particularly the exercises I had to do at home between visits to the outpatient PT department at the local hospital in Port Jefferson. This time around, my dad implored me to try walking without the crutches I had been leaning on since being liberated from my plaster prison. At first, the idea of walking without the crutches seemed to work. I was walking without any aids and, while it hurt to do so, I was beginning to see progress.

Right around then, my mother's friend and our former babysitter Audrey offered us the use of her motor home at a campground she owned, and my mother, two brothers, and I took up residence for a long weekend getaway. I wasn't really happy we were going, but because Mom wanted to do it for my brothers, we went.

Always resourceful and ready for action, I asked Audrey if I could work at the campground's general store. I would do just about anything to make the time pass. And making a few bucks in the process didn't hurt either. Audrey loved the idea. She gave me a job where I did anything needed. I helped customers—sold the bug spray, citronella candles, and propane—and lifted everything, carrying bags of ice and moving stuff around. We returned home on a Sunday and on the very next morning when I woke, I couldn't walk.

One of my hip joints had filled with synovial fluid, much like "water on the knee" but on the hip. Basically, my hip's synovial fluid, which typically helped cushion it, had built up and inflamed the area to the point where my hip literally was pushed out of its socket. However, I bit my lip and thought I'd just grin and bear the pain, even though I couldn't move.

"What happened?" my mom asked from the top of the stairs. "What did you do?" I hadn't done anything. I just couldn't walk without writhing in pain.

"Well, if you can't walk, that is obviously a problem," she scolded. "We have to get you down to Baltimore."

So she made a phone call, and the next day we hopped into the car for the trip to Dr. Kopits's office. There, he did an arthrogram, which was like a moving X-ray, where they stick needles in your leg in order to fill the space around your joints with dye to show the contrast between the bones and soft tissues. Once the dye is in place, the doctor could visualize the joint movement and see where the problems were.

It was very painful, because Dr. Kopits did it when I was awake. In fact, it was a nightmare, as I was already in so much pain. Here he was, sticking six- to eight-inch-long needles into my leg, then injecting dye into it, and then manipulating it. At one point, I flexed my quad muscle so tightly that I bent the needle while it was in my leg. But it had to be done, so we both persevered. Dr. Kopits attempted to drain the fluid he found in my hip while performing the arthrogram.

He was able to remove nearly three cups of synovial fluid before he stopped, as my screaming necessitated the procedure's end. He resumed the next day, when I was under anesthesia.

After the procedure, I landed in a hospital bed on thirty days non-weight-bearing bed rest. The timing couldn't have been worse. The eighth-grade dance was coming up, and I was stuck in the hospital. I had even gotten a date and gone in on a limousine with my stepbrother and another friend, Glen. I had paid for the tux, the corsage, and my portion of the stretch limo with money I had been saving from mowing lawns. So, now, I lost the money, I didn't get to go on the date, and my stepbrother and friend got to use the limo for the four of them instead of the six of us.

Well, realistically, my "date" was kind of a stretch. There had been a girl I wanted to take. She was a cute, petite little seventh grader. I had asked her to go to the dance with me over the phone, and she had said yes, but that she would have to talk to her mom. When she laid down the receiver, I could hear her mother saying, "That is not that short boy, is it?" Her mom quashed it because of my size. The feeling I got hearing that reminded me of my first "girlfriend," who kept our relationship for nearly three periods of school before the peer pressure related to being associated with me got to her and she broke up with me. Of course, I shouldn't make too much of it. After all, in middle school, having a girlfriend meant having a crush on someone and asking her to be your girlfriend, maybe obligating her to go to a dance with you, but nothing more.

Now the girl I had asked out hadn't rejected me, but her mother had. I ended up inviting Doreen, a Little Person I had met through Little People of America who was a few years older than me and lived in Selden, a couple of towns over. Doreen had said yes, but I knew she was doing me a favor. I didn't think she really liked me. She was one of the first people I had a crush on who was a Little Person. She was in eleventh grade and I was in eighth grade, so being with her at the dance would have been a little awkward for her anyway.

But going to the dance was not going to happen. I had to be 100 percent non-weight-bearing—I couldn't stand up, I couldn't get off the bed, I couldn't go to the toilet, I couldn't look out the window, and I couldn't go home. All I could do was lie in my hospital bed, 250 miles away from my family and friends. As if that weren't bad enough, the little bums, aka my friends, called me from the limo on the night of the dance to gloat. "Wish you were here," they yelled into the phone.

I HAD NO friends and no family in Baltimore, and I was miserable. I completed all of my homework for the remainder of the year, watched a lot of movies, and sulked. I was so frustrated with my circumstances that I took out my frustration on one of the nurses taking care of me. I yelled at her and smacked my backscratcher against the bedrail. For that, she took away the A/V cart, raised my bed to an extreme height and unplugged it from the wall, turned off the lights in the room, pulled the curtain, and closed the door. It was a horrible feeling. Everything was totally out of control, I had no recourse, and I had nobody to tell. It just couldn't get worse.

My hip never did get better. It would not be coaxed back into the socket, and for the next two years I was on crutches. By the time I got to tenth grade, both hips were in need of surgical repair. My right hip had become dislocated and the left was partially dislocated.

So, when I was fifteen years old, Dr. Kopits recommended we try a tricky reconstructive surgery called the Durke procedure. The goal is to reshape the femoral head and the socket of both hip joints. Very invasive, very painful, and a very long surgery—also very often unsuccessful. But it was used as a last-ditch effort to avoid early adulthood hip replacements on both my hips. These bilateral hip reconstructions were huge surgeries, ten to twelve hours each. I had to be fitted for a "bean bag," a kind of orthopedic prop to help keep you in one place without pressure sores developing while they are leaning on you and cutting open your leg. So there was lots of preparation, four or five weeks in the hospital, a full spica cast, then ten to twelve weeks in the cast, and another ten to twelve weeks' worth of rehab after that.

The ten or twelve weeks in the body cast were at home. My house had two stories, and all the bedrooms were on the second floor. Mom always set up my hospital bed in the living room, which was generally off-limits to kids. It was saved for holidays and special occasions such as Christmas and times we had company at the house. Other than that, we weren't given full access, so being able to sleep in there was kind of a treat. We had a den adjacent to the living room, which was where the TV and couches were and where the family hung out. So I wasn't really encroaching on anybody's normal living space, and my mom could conveniently slide the entire hospital bed behind the wall if she wanted me to go to bed.

As I got older, I figured out a way to just pull the whole bed with me in it back to the den, so Mom gave up after a while. If I wanted to watch TV until one o'clock in the morning, there wasn't much she could do to stop me.

I spent most of my recuperation period in the hospital bed. I had a triangle that I could pull myself up with, and I had a hospital tray to keep my high-in-demand sundry items such as multiple issues of *Mad Libs*, my urinal, a box of tissues, and my CB radio. I would do most things on my stomach, such as eat, do homework, play video games, and talk on the CB. I washed my hair in bed by using a large plastic bag, like a garbage bag, and leaning a little bit out from the mattress. I did get out of bed daily. We had a reclining wheelchair that allowed me access to the other rooms on the first floor. Navigating through the narrow thresholds between rooms was always a trick.

I even performed my frog dissection at home, in my cast. Mr. Berry, my tenth-grade biology teacher, had brought the frog to my house, along with the wax-filled tray, pins and flags, a scalpel, and a pair of scissors. We kept the frog in the fridge overnight so I could complete the task the following day. Needless to say, Mom was not happy with Mr. Berry or me. Eventually my cast would come off and life would return to "normal." As you might imagine, Mom was as anxious as I was for me to complete my stint at home and start my therapy—but most of all, to stop dissecting amphibians and leaving them in the fridge!

CHAPTER NINE

Jen

NO DATE FOR THE DANCE

THE HARDEST TIMES FOR me growing up as a Little Person were during my coming-of-age years, those interminable teenage years that few of us remember fondly. These were the years when it seemed very important to fit in, be included in the big social events, and of course *date a little*. It was difficult never having a date to the middle and high school dances. I still went as part of a larger group of friends, and that was fine, but when the slow songs came on, I'd end up sitting along the side of the gym. I usually tried to find someone else who was also on the sidelines to talk with, but with the loud music and height discrepancies, that wasn't always easy. Over time, I realized there were other ways to enjoy attending dances and social functions without a date—be the party planner! So I became active in student government. Because I was the class vice president or secretary and in charge of planning the prom or fall dance, I *had* to go, date or no date. When the slow songs came on, there was usually a "job" to do: check on food, the DJ, or decorations.

I remember coming home after one high school dance and crying profusely, having been the only girl there who didn't have a date. I went into my parents' room and collapsed onto their bed. "I am *never* going to get a boyfriend, and *no one* is ever going to kiss me!" I ranted in despair.

"What are you crying about?" my mother demanded in a "why are you feeling sorry for yourself?" tone. "You are so lucky, and you have so many wonderful friends. There is so much going on for you that is good, and sitting here sulking is a huge waste of time."

My mom was always tough, mostly in a supportive way. It seemed her way of dealing with my teenage angst was with tough love, which she hoped would translate into thick skin. "Stop having a pity party!" she'd say, almost making me feel bad about feeling sad. Even though I knew that was just her way of trying to deal with my emotional pain, it could sometimes be hard because at that time, that moment, all I wanted was just one night to sulk. But my mom would list all the things I had to be thankful for: my health, my academics, my friends. Just because I couldn't get a date to the dance, it was not the end of the world. I should evaluate my priorities and get perspective, and I shouldn't really cry over something as unimportant as a date to a dance. "You have plenty of time for that," she'd reason. "You don't need to worry about that now."

I am sure it was really hard for her to see me feeling rejected or sad, so she tried to encourage me to be very tough. Being stoic was actually her way of supporting me. Both my parents always pushed me to not let my size get in the way of anything I wanted. My mom has always told me, "Jennifer, you can do absolutely anything you want." She truly believed it, and because she did, I did, too. It didn't mean I didn't have my fair share of good cries alone at night. Fortunately, in the light of day, things always looked brighter.

AT SCHOOL, I didn't let my short stature stop me from becoming a member of the cheerleading squad in the seventh grade. I even found the nerve to try out for the freshman squad when I moved from St. Charles to Bishop Moore High School in ninth grade. To this day, I still can't believe I made it, although I think they had a "no cut" policy and anyone who tried out made it. The following year, the whole cheerleading thing was becoming less pep club and more competitive sport, and I had found new interests, such as student government, so I didn't try out again. I didn't think I was cut out for something that was too hard physically. I stayed active doing other things instead.

Although there were a handful of kids who switched to public school going into high school, most of the kids from St. Charles went to Bishop Moore High, the only Catholic high school in Orlando. It had quite a few students, as all the parochial schools in the area fed into it. Luckily, it was actually located on the St. Charles property, so I didn't have to travel any farther than I already did. It was beside a lake, and we had mass under the pines there every Friday. It was truly a beautiful campus.

I was never really in the popular crowd, but of course everyone knew who I was. I did have a great group of friends. Some of them were the more studious type, like me, and others more eclectic individuals who were not afraid to be their own person. I was quite friendly with everyone. I was someone who could hang in different circles if I needed to. I liked it like that. I could be as involved or uninvolved as I wanted. I wasn't interested in drinking and all that other stuff so many teenagers dabble in. I never tried a single drug, and my first sip of beer wasn't until college. I was a "good girl" in high school. I was fortunate in that nobody would bully me for being a goody-goody.

At Bishop Moore, I got involved in lots of extracurricular activities, including meetings of our Christian community service association and other clubs and organizations, that took place after school. I have always been a bit of a social butterfly and loved going out. Being involved in all these activities gave me an excuse to be social and have fun with friends.

Although procuring dates for functions within my school didn't often work out, I did have a date for one dance in middle school, arranged in part by my parents. After my "no date ever" breakdown, my mom had introduced me to another young man my age with SED from our Central Florida Chapter of Little People of America (LPA). Years earlier, my parents and I had been involved with the local chapter. Usually, these gatherings had been social get-togethers like a potluck dinner at someone's home or outings around town. Sometimes, we'd play mini golf. However, as I got busier with school and with my summers of surgery, our participation in LPA had become less and less frequent.

Now that I wanted to have a "date," I was willing to become involved in LPA again. It seemed to be a pretty common theme within LPA that young people got reinvolved or involved for the first time when the goal was to find a date or mate. I ended up going on a blind date with a boy named Norberto, who was about my age and lived about an hour and a half south of us. Even though his name was Norberto, everybody called him Alberto, except for my grandmother, who called him Alfredo. His parents drove him to Orlando, and we went on a real date, first to dinner at McDonald's and then to a movie, *The Naked Gun*. Okay, before judging, McDonald's may not be the most romantic spot for a first date, but we were only thirteen and accompanied by my dad. We had such a nice time that I then invited him to go with me to the homecoming dance, which he accepted. I wore a black and white party dress for the occasion. At the end of the night, he gave me a peck on the cheek. He was cute, nice, and well-mannered, but his undoing was giving me a piece of jewelry etched with the insignia of the Playboy Bunny. That was the end of that.

Bishop Moore High School, like St. Charles and the other parochial schools, didn't have the resources that the public schools in Orlando did. The popular public high school had its own theater, a marine sciences department with all the latest technology, and a connection with NASA, so students could take really exciting electives. My school offered just the basics, but it did do the basics really well.

We didn't have air-conditioning or an elevator, either. Even with the Americans with Disabilities Act, which passed halfway through my time in high school, this was a private school, so it didn't have to be in full compliance. The school was only two stories, but there were lots of steps, even on one level. Because steps were so difficult and taxing on my legs, someone would often carry me up the stairs between classes. Usually, it was one of our younger teachers or my good friend Chetna. She was a petite girl herself, so it was amazing that she could even lift me up.

Academically, Bishop Moore was very intense. In ninth grade, I pulled my first "all nighter" with Chetna studying for Mrs. Thanski's world history final—an all-essay exam. I studied my butt off all four years, taking four AP classes in my senior year. That was the year I got my only C, which was in AP calculus. Our teacher, Miss Brown, would say, "If you don't get it, you don't get it." Eighty percent of the class got a D on the midterm. Even with my disappointing final grade, I still got a four on the nationwide AP exam, allowing me to get college credit for that course. By the time I got to college, I had enough AP credits to be almost a full year ahead.

In my junior year, I started looking at colleges. I always knew I was college-bound, but I had to choose a school that would be the right fit for me. I really wanted to go out of state, but my parents preferred that I stay close. I really liked Johns Hopkins, especially as I thought I'd end up in the sciences and was familiar with it, having been a patient there all those years. For most of my childhood, I had loved marine science and wanted to be the next Jacques Cousteau. When I was eleven, I was so obsessed that for my birthday my family redecorated my bedroom in an underwater theme, with pictures of sea life on the walls, statues of manatees and stuffed dolphins and whales on the shelves and surfaces, and a marine-themed Ken Done comforter and matching sheet set on my bed.

My mother, though, was not a fan of the idea of my becoming a marine biologist. "I'm afraid you would be shark bait," she joked. I think she truly feared my being eaten by a shark or a whale. Of course, she also knew that although I loved the water, I was never successful at truly learning how to swim with my head above water. She was happy when I started seriously considering the University of Miami, not because it had a great reputation for marine science, but because at least it was in the same state. Aside from her fears for my safety on a *Calypso*-like boat and the physical demands of being a marine biologist, she also worried I wouldn't be able to support myself, because there is not a lot of money in that field. My parents wanted me to become a geneticist or get a PhD, something where I would be using my brain and not my body. I think because my mom spent so much of her work life waitressing, a physically demanding job, she never wanted a similar future for me, given my physical limitations.

In the end, I did choose the University of Miami. It had a great marine science program and gave me a substantial scholarship. Also, Chetna, my best friend, was going to be there, and we had agreed to be roommates, so I wouldn't have to start off with no friends. The beauty of having Chetna as my roommate was that she already knew the campus. She had spent her senior year at the University of Miami as part of a special dual study program that enabled her to earn credits as a high school senior and a college freshman at the same time. Technically, she was still a member of our senior class at Bishop Moore and took part in our end-of-year ceremonies, but she had already been at the University of Miami the year before.

High school graduation was a blast. All my relatives were there for me, including my mom, my dad, my brother David, my grandma, and Aunt Chrissy. The graduating class wore white caps and gowns for the ceremony. Needless to say, my gown needed alterations. We gave the company my measurements, and they basically took an average white gown and shortened the arms and the length, but didn't adjust the width, so it looked like a halter top for an angel. My grandmother wound up altering a new one for me, so I could receive my high school diploma looking dignified, in a gown that fit me. That was when I learned "custom ordering" did not necessarily mean *custom*.

Besides the ceremony for the entire senior class, there was a smaller celebration for everybody who graduated with honors. Both Chetna and I received honors and awards. In the middle of the festivities, I was floored with some really bad news. Chetna had just learned that she was not going to be at the University of Miami in the fall. This was devastating news for both of us! We were best friends and had supported each other through many challenging times in high school.

Now, I would have to start there without my best friend and a roommate. I was definitely disappointed for both of us, but I knew I could do it. I hadn't let anything hold me back yet.

CHAPTER TEN

Bill

BRaInS OVeR BRawn

THE PROPORTIONS OF A Little Person are often different from those of the regular population. Most Little People stand approximately four feet tall, with some taller or shorter than that. Our dimensions vary greatly. Some are more proportionate, some are stronger, some have joint laxity (or overly loose joints), some have arthritis, and some aren't able to walk due to the severity of their skeletal deformities. Depending on the type of dysplasia, other complications are part and parcel of the skeletal issues. For instance, with the type of dwarfism Jennifer and I have, a third of the people diagnosed will exhibit hearing or vision loss or both before adolescence. Another third will present with these issues before they are done growing (by approximately twenty-one years of age). And for the lucky one-third left, the statistical chances of congenital-related hearing or vision loss are greatly reduced.

When I was eight, I had a very slender build, thirty-six inches tall and thirty-six pounds. But when I hit puberty at ten or eleven, I went from petite to massive for someone with skeletal dysplasia. I only grew about ten inches between ages eight and fourteen, but I doubled in weight. By high school, I was eighty-eight pounds with a forty-inch chest, and I stood forty-six inches tall. I was like Popeye, with tremendous upper-body strength.

I was working out, so these numbers didn't happen by accident. My gym class consisted of working out in the weight room for forty-two minutes a day with the "special" gym teacher, Mr. Musso. If the line was short at lunch, I would eat my French bread pizza and I would go back down to the weight room to lift for twenty more minutes. After school, I would train with the high school football and wrestling teams. At my peak, I could bench a couple of hundred pounds in the gym. I didn't build my upper-body strength just to prove myself to my classmates. I needed it to get myself around. And, for the first time, I was able to excel in a sport. Actually, I was good at badminton, too, but that wasn't as competitive as weight lifting.

After that stint in the hospital in eighth grade where I was remanded to bed rest for thirty days, I didn't have the ability to walk without crutches for the next five or six years. And because of those years on crutches, my back and chest just became huge. And with that many years with crutches, I learned a trick or two. I could lift myself off the ground, using only the crutches to walk.

Meanwhile, my dramatic shift in proportions made finding clothes more of a problem. Casual clothes were okay. I wore mostly T-shirts, sweatshirts, turtlenecks, and jeans. In high school, my mom had a couple of suits made for me. I'd go and pick an adult-sized suit at Macy's, and the tailor would have it cut down. The tailoring would end up costing more than the suit, so a $150 suit would be $500 by the time the alterations were finished. That was the price you had to pay to look good.

I got along with most of my classmates in high school. I was friends with the smart kids because I was in a lot of enriched classes throughout high school. I got along with the jocks thanks to my time in the gym during and after school. I would pitch quarters with the burnouts while they smoked their cigarettes behind the school. I was also friends with the geeks, the class clowns, and the cool kids. And while I was able to easily navigate between different cliques, I never identified myself as part of any one of them. It appeared, to me at least, that everyone included my stature in their assessment of whether I was part of the group or just there for attendance. My personality was a bit more chameleon-like, but my stature made me different from everyone.

It is sadly ironic that as teens, and even as adults, we often try to find our own identities by desperately trying to be like others and accepted by others. When you think about it, most of us spend that critical time of development trying to blend in with everyone else, not realizing that what we really want, and what is really in our very nature, is to stand out from the crowd. The qualities and characteristics that distinguish us from everyone else are the qualities and characteristics we will often go to great lengths to minimize or suppress for fear of being stuck with the most deadly label of all—"different." Ferris took his "different" and ran with it, all the way to lip-synching the Beatles on a downtown Chicago parade float. I, like a lot of adolescents, tried to suppress and minimize my "different," because, to me, "different" meant I was unworthy.

My high school years were punctuated with good grades and lots of pranks and class clown behavior to garner attention. For instance, I had to ride the elevator to my courses on the second floor of the building, so my stepbrother and I may have sabotaged it a couple of times to get us out of class. There was also the time I locked the principal out of his office and took over the PA system. Of course, I got a day of detention for that. I was definitely a goofball.

The "goofball" part was mostly for attention. I enjoyed making people laugh, but in reality, I considered myself an outsider looking in. If I went to a party, it felt as if I was looking in from the window. Over time, my attitude changed, too. I wanted to attend for the sake of attendance, but I didn't want to be there, either. I probably tolerated the social awkwardness by overcompensating by drinking too much. I was lucky that I was funny, but I often wanted to be out of the party as quickly as possible, too. Like most kids, I drank in high school. Mom and Dad both knew about it, and they weren't very happy. They tried their best to punish me and thwart me at every turn, but sweet sixteen parties were conveniently held where parents weren't. I built up a tolerance to alcohol, but too often I would indulge in a foolish attempt to keep up with my friends or to escape from the party by overindulging and ending my party early.

Believe it or not, I got into my first bar when I was only twelve years old. The sign over the door said "No admittance under the age of 25," but I went in with a group of Little People after an LPA chapter meeting. These meetings were open to all ages, and they were not about recovery and AA, so if people wanted to go out for drinks or continue socializing afterward, they would. In fact, in my teen years, most of those in our chapter of LPA were of age and the whole point of the meeting was to decide where to go out for cocktails. My drink of choice was a bay breeze. Mostly juice, very little booze, but I just loved the fact that bartenders couldn't tell if I was over or under age twenty-five!

I started learning to drive when I was fourteen, even though the legal age in Suffolk County was sixteen. Cars had always been a fascination of mine. Driving was something I knew I could do well, ever since I had first sat behind the wheel of my go-cart. Of course, the only thing standing between me and the freedom of the open road was about ten inches of space between the bottom of my sneaker and the gas pedal. (Who uses the brake, anyway?)

TRUE TO MY age, my first driving experience ended with me in hot water. Mom had a company car she used for work, and another, slightly older car she had purchased a few years earlier, a silver Dodge Omni. It was an ugly four-door plus a hatch, and we affectionately referred to it as the "egg-mobile." It was a weak 2.2-liter, four-cylinder engine. Zero to sixty in ten seconds! Anyway, Mom had left the keys to the Omni at the house and gone to work. I decided today was the day—I was going to go for a ride. I went out to the driveway, got into the driver's seat, and started the car. Mom had let me "warm up" her cars for years, so I knew my way around the vehicle. I adjusted the rearview mirror all the way down, so I could see out of the back window while lying down on the seat, arms up toward the steering wheel and feet on the pedals. Imagine using the rearview mirror as a periscope with reverse as your only gear. I proceeded out of the driveway and began making my way down the block, backward. I noticed a car coming from the opposite end of the street. It was Mom, in her other car. She was home early. I pulled over, put the car in park and walked home to greet her and accept my punishment.

It was clear that since I wasn't going to get much taller, I would need to come up with a safer way to drive a car. When I turned sixteen, I reached out to the folks at BOCES. I had heard that New York State had a program for students with special needs called BOCES, the state's Boards of Cooperative Educational Services. These schools are actually branches of the public school system and are not "special schools" per se. They offer an incredible number of courses and training that just wouldn't be possible in a standard high school—unique, in-depth programs in the arts, vocational training, literacy programs, speech and occupational therapy regimens, and lots of classes for students with disabilities. Through BOCES, I was provided a drivers' ed instructor who could teach me how to drive. I sat in the driver's seat, and my first "legal" experience was using pedal extensions. I drove down the block from my house, made a right turn onto a neighboring street, and pulled to the side. My first half-mile in the car was jerky, unsure, and I was nervous. I didn't trust my legs well enough to have confidence in them for something so serious. So I asked to switch to hand controls. I put on the blinker to merge onto the road again and away we went. It was as if I had been using hand controls all my life. It was smooth, my stops were perfect, and my control was masterful. It was weird. Even the instructor was a bit surprised at my performance. Like a proper teenager, I got my license as close to my sixteenth birthday as possible. Also like a proper teenager, I was a little reckless. Mom was generous and gave me her old Dodge Omni to use. It was a great car for a sixteen-year-old—it was a car, and it was mine. It afforded me the freedom all teenagers want. And I was a good—dare I say great—driver.

Ultimately, I killed that little Dodge Omni by doing a neutral drop, while going in reverse down a hill at forty miles an hour. The tires smoked and screeched, and that was the last time that car moved any faster than your average lawn tractor. I retired Mom's car to the driveway and sought out a new old car to abuse.

In high school, there was a special program that helped kids with special needs interested in getting a job find work. At the job fair,

I found a position I felt was suitable, summertime janitor in my old elementary school. It was a great job—manual labor throughout the hot summer in a building without air-conditioning. Our task was to clean the entire school in preparation for the following school year. We would clean and remove the gum from under the desks, dust everything, wash and paint the walls, strip and wax the floors, repair all of the lights, clean the bathrooms, and put a fresh coat of polyurethane on the gymnasium floor, among other things. My first summer there, we were a motley crew of workers. I wound up keeping the job after the summer. In fact, I worked all four years of high school in the same job, as an after-school janitor. I would push a broom, mop floors, wipe down twenty to thirty desks and counters in every classroom, and clean ten bathrooms every night, all while on crutches. I figured out a way to push a drag mop down the hall and pin one crutch under my arm at the same time. Looking back, I don't know how (or why) I did it.

I was also a volunteer at two hospitals in the area, kind of a male version of a candy striper. One of my favorite jobs was working at the live animal facility at Cold Spring Harbor Labs in Cold Spring Harbor for a couple of summers. On top of that, I worked in a gas station, which proved useful, since my cars were pieces of junk, and I was also able to avoid asking Mom for money. I was picking up lots of information about cars, my favorite hobby, to boot. I always liked tinkering with things. When I was young, I took apart and rebuilt toys. But I slowly graduated to bigger things, like appliances and engines.

My height never held me back. If I wanted to take on a job, I did. If I wanted to jack up my car and change the spark plugs (weekly), I did it. The beauty of not being handed everything is you appreciate what you have and enjoy working for what you want.

By the time my senior year came, I was definitely ready to finish it up and leave home for college. My grades were really good, my test scores were admirable, and I was in the top 10 percent of my class. I liked the challenging courses, especially the three years I spent in the Westinghouse Preparatory Class. The goal of the class was independent scientific thought in preparation for the Westinghouse Science Talent Search (now called the Intel STS). I accomplished more in that class than in any other class I took—figuring out unique ways to determine the amount of water contained in the average tomato, designing a self-sustaining environment for a Mars colonization project, and developing a renewable energy source employing carbon dioxide reformation and methanation, a project that went all to the way to the New York State Energy Competition finals. While I didn't become a finalist in the Westinghouse competition, my project, which was a sociological study on the effects of dwarfism in deference to human development, helped me to better understand some of the challenges I would soon face as an adult, outside the protective walls of high school or my hometown.

In my senior year, I ran for student council president and gave a popular girl in our class a run for her money. In the end, she edged me out and won the position by a fraction. Hindsight is 20/20, but our class would likely have benefited from my presidency, particularly for alumni-related activities. I think I would have been a better class reunion organizer, but that's just me.

When it came time to enumerate my extracurricular activities on my college applications, I needed extra sheets of paper. I was part of a group called Bring Unity To Youth (BUTY), an organization created by my fellow club members and me to help break down racial barriers. I was also a lead member of the Science Debate Team and part of both the high school band and the marching band on two instruments, the trumpet and the French horn, all four years. I even taught chemistry when our teacher, Mr. McCafferty, had to take a leave of absence to care for his ailing wife. He taught me the lesson plans in advance, and then while the substitute teacher babysat the class, I taught the lessons, so we could all pass the Chemistry Regents (I believe the topics were Stoichiometry I and II). So I had impressive assets going into the application process.

I applied to seven schools, getting into all of them, except for Johns Hopkins. They all offered me scholarships, some full, some partial, but with enough money on the table to make the choice mine. I ultimately chose New York University in Greenwich Village for two reasons. The first was the scholarship. Nearly a full ride to a top institution! Second, NYU has many of its classes in buildings with elevators. Where most campuses are on acres of land, sprawling quads, and so on, the urban jungle made for less walking and greater convenience. The only accommodation I really needed, besides the elevators, was a footstool in each of my labs, biology and organic chemistry.

I thought living in the city might be taxing, but when I first crutched the neighborhood around NYU, I felt great. I had never been away from home before, except for the hospital stays in Baltimore, so to go to school in the big city seemed like the adventure of a lifetime. I had only been to New York without a parent once before, on prom night, where our group of friends and respective dates went to the Catch a Rising Star comedy club to see a performance. Other than that, the closest I had come to Manhattan alone were the infrequent trips to Brooklyn to visit my aunt and uncle and a trip to see *Joseph and the Amazing Technicolor Dreamcoat* with my aunt Diane as a wee lad.

My social habits carried over to college. The problem was that in college, it was easier to get away with dumb behavior, because I wasn't accountable to my parents. My downward spirals were certainly more aggressive, so if I was in a depressed mood, I was way more depressed, and having unfettered access to bars and alcohol didn't help.

College for me was both better and worse than high school. It was one of those things where I had the freedom to be who I wanted to be, but I wasn't so sure I liked who I was becoming. I was hanging around with people who were good looking and did well in school seemingly without trying. My trying to keep up with this crowd might not have been that healthy for me. Everything seemed to come easily to them, which made me feel inadequate. Of course, you find out later on that not everybody was as happy as you thought they were. But to me, college was about getting good grades and having sex as often as possible, and I wasn't doing either to the degree that I wanted to.

I selected biology as my major and chose to live in the dorms at Goddard Hall on the corner of Washington Square East and Washington Square South. Most of my classes were held in the Main Building on Washington Square East and Waverly Place, literally one hundred feet from door to door. I did go to class some of the time, but like most kids in college, my schedule was more aggressive than I could keep up with, so I slept through classes that started before 10:00 a.m. My focus was not where it needed to be, but instead was directed at making friends, partying hard, "experimenting," and finding a girlfriend. Going to class seemed to be the last thing on my mind most of the time.

Parties were different in college than they were in high school. Going to bars was easy, my friendships were new, and the landscape was very fresh and exciting. But the attitude most people had about my stature wound up being eerily familiar to me—I was often rejected, just like in high school. Being in the biggest city in the world and being in Greenwich Village did have its advantages. No one stuck out as the coolest, the prettiest, or the smartest. Everyone was different, or was trying to be. And in the world where everyone was trying to be unique, I just wanted to blend in. Unfortunately, my unwanted and unearned celebrity transferred from high school to college seamlessly. I was called "midget," I was teased, I was ignored, I was threatened, I was chased, I was beaten up.

One day, while walking across Washington Square Park from Hudson dormitory to mine, I was hit in the cheek by a small object. At first, I thought it was an acorn from an angry squirrel. I looked around and found a penny on the pavement. Then, from the not-so-distant open-air patio of the second floor of the Loeb Student Center, right across the street from the park, I heard the word "midget" being shouted in what would presumably be my direction. My suspicions were confirmed when another bit of change was tossed at me. To me, it looked like eight young men were leaning over the railing. Correction—eight ignorant classmates at NYU were sitting atop the building I went to every evening for dinner. So, even though I was outnumbered eight to one, I could not let this one go. Instead of picking a fight that would undoubtedly end with my getting a bloodied face or worse, I used my head to address my bullies. I approached two police officers patrolling nearby and explained that a gaggle of fools was making derogatory comments. I told the officers that I had been assaulted and feared I was in danger of bodily harm; and that I was being harassed; and that I would like them to be arrested. The eight students were taken into custody and removed from the building. I never pressed charges, and I was never confronted by any of them again. Sadly, that was just one of many instances in which one or more people saw fit to harass or insult me.

For the most part, these experiences were fleeting. I would

hear a comment, a whisper, the word "midget" shouted from across the street or down the block, and I wouldn't think anything of it. I wouldn't let it bother me for more than a few minutes. However, it turned out that the subconscious, cumulative effect of hearing these comments, being bullied, being excluded, and being made to feel inferior culminated in a single swift action to end it all.

I had been in college for about a year. It was the fall of 1993 and I was returning to NYU as a sophomore with an established group of friends. Unfortunately, I also returned to just as much ignorance as I had left the summer before. I continued to hear comments and whispers, and watched as people pointed and laughed at me. I tried my best to ignore the negativity hurled my way. I was doing better scholastically and kept reminding myself I had a promising future. But I couldn't shake the feelings of loneliness and despair.

From my vantage point, my classmates seemed to have it all together. In fact, my emotional turmoil and struggle with my self-image made it seem like even the avant-garde film school students were better adjusted than I was. I was socially active, but did not feel socially connected. I really wanted a girlfriend, a Ms. Right or even a Ms. Right Now.

I would go out to the bars frequently in a failed attempt to find a companion. My friends and I would play pool and drink pints of Guinness at Dempsey's, a local watering hole in the East Village. I would always arrive home alone and often fairly intoxicated. Even then, I might extend the party a little bit longer in the dorm and inevitably wake up feeling miserable.

It wasn't just a hangover. My depression and self-loathing were finally coming on strong. I was really feeling defined by my stature, and I felt inferior to the people I lived with, studied with, and partied with. I found myself wondering if their friendship and kindness were acts of charity or sympathy. Subconsciously, I had bought into the "worthless" label.

One night, all these feelings finally pushed me to the brink. I lived on the third floor of the dormitory, my room facing the Fourth Street side of the building. Outside my window was the ledge, a two-foot embellishment all the way around the building between the second and third floors. It was dark in my room, my roommate was out for the night, and most of my friends had company for the evening or were partying down the hall.

I decided I was tired of hearing the word "midget." I was tired of being in a group and yet somehow excluded. I was tired of the stares, the pointing, and the laughing, and I was tired of being alone. I wanted a companion, a girlfriend, someone to fool around with. I wanted comrades who didn't make me wonder whether they were sincere when they said they were my friends. I opened the window, and I stepped out onto the ledge.

It was a good thirty feet down to the street. There was a small tree on either side of my window and a few cars parked at the curb. It was cold, there was a slight breeze, and the streets were barren. I could hear the music from other dorm rooms and kids laughing and having fun. Taxis sped by and police sirens blared in the distance. I stood up and leaned against the wall next to the window. I looked down to the place where I might die.

Many thoughts were going through my head. At first, I wondered what would happen if I hit the tree or the car, or I just didn't die. I thought about how embarrassing it would be if I failed at taking my life. I chuckled for a moment, and then I thought a little more about what I was doing. I remember thinking my mom would be pissed and my dad disappointed. I thought a bit more about how I'd miss my brothers. And then I realized that I had a lot more to live for than fleeting relationships and being accepted by a few people I hardly knew. I began to realize that I'd miss it, life. And I took a step back from the ledge.

No sooner had I done that than a friend of mine came to the window. He offered me some company and had a couple of beers and cigarettes in tow. He came out onto the ledge, we sat down, and we had our beer. I didn't bother to explain why I was out on the ledge, and he didn't ask. But I'm fairly certain he knew.

IT'S FAR EASIER to explain what it was that led me out onto that ledge than it is to theorize about what it was that caused me to climb back in the window. What I concluded is that I was (and still am) fighting off the negative labels that were (and still are) imposed on me.

Although I ultimately decided to climb back through the window, it wasn't until years later that I asked myself what it was that made the difference in that moment. It had to do with self-worth. Despite the cruelty of a world where everyone is categorized, aggregated, and labeled for convenience, if nothing else, my family, my parents, and my brothers had constantly reinforced my value and built up my self-image. However, their influence and support had not been enough to completely drown out the negative self-image and labels that emerged during my adolescence. And clearly, it wasn't enough to keep me from climbing out onto the ledge. But their voices were enough, in that critical moment, to help me conclude that despite the attractiveness of the idea of ending the pain in a single leap, it was not worth giving up the new day and the hope that things would get better.

• • •

MY MOTHER KNEW that I was "different," but to her I was not different in a negative way; to her I was different because I was interesting and uniquely gifted. Whenever we discussed my stature or the challenges presented by my height, she would remind me, "There was a reason you were made this way."

"There was a reason you were made this way" remains my mantra. From a spiritual perspective, this translates to "God doesn't make mistakes." I can't help thinking how much happier vulnerable school-age people would be if their teachers and coaches and others in mentoring positions, by both word and deed, reinforced the idea that it's not only okay to be different, it's awesome and admirable and courageous and heroic. It's your differentness that is your destiny and your happiness, and your differentness is what makes the world more interesting.

THINGS GOT BETTER after that night on the ledge. Now that I had decided to live, I worked harder at doing things that made me feel good. I even got a girlfriend, my first real relationship. She was average size, which made it even more interesting. She was a fellow student at NYU, although she was a class or two behind me. She was from Pennsylvania, but she lived across the hall from me in the dorm.

We went out for almost two years. We even lived together for a little while in her nine-by-nineteen basement studio apartment in a prewar building in the East Village. It shared a backyard with the Alpha chapter of the Hell's Angels, and with the boiler room directly underneath the studio, the "hell" part took on even more relevance. The black and white checkered floor was warped from all the steam. I still kept my campus housing to have a place to study and keep my books.

This was my first legitimate relationship, and my girlfriend and

I had a really good time. We would go to the movies, out to dinner, or hang out with friends. She was a bit of a musician, and she was learning how to play guitar while I enjoyed listening. We were both sci-fi geeks and would stay up watching *Star Trek: Next Generation* or *Deep Space Nine*; or sometimes the lighter fare of *Northern Exposure*. We'd wander the open-air art fairs in Washington Square, go to parties, concerts, and bars, eat at inexpensive restaurants, and study, of course. It was a really fun time.

When things started to fall apart, I still thought having a relationship was better than not being in a relationship. Maybe I was worried that she was my only shot. Even when I got wind that she had cheated on me and I felt that kind of devastation, I wasn't ready to call the whole thing off. My insecurity made me willing to accept things I shouldn't have. Despite having worked on my confidence, I still lacked the feeling of self-worth that would allow me to believe I could be loved. Ultimately, it's all timing, and when that relationship finally ran its course, it meant there was room for someone else.

In the spring of 1996, I graduated from New York University with a bachelor of arts in biology and a minor in chemistry. The ceremony was held in Washington Square Park in the pouring rain. The only people under cover from the elements were the speakers, Steven Spielberg, Robert De Niro, and the wife of the late Jackie Robinson, along with NYU professors and administration, who were sitting on the protected stage. The sea of students took up any open space around the park's central fountain, a stone's throw from the famous Washington Square Arch. My family was somewhere in the crowd beyond the sea of sloppy wet purple mortarboards and gowns, also known as the graduating class of 1996. After graduation, we all sloshed through Washington Square looking for each other, then headed out to lunch before I returned to do the "better" things saved for the graduates themselves.

That summer, after NYU and before any other plans materialized, such as applying to medical school as I intended to do, Dr. Kopits offered me an internship with him. It was a huge honor. He only chose one student a year to shadow him. I moved to Baltimore for the summer. I lived at the Pierre House, the convent that had been converted into housing for family members of children having surgeries. My parents had both stayed there multiple times when I had surgery. But this was my first time as a guest. I didn't even have to pay the ten-dollars-a-night room and board.

I spent twelve weeks in Baltimore, working extremely long but fulfilling hours. I got up at 6:00 or 7:00 every morning and reported to Dr. Kopits by 8:00 a.m. On surgical days, our start time in the hospital was as early as 6:00 a.m. He allowed me to do just about everything. I was present with the patients during office visits; I went into the OR and assisted the surgical team by holding retractors or suction hoses; I even helped with a hip reconstruction, the very same procedure that I had undergone with Dr. Kopits, but this time I was on the better side of the surgical drape.

It was both surreal and funny. My insight, having been the patient as many times as I had, was amazing. As I stood by Dr. Kopits's side, I remembered my times going into the operating room as a patient and being put under with the anesthesia mask. Now, I was watching my patients falling asleep and turning into rag dolls on the table. Dr. Kopits allowed me to help plan the surgery, from X-ray to execution, which was nothing short of amazing. I was working with patients during clinical evaluations. Dr. Kopits and I would talk about what we were going to do as we looked at the X-rays, MRIs, and all the other imaging pinned to the light board, and we'd go through our plan. It was educational and lots of fun.

While I was in Baltimore, I started seeing someone, a Little Person who was volunteering at the hospital in Dr. Kopits's unit, Two North. Like me, she was also a former patient of his. She was on the floor volunteering, and I was participating in rounds with Dr. Kopits, visiting the patients who were on the floor for surgery or PT. I asked her out for a drink, and we hit it off. Her name was Charla. Even though we both knew this was a summer fling, she was really great and certainly helped me realize that my relationship in New York was over.

A "matchmaker" named Diane, who worked with Dr. Kopits as his long-time nurse practitioner and right-hand man, had another woman in mind for me. She told me about her when I was in the office after rounds. She was very excited. "I have someone I think will be perfect for you," she said gleefully. "There is this really cute girl down in Miami named Jennifer. She is wickedly smart and she is going to Johns Hopkins Medical School in the fall. She has blond hair and blue eyes, is cute as a button, and you will totally love her."

With that, she took me over to the photo wall where Dr. Kopits had hundreds of pictures of his patients. She proudly pointed Jennifer out on the wall. Diane was right. She really was a strikingly beautiful young woman. I didn't realize that she was the Jen I had met in the hospital when I was ten.

I wasn't in the mindset to do much with Diane's match for me. At that point, Jen wouldn't even be in Baltimore until I had already gone back to New York, where I was still semiliving with my girlfriend. Did I really want to talk to this girl who lived in Florida, soon to be studying in Maryland, when I lived in New York? It just didn't seem feasible. I was twenty-one and not really thinking about anything long distance or long-term.

What I didn't know was that Diane had told Jen about me the year before when she had been Dr. Kopits's summer intern. Oddly, Jennifer had been offered and accepted the very same internship the year before. I loved it when I finally heard the story. "There is this guy named Bill," Diane had told her. "He is up in New York going to NYU. He is smart, cute, and funny, and he is working over at Cold Spring Harbor Laboratories right now. He might be going to med school in a couple of years. You'd love him." Jen said no, she was too busy. Her friends were in Florida, where she was going to the University of Miami, and she had to focus on getting into medical school. She had blown it off.

So, I finished up my internship, returned to New York, and began looking for a job after I decided I didn't want to go to medical school after all. I didn't think I was smart enough, but I probably had a couple of other issues, too. I wanted to make money, start enjoying my life, and get away from academics. But Jen was now on my radar.

RIGHT: Billy on the beach. Clearly I need to work on my tan and maybe get a procedure to straighten that right leg. The curls were natural.

ABOVE: My mom and dad, along with the boys, shortly after Joey was born. Notice I am the only one looking at the camera. At least someone was paying attention.

ABOVE: Mom's dad (aka Grandpa) and his three grandsons. Notice, again, I am the only one looking at the camera.

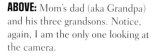

ABOVE: Bill and his first motorized wheels. Full tank of gas, bald tires, and no rules!

RIGHT: One of those pictures Mom makes you take and you only appreciate twenty-eight years later.

ABOVE: Mom and Jen on the front stoop—
contemplating the spirit of everything.

ABOVE: Jen and Grandma Shipman.

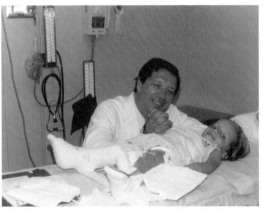

ABOVE: Jen and Mom on a presurgery
trip to Washington, D.C.

ABOVE: Jen and Dr. Kopits, with my cast cut open so
he could take a look before sending me home for a
couple of months.

LEFT: Jennifer and her little brother, David.

ABOVE: From left to right, family friend Susan Taft, Jennifer, and Jen's aunt Chrissy. This was from Susan's wedding. My aunt was the maid of honor and I was the best man!

ABOVE: Beloved Aunt Chrissy.

LEFT: Bill's mom and the back of his head.

ABOVE: Jen striking a pose on the beach.

ABOVE: From left to right, Jennifer's aunt Barbara, mom, and aunt Chrissy.

ABOVE: Jen along with Mom and Dad at graduation from the University of Miami in 1996.

ABOVE: Officially Dr. Arnold, on her day of graduation from the Johns Hopkins Medical School.

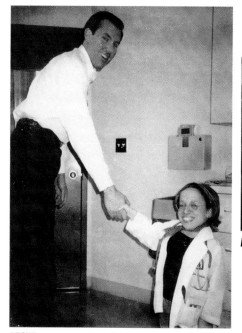

ABOVE: Dr. Kopits and Dr. Jen at her graduation dinner.

ABOVE: Doing rounds with Dr. McKusick, who took this photo. I'm shaking hands with one of his patients here.

RIGHT: Jen and Mom at the grand opening of the new Simulation Center at Texas Children's Hospital.

LEFT: In my apartment in medical school in my short white coat.

ABOVE: Jen and Diane (aka The Matchmaker).

ABOVE: This is the first-date weekend. Here we are at Jen's birthday party hosted by her BFF, Lakshmi.

ABOVE: Jen's brother, David, with his girlfriend and soon-to-be fiancée, Lisa, at our engagement party.

ABOVE: The proud dad gets to walk Jen down the aisle.

ABOVE: The boys. Everyone except for the father of the bride accounted for. He's probably doing a last-minute background check on me.

LEFT: Us on St. Pete Beach on our wedding day.

RIGHT: Us walking "into the sunset."

ABOVE: Someone must have said something funny!

RIGHT: My beautiful mom in her lovely dress. May I have this dance?

ABOVE: Will and Zoey in our driveway, hoping for rain!

LEFT: Just a good picture of Jen. Isn't she pretty?

RIGHT: Dad and Debbie and the five boys.

ABOVE: What happens in Houston stays in Houston.

LEFT: Zoey and Will in one of the modules in the NASA International Space Station . . . the one in Houston, not in space.

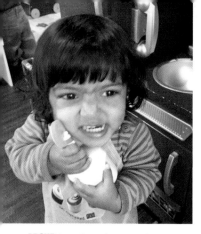

ABOVE: Zoey loves her cupcakes. Even the plastic ones.

RIGHT: If Zoey tried to smile any more, her teeth might crumble. Happy Valentine's Day!

ABOVE: Comparing wheels.

LEFT: Zoey getting in some reading before bed.

RIGHT: Rocky and Maggie.

LEFT: Will and Zoey taking a stroll through the leaves in front of our house just before Christmas 2014.

CHAPTER ELEVEN

Jen

MIAMI OR BUST!

MY FIRST DAY AT the University of Miami was stormy—literally. Freshman orientation was supposed to be Monday, August 24, 1992, but it was canceled suddenly and dramatically. Instead of picking up our class schedules and meeting our hall mates, we were dodging Hurricane Andrew, the most fearsome storm to hit South Florida in nearly three decades. It crashed into Miami with winds whipping up to two hundred miles an hour. The Category 5 storm, one of only four to ever make landfall in the United States, blew apart buildings, flattened houses, and obliterated the power grid, ripping power lines right off the poles and blowing up transformers. Twenty-six people lost their lives and more than 250,000 were left homeless. Fires burned around the city, but fire departments were helpless, as the storm surge had put thousands of miles of roads and highways underwater. Not only was freshman orientation canceled, but the whole university was shut down in a state of emergency and the administration was desperately trying to evacuate all sixteen thousand students. Many of the residence halls were official hurricane shelters, so students on or arriving on campus were being moved to these residence halls for the night. There were even local residents in the Coral Gables area coming to the residence halls for shelter.

Because it was going to be my first day of college and because I was so excited, that Sunday morning before orientation, I convinced my parents to keep driving south from Orlando to Miami despite the fact that the Florida Turnpike had a steady flow of traffic moving in the opposite direction.

Once we got to the campus, it was clear that the hurricane was headed our way. The college staff invited parents and students to stay, but because my dad had to work the next day, he wanted to head back. Of course, I wanted to stay. No matter where weather forecasters project a hurricane's landfall, they aren't always right, and there was no chance that I was going to miss my freshman orientation activities if Andrew happened to hit farther north, sparing Miami.

My parents spent the afternoon moving me in and then reluctantly departed. After they left, the resident assistants (RAs) of my dorm, Mahoney Residential College, called a meeting to discuss the hurricane plan, as it did indeed look as if the eye of the hurricane was making a beeline for Miami. We were asked to fill our tubs with water and move anything we didn't want to get wet four feet off the floor. Everybody who was on a high floor or at the ends of the building was moved to lower and more centralized rooms, should the ends or upper floors of the building collapse. Looking back on it now, I can remember how scary it was to have my first night away from home at college in a terrifying Category 5 hurricane. At the time, however, I think I was just in survival mode once again, ready to take on whatever came my way.

It took my parents eight hours instead of the typical four to get home. By the time they got there and realized that Andrew was indeed headed directly toward me, my mother was furious at their decision to leave. But it was too late to change anything now.

Conditions on campus deteriorated as the night wore on. At about 3:00 a.m., we were all evacuated from our rooms to the halls to weather the storm, and we sat in the dark except for our flashlights until dawn. The entire residence hall, seven floors of concrete, shook four times in the severe winds. We were not allowed to open the doors to our rooms because the rooms had the old-school Florida crank windows, so they weren't airtight, and we might be sucked out if a window had broken and we didn't know it. When the actual eye went over us and the winds suddenly calmed, we were allowed to enter the RA's room to use the toilet, so thirty of us used the toilet in twenty minutes, without the ability to flush—not pleasant! One of my fellow incoming freshmen was a girl whose father was a professor at the university. She had chosen to stay in the dorm while her family stayed in their home in Kendall, about fifteen miles south of us. We listened to some of the radio reports that Kendall was being hammered, and she essentially cried much of the night. I had spoken to my parents before we lost power, but now that talking to them was not an option, I imagined how very worried they must be at home. There were no cell phones in the early nineties, and no electricity meant no phones.

When dawn broke, the storm had passed, and we were finally allowed to return to our rooms. Even though my room was located on the fourth floor, it still had four inches of water in it from the sideways rain that had come through small leaks around the windows, even though no windows in my room were gone. My room was in good shape compared to most of those on campus. We had no running water and no electricity, which meant no air-conditioning. The storm left Miami in a more oppressive heat than usual for August, as it had deposited every ounce of tropical humidity it had picked up in its track across the Atlantic right on top of us. Food was being rationed, the toilets in all the dorms were overflowing, and there were no stores or canteens open to get supplies. With the elevator out of service, I had to walk up and down four flights of stairs in the dark, as there were no windows in the stairwells, and this was beyond challenging. My parents couldn't come to get me because all the roads heading south were restricted to emergency vehicles. Thank God for my friend Chetna. Even though she was no longer at the University of Miami and she wasn't my roommate as planned, she knew tons of people and started calling around until she finally found an upperclassman who was going to Orlando and could take me home.

Once there, I found out just how stressed my family had been. It turned out my mom had been up all night glued to the Weather Channel and on the phone with my aunts Chrissy and Barbara. I think that was the closest my mom ever came to wanting to kill my dad for leaving me there—yikes!

I started the University of Miami excited to be a "Hurricane," the official name of the sports teams and, by default, the student body. Instead, I actually went through one! So, I was truly a University of Miami Hurricane!

As it turned out, the campus was shut down for two weeks for the massive cleanup. But once my fellow twenty-five hundred freshman classmates and I finally settled in, I liked what I saw. I was extremely happy there from the start. I became very active in student life and joined as many clubs and civic organizations as I could handle. When I wasn't in class, my friends and I loved going out to the beach or dancing in South Beach. I became a big fan of reggae and loved going out to the Hungry Sailor for dancing on Thursday nights with my friends. I was active in student government and was in the Presidents 100 Club, which was a prestigious group of one hundred specially selected students who helped plan the events for the president of the college.

Early on in my freshman year, I applied for a sought-after RA position in my residence hall. To my delight, I was one of only a handful selected. It really was a wonderful position, and there was so much involved in being an RA at U of M. RAs started school two weeks early for leadership, diversity, and emergency-skill training. Not only was I responsible for supporting and overseeing a group of twenty or more fellow students on the floor, but I had to learn how to identify drugs and how to handle emergencies. RAs were often on night duty, so once every few nights it would be my turn to walk around the halls at midnight, looking for problems and making safety checks for working fire alarms and fire escapes. When on duty, I carried a pager and was on call for any emergencies. One night, one of my residents had a psychotic break and was circling the dorm, barely dressed, speaking nonsense, and threatening to hurt herself. I had to counsel her and keep her safe until campus police and the residence coordinator arrived. Fortunately, I knew her, and she trusted me and I was able to move her to the lobby until more help arrived. The benefit of being an RA was that my room and board was paid, and I also received a small monetary stipend, which was helpful for maintaining my social life and indulging my love of clothes and shoes.

I was an RA for two years before rising in rank to a PA (program assistant) position my senior year. There was one PA per residential college. It was a pretty competitive position that involved programming all residential college activities and social events, such as trips to the opera and the college's participation in university-wide activities. I had an office in the college's administrative area and really enjoyed this position. To this day I still love to plan a good party!

For my personal transportation around campus, I still used a scooter to get to and from classes. I had the "Rascal," a motorized scooter that replaced my "Pony" from high school. I always had some assistive device for long distances, but I didn't use it socially. I had a couple of good buddies who used to hijack it and ride it down the halls. On rainy days, there would always be two guys hanging on the back as I high-powered it at its fastest speed, five miles an hour, across the campus.

Being on my own for the first time in college was wonderful in the most extraordinary ways. I had reinvented myself and was becoming more self-confident, more outspoken, and happier than I had ever been. I had developed even closer friendships than I had in high school. I became a part of a close group of four friends, Sonal, Suketu, Walter, and myself. I first met Sonal in a biology class. Then we met Suketu and Walter, who both lived on my floor. The four of us became inseparable. We studied together, ate together, and of course went out dancing, to concerts, and shopping together. I had never felt so secure in friendships before, and thankfully, this foursome didn't end until we started to lose touch long after college ended.

While things were changing back at home with my parents reuniting, I was trying to identify my career path. I was majoring in biology with a plan to double major in marine science with the goal of becoming a marine biologist. During the second semester of my freshman year, I had my own pivotal moment. I decided I would become a doctor instead. This epiphany came during a conversation I was having with my aunt Chrissy.

"What about medicine?" she asked one night while we were catching up on the phone. I trusted Chrissy's opinion more than anyone's. I was open to her suggestion, as she had faith in me, knowing me better than anyone.

Essentially, my whole family had wanted me to be anything but a marine biologist, and feared I would be eaten by sharks. On a field trip to the Florida Keys during my oceanography class, I had gone into the water to survey a one-square-meter area for the purpose of counting the fish and plankton. I had a rope tied around my waist, because my instructor was hoping to prevent my drowning, as I am not buoyant and typically sink like a rock. He succeeded, but I came to realize that it was likely not only physically impossible for me to be the next Jacques Cousteau, but in realistic terms, marine biology was not as romantic as I had thought. I would probably end up being in a lab all the time working with plankton, whereas I really liked working with people.

Medicine was definitely a more "people" career, and with that I changed focus. Because a lot of my classes counted toward premed, I was able to complete my minor in marine science and get a double major in biology and psychology. In the end, I realized that I was more of a people-person than a lab rat.

Aside from my academic decisions, my sophomore year was filled with more personal difficulty. My maternal grandma, one of my favorite people in the world, who had played such a huge role in raising me, died that year. Her medical crisis began in August, right before I went back to U of M. She had gone to the hospital for a routine colonoscopy when they discovered she had a few polyps. It was nothing too concerning. I had accompanied her to the procedure right before I went back to school.

Back at home, she had started experiencing fevers, chills, and blood in her stool. Because I was back in Miami, everybody kept me in the dark, thinking that she would get better and that it was better to not disrupt my studies or stress me out. It turned out the gastroenterologist had punctured her colon during the exam.

For too long, the doctor dismissed the symptoms when she called him. She had followed his advice and remained at home to rest. One day, about a week after the procedure, my mother found her lethargic and weak and rushed her to the ER, when she was found to be in septic shock. In the ICU, she arrested three times. The doctors noted that if she had remained at home much longer, she likely would have died.

Even though they saved her life, her condition was still really grave, and she was intubated in the ICU for months, suffering more complications from sepsis than I can describe. As soon as my family told me, about three weeks after she was admitted, I took the first flight back to Orlando to visit her.

By that point it was clear she would be in the hospital for some time, and I went back almost every two to three weeks to see her that semester. After a roller coaster of days in the hospital, my grandmother had a tracheostomy placed and lost digits from her hands, but was stable enough to be transferred to a nursing facility to continue to heal. It wasn't until Thanksgiving weekend that she was actually coherent and able to talk with all of us via her trach tube. I remember telling her I just got 100 percent on my physics final, and she was happy and proud. I was very relieved to be able to spend time with her when she wasn't sedated.

Unfortunately, Thanksgiving weekend was the last time that I saw my grandma alive. I was only going to be back in Miami for two weeks to finish final exams, and I had hoped and prayed she would be okay until then. However, one afternoon as I rode my scooter into the Mahoney lobby after one of my finals, my boss, Gay, the residence coordinator, saw me at the front desk and pulled me back into her office.

"I have really bad news," she said, and I knew immediately what it was. She didn't need to say anything else. With tears running down my face, I went back to my room, packed my bags, and flew home that very evening, December 5. I had one final left, organic chemistry, but that didn't matter anymore. To this day, I have kept in touch with Gay. At a conference for student life that I recently attended, she told me how hard it was to deliver that news.

My grandmother's service was held at a funeral parlor in Orlando. Between family, friends, and her coworkers from Disney, there were more than sixty people in attendance. Family I had never met traveled from all over the country to be there. My mom gave the eulogy as Chrissy, Barbara, and I comforted each other through our tears in the front row. I had the rest of winter break to mourn her death and spent much of that time with my aunt Chrissy. It was definitely the loss of our family's matriarch. That Christmas was the worst I ever had. We didn't even put up a tree.

The second semester of sophomore year came and went. I made up my organic chemistry exam and tried to keep up with my schoolwork, as I know my grandma would have wanted me to. At the end of the year, I had another surgery, this time on my knee. It took place in the early summer between my sophomore and junior years. I was laid up in my parents' house in a leg cast for the entire summer. They were now living in Pensacola, where they had relocated for my dad's work. Although I liked the house, a cute two-story traditional house on the intercoastal waterway, I was in no position to enjoy it. My brother, David, was now thirteen and had been dealing not only with the death of my grandma that year but also changing schools, a tough time for him as well.

From my perspective, being in a new home and recovering from surgery after what had been a few years' reprieve without it was tough on everyone. After getting used to being so independent at college, it was hard to be back in the vulnerable and dependent position of being in a cast.

I had to rely on others for assistance again for everything, including using the bathroom. I remember one incident in which my mom was out, and I inevitably had an emergency. My brother was the only one home, and there was probably no worse age for a brother to be when he needed to help his sister with the duties I required—assistance getting into the bathroom and onto the throne. I was in a wheelchair, so I could get to the bathroom door, but I just didn't have the strength to lift myself onto the toilet in a very tiny powder room, the only bathroom on the first floor. An argument between David and me quickly ensued, as he was so grossed out by the idea of lifting me onto the toilet, and he almost refused to do it. I was equally angered by the fact that I had no choice but to beg him for assistance. We were both yelling back and forth for what felt like hours. Finally, he did give in and helped me onto the throne. It was not a good time to have a battle of the wills between two siblings. In fact, it was torture.

My brother and I have always had a typical sibling love/fight relationship. David could treat me like a princess, as when he would help carry my books to school when we were in grade school together, but as a toddler, he could also destroy my bedroom during a temper tantrum. Of course we love each other and would do anything for each other, but we had our share of fights. I am sure it was hard for him growing up as a sibling of a child with such complex and frequent medical needs. I was almost seven when he was born, so we really grew up separately and very differently.

In my third year of college, I was already applying to medical schools and taking my MCATs, the standardized tests for medical school admission. My preferred fields of medicine going into the application process were pediatrics, maybe genetics, and maybe ophthalmology. I agreed with my parents that I needed something that would not wear me out physically. Pediatric orthopedic surgery was a thought, being so near and dear to me, but orthopedic surgery was an exceptionally physical field and likely not in the cards for me.

Like many of my other pre-med friends, I applied to thirty-plus medical schools, because it is such a competitive process. My application was strong, but I knew I was going to be in a pool of many talented and high-achieving students. I highlighted activities on campus, my involvement with student government, and my memberships in the Leadership Honors Society and the Presidents 100 Club. I had above a 4.0 GPA, and my MCATs were good, although not spectacular. In my essay, I wrote about the fact that I wanted to be a physician in order to give back, since the medical community had done so much for me as a Little Person. All in all, I thought I had a good chance. More than thirty applications was a lot.

After the initial application, the next step was to wait for secondary applications from the medical schools themselves. If your primary application had made the initial cut and the med schools wanted another level of material to keep you in the pool, meaning they were *potentially* interested in you, they would send you a secondary application. I received ten secondary applications and I was still feeling optimistic. Now came the wait for the third level of screening, the invitations for a face-to-face interview.

When my friends started getting invitations for these interviews and I didn't, I became very concerned. Not one of the ten schools where I was still in the pool was reaching out to me. They weren't rejecting me per se, but any med school applicant knows that no news is bad news. I knew the credentials of my friends were exactly on par with mine, so the only difference I could think of was the fact that in my essay, I had disclosed that I was a Little Person. I feared this might be working against me. Specifically, many of the schools' brochures had a disclaimer—that they reserved the right to not accept any applicants who did not meet the physical, mental, or emotional requirements for practicing medicine.

I started second-guessing myself. Perhaps becoming a doctor was simply not in the cards for me, and I should consider another path. I even entertained pursuing a career as residential coordinator. I loved being an RA and given the fact that I enjoy working with people so much, that might be a really fun and rewarding career.

After a few weeks, Dr. Foote, the president of the university, came up to me at a Presidents 100 event. Aware that I was applying to medical school, he wanted to know how things were going. "Have you interviewed here yet?" he asked. When I told him no, he seemed surprised. I didn't want to lie, but for some reason I felt bad telling him I never got an interview. In fact I had already received my rejection letter from U of M. "It's okay," I said, not daring to look heartbroken.

Two days later, I got a call from the School of Medicine offering me an interview, so obviously Dr. Foote had made a phone call. I had very mixed emotions about getting this interview. Although I greatly appreciated the effort and support I had from Dr. Foote, I wanted to get into medical school on my own merits, not because the president had made a phone call and brought me to someone's attention. Because I didn't want to disappoint Dr. Foote and because I had no other prospects at the time, I accepted the invitation to interview.

At the University of Miami interview, I faced the hardest set of questions I have ever been asked, but not for the reasons you would think. The two physicians conducting the interview, a trauma surgeon and an internal medicine doctor, wasted no time in addressing the elephant in the room, and the interview quickly became focused on my size, or lack thereof.

How, with my stature, was I going to take care of patients? How did I drive a car? If I became a trauma surgeon, how was I going to be able to do all the things required of me?

I actually felt under attack. "I am not going into medicine with any interest in putting a patient in harm's way," I replied. "That would defeat the purpose."

I told them I didn't want to become a trauma surgeon. I knew this specialty was the "it" field at that time, popularized by TV shows like *E.R.* In fact, my pre-med friends and I loved to get together to watch *E.R.* whenever we could, hoping George Clooney would save the day. In my mind, however, I knew that it might not be practical for me to crack open the chest of a fifty-year-old motor vehicle accident victim, but I never wanted to do that anyway. When a patient came into the ER, there were many roles for physicians, and no one person saved a life in a vacuum. These were well-coordinated, well-trained groups, and it wasn't a single doctor (George Clooney, please) responsible for resuscitating a patient, like on TV. I had no doubt I could perform any one role with a step stool. I could manage the airway, get access, or even lead the code. I also explained that my interest was nowhere close to becoming a surgeon. I was envisioning a career in pediatrics, ophthalmology, or genetics.

The grilling didn't stop there. *If you get into medical school, you have to be in top condition, physically and mentally.* According to the surgeon's philosophy, to enter the field of medicine, all candidates should be physically and mentally capable of performing any role in any field. This idea that a medical student, a future physician, must be "pluri-potential," capable of working in several different roles, is fortunately going by the wayside, and medicine is opening its eyes to the fact that many talented individuals are being overlooked because of this thinking. Now more than ever before I am seeing physicians with disabilities entering the field.

I never believed a doctor had to be capable of being *every* type of doctor there was—a neurosurgeon, an ER physician, a pathologist, a general practitioner, an endocrinologist, and so on.

When asked specific questions related to my physical abilities, I was honest and confident. I told them I could drive a car, I would carry my own step stool around, I have a scooter that I would use for distance. I felt that I could learn and participate in all fields of medicine during medical school, but that I would never want to choose a specialty in which my physicality could put a patient at risk.

By the time I finished my cross-examination, I was beet red, and not even sure I wanted to go to that medical school anymore, even if I did get in.

The following week, the unbelievable happened. I was invited to the Johns Hopkins School of Medicine for an interview. This time it appeared to me that I was invited on my own merits. Not that I hadn't appreciated Dr. Foote's effort on my behalf. I thought he was a great president, and I absolutely loved the University of Miami.

Because I had been a patient at Johns Hopkins Hospital for ten years, from the age of two through the age of twelve, and still knew a few people, such as Dr. Victor McKusick, who had diagnosed my skeletal dysplasia, I didn't tell anyone from there that I had applied. The only person from Hopkins I told of my visit was Donna, who had morphed from being my favorite nurse to being my good friend. I didn't even tell her until after I received the invitation to interview. In fact, the reason I called her was that I wanted to see her while I was in town.

After my tumultuous interview at the University of Miami School of Medicine, I was nervous about my interview at Hopkins. However, much to my surprise, the interview was fantastic. I met one-on-one with a single physician, a pediatrician. He didn't start interrogating me about my limitations. Instead, he asked me about why I wanted to become a doctor and things relevant to the study of medicine. He asked about my interests and extracurricular activities. He never even brought up my stature. At one point, I was beginning to wonder if he even realized I was a Little Person! Of course he did, but it felt strange that he wasn't bringing it up. So I had to bring it up! I thought if he had concerns and was afraid to ask me about them, I wanted to address them head on!

"I will need a step stool to see patients," I told him offhandedly.

"Yes," he replied, "that makes perfect sense."

"And I will need a scooter to make rounds," I continued. "Is that okay?"

He said that a scooter sounded fine to him. The interview ended with him showing me pictures of his kids. Wow, what a different experience. The interview was easy, almost too easy. I thought it had either gone great or gone horribly, but I could not predict which. After the interview, I went on a tour with about twenty other applicants. We went all over the hospital. My favorite part of the tour was the "dome," where our guide explained how Sir William Osler and other physician icons used to go around the dome, examining and discussing the patients in each of the rooms. That is where the term "rounding" that every medical institution now uses comes from. Doctors "round" every morning, seeing all their inpatients and making the plan of care. Because this practice began at Hopkins due to the circular configuration of patients' rooms, the term "rounding" was born. After touring the hospital and remembering my experience as a patient there, I was in awe of the institution. How amazing would it be if I got to be a medical student where I was once a patient? As much as I wanted this, I truly thought that it was an unattainable dream.

Well, that is what I thought, but I guess dreams can come true. One week later, I got a phone call from the dean of admissions, offering me a position in the Johns Hopkins Medical School Class of 2000.Wow! A personal phone call and a spot in the School of Medicine! I happened to be with one of my good friends, Brian, when I got the phone call. He was so happy for me, he literally picked me up and we spun around my dorm room.

I learned, too, that my connection with the hospital as a former patient was irrelevant to my acceptance, thank goodness! Dr. McKusick didn't even know I had applied or was interviewing until well after the fact, when he learned I had been to Baltimore from a colleague and heard that I "may have made it to the second step" in the application process. He must have found out the day I got the acceptance call from the dean, because when he called my house to tell my mother that he had heard I was interviewing there, he warned her it was tough to get in, because Hopkins only accepted the "cream of the crop" from a pool of applicants from all over the world. He said I should feel good about the interview, but not get my hopes up.

My mother knew I had already been accepted, so when she told me about this phone call, I knew that I had been accepted on my own merits. Dr. McKusick couldn't have been in on it. It was an incredible confidence boost for me to know that the people who knew me growing up had nothing to do with my getting in. I hadn't even seen Dr. McKusick since I was a kid.

When I started medical school, there were almost no physicians who were Little People. I knew of only two, one being Dr. Michael Ain, who started at Johns Hopkins Medical School two years before me as an attending physician. He is actually a pediatric orthopedic surgeon and specializes in patients with skeletal dysplasias. The other Little Person physician I know of is Dr. Kenneth Lee, a pediatric gastroenterologist. Both of these doctors are male and have achondroplasia, which is very different from my dysplasia. People with this type of dwarfism are often taller and can have fewer orthopedic complications. I might be the first female Little Person physician, but I cannot be sure.

It turned out that despite the stressful interview at the University of Miami School of Medicine, I was also accepted there. A part of me really wanted to go to the University of Miami, because so many of my close friends were going to medical school there. However, ultimately, I had to say yes to my dream school. I knew I could never feel good about going to a school where I believed that some of its faculty doubted my capabilities. I realized it would only intensify the feeling that I needed to constantly prove myself. Still, I had a little bit of anxiety telling the university I wasn't accepting the offer.

There were about three thousand people in my graduating class that May 1996. There was a smaller, separate graduation ceremony for the individuals who were in the honors program. There, we each got to personally cross the stage and receive our diploma when our name was called. My parents were proud members of the cheering families in the audience. My aunts, my brother, and even Dr. Kopits had made the trip to see me graduate!

I was called up to the stage to be presented with my honors medallion by the vice provost, Dr. William Butler, whom I knew fairly well from my involvement in student life. He said "congratulations," and then leaned down to give me this big, weird, awkward kiss, which was like on the top of my head. He then went on to laud all of my accomplishments, resulting in an enormous round of applause. He finished by saying, "The only mistake that Jennifer made at the University of Miami was not staying to go to our medical school."

CHAPTER TWELVE

Bill

HOT RODS and CUSTOM SUITS

AFTER MY INTERNSHIP WITH Dr. Kopits in Baltimore, I returned to New York, packed up whatever belongings I still had in my ex-girlfriend's East Village apartment, and moved back to Mom's house in Port Jefferson. It was time to find a career. Most graduates with a degree in biology in the mid-1990s looked to the pharmaceutical industry, which was exactly what I did.

I sent my CV to every single pharmaceutical company out there— Bayer, Bristol Myers Squibb, Abbott Labs, Forrest Labs, Wyatt, Johnson & Johnson, Merck, Pfizer, Zeneca, SmithKline Beecham, and so on, hoping to land a career in pharmaceutical sales. Besides a BA in biology from New York University, my clinical experience with Dr. Kopits that past summer was enhanced by a junior year internship at the Cold Spring Harbor Laboratory in Cold Spring Harbor, New York. The lab was one of the top research institutions in the world in the fields of genetics and molecular biology, and I had the privilege of working with the best scientists out there. I was working in the live animal laboratory, drawing blood from rats, mice, and rabbits, cleaning their cages, and feeding them. I was also assisting the scientists in performing laboratory experiments and dissections.

Once my resumes were out, I looked around for temporary employment while I waited for calls from potential employers. My father had a friend who owned a private security company, and he offered me a job as a security guard, working the midnight shift at an abandoned warehouse in Riverhead. A small aside, this friend, Jay, was a former police officer who had worked with my father and had been my childhood jiujitsu instructor growing up. Anyway, the pay wasn't very good, but the hours guaranteed that I would be available during the day for interviews for permanent jobs.

I was pretty excited when I got my first couple of requests for interviews. I got a few callbacks, but nothing materialized. At first, I wasn't surprised to not get a second interview—it happens to a lot of applicants who are starting out with little or no sales experience. But after ten or so interviews, optimistic patience became realistic disappointment. Although I looked great on paper, my in-person meetings ranged from bland and very uncomfortable interactions to blatant prejudice.

One particular interview at a publicly traded pharmaceutical company blew me away. I pulled out one of my new outfits, a gray pinstripe suit, white shirt, and power tie. I drove from my house on Long Island all the way to the company's corporate headquarters in New Jersey, at least a two-hour drive without traffic from Port Jeff.

My interviewer met me in the lobby and almost immediately I could read by his face that he wasn't going to give me much time. He was a bottom-tier sales manager with an outwardly cocky manner. From his expression, I could tell he would rather be showing me to the exit door. Nonetheless, he dutifully led me past the elevators and down a long hallway to an in-service classroom, where he administered his version of an interview—a few basic questions that had no relevance to the job for which I was applying. He didn't ask me anything about myself, or why I wanted to get into pharmaceutical sales, just a couple of offhanded generic questions about the company's products, and even these questions came out totally flat. I didn't even get the often recycled "Sell me this pen" sales question. Then he abruptly rose to show me the door. "Unfortunately, you don't have the look we are looking for," he told me as he escorted me out of the building. *THE LOOK!*

His remarked floored me. I was *totally* groomed and dressed in a fancy, never-been-wrinkled gray pinstripe suit, just like everybody else I had passed on the way to the "interview."

"What do you mean?" I asked, acting completely baffled.

He glanced around, as if he was suggesting that I observe all these guys around me, who were six feet tall, in snappy suits and polished shoes, maybe off to model for the cover of *GQ* after work. The girls, too, were gorgeous. In retrospect, it looked more like a fashion show runway than a hallway in a corporate office. *You had to be cookie-cutter good looking* was what he was suggesting, and I didn't fit that bill. The "corporate look" the firm was looking for did not look like me. He didn't say it, but his insinuation was that I was of lesser value than my resume conveyed due to my appearance. This creep didn't even want to know what I could bring to the table. It was one of the most outwardly prejudicial acts with relation to my stature I had ever encountered. I was infuriated that, in a professional environment such as this, and in the grander world of medicine, it could be conceivable, let alone condoned and encouraged, to filter prospects based on their physical disability.

As appalled as I was, I didn't let it deter me. This would not be my last disappointing experience, and why would I want to work for a bunch of ignorant fools, anyway? In another gem of an interview, the hiring manager told me he was afraid I might not be capable of the heavy lifting the job required when dropping off sample boxes to doctors' offices. And my all-time favorite excuse anyone gave me was that there was concern that I might not be noticed in the waiting room, which perplexed me.

"What do you mean I might not be noticed?" I asked, thinking he must be kidding.

"How are you going to get noticed by the receptionist?" he asked, as if my size made me invisible. He added, "People might assume you're a patient." As if every man who goes into an OB/GYN office that is short in stature must be there for treatment. While I was certainly frustrated with these idiotic comments, I accepted that these people weren't for me, and just kept looking. If this was the caliber of individuals I would be working with in this industry, the industry I wanted to be in, I realized I had better get used to this stuff . . . or start looking at other options.

About fifty interviews later, I finally met with success. I faxed my resume over to an ad I saw in *Newsday*, our local newspaper, and to my delight, I got a call from a man named Michael Sperduti at a company called Triad Medical, Inc., a national distributor of infusion products, devices, and pharmaceuticals to the home infusion marketplace. He wanted to begin with a cursory interview with me over the phone before he took it to a face-to-face.

"Tell me what you are looking to do," he began, and satisfied with that, he went next to, "Tell me about college." After thirty minutes of in-depth dialogue, we finally arrived at the end, at which point he set up an interview. "I would love you to come in tomorrow at eleven o'clock to meet with me. Does that work?"

It worked for me. The next day, I hopped in my car, a Cold War–era 1987 Pontiac 6000 SE station wagon with a few dents and a touch of "spy hunter"–like smoke coming out of the tailpipe. I hadn't needed a car at NYU, so this was a legacy vehicle my dad had provided me while I was back from college and looking for a career. This was the beast I drove all over the tristate to my many interviews. And it was the vehicle I drove to Deer Park, about forty minutes from Port Jefferson, for my interview with Michael.

"Hi, my name is Bill Klein," I told the receptionist at precisely 10:52 a.m. "I have an eleven o'clock interview with Michael Sperduti."

She handed me a clipboard with the application and a pen and directed me to fill out everything. As I was sitting down in a chair to do just that, she was disappearing into a back office to alert Mike that his eleven o'clock interview had arrived. I only learned later what she had *really* told him. She had come running into his office in total confusion and said, "You are not going to believe this. There is a midget in the waiting room filling out an application!" Apparently, this was the first time she had interacted with a person short in stature. She seemed a bit more nervous than me, and I was the one applying for the job!

When she came back to her desk, I could see that she wasn't as bubbly or exaggerated in her motions as she had been initially, although she wasn't rude. "Come this way," she directed, motioning for me to follow her to Michael's office.

Michael was a stout, dark-haired guy, standing just under six feet tall, well-groomed, with wire-rimmed glasses and a firm handshake.

"Let's talk," he said, signaling for me to have a seat across from him. We talked about everything from football to college, from health care to personal goals and aspirations.

"I hired you on the phone, because your phone presence was phenomenal," he told me. "That's what you need in this job in order to succeed." I appreciated Michael's candor. He had been impressed by my personality and my presence, my ability to "sell" myself over the phone. He wasn't going to object to my height. After all, he was hiring me based on my qualifications and his confidence that I could do the job well. Not to mention that this job was an inside sales position, so while appearance and professionalism were important internally, no one cared or knew how tall I stood on the other end of the phone.

At the end of our interview, Michael offered me the job, and then invited me to lunch at Pace's Steak House to celebrate. It was where he took all his new hires.

With the business of the day out of the way, we headed to lunch. Mike asked me to drive, which was my pleasure—since I loved being behind the wheel of any car, even mine. We walked over to my big maroon wagon in the parking lot. He looked surprised that I had chosen this size vehicle, and even though I hadn't necessarily chosen it, the wagon did the job well for me.

I opened the door for him and ran around to my side of the car to hop in. He was a bit stunned at the acrobatic, fluid motion I made to hop into the car. He put on his seatbelt and sat, with anticipation, wondering how this was all going to work. He didn't seem to mind the antiquity of my car, but was excited like a kid getting on a roller coaster for the first time. I was beginning to see that this was my kind of guy, someone who didn't judge things or people on nonsense criteria, like height or make and model!

Now, I mentioned previously that I had learned to drive with hand controls, as I wasn't all too confident my legs were trustworthy enough to depend on while behind the wheel. What I didn't mention was that by virtue of driving with hand controls, my ability to multitask was limited—or so you would think. My left hand operated the wheel spinner, like the one found on the steering wheel of big rigs. My right hand was for the hand control, which had two functions, depending on which direction I moved in. The gas pedal was depressed, and the car accelerated when I pulled it toward me, and the brake would engage when I pushed the hand control toward the dash. You would think that with both hands occupied, there was very little I could do other than drive. But that was only if you were a mere mortal!

I smoked cigarettes back then, and lighting up meant abandoning the wheel or the gas/brake to grab my smokes and lighter. It got a bit crazier when I abandoned the wheel and the gas/brake to light up. And who didn't like coffee with a smoke on the way to work? Yup, the average morning ride in the car involved this juggling act between coffee, cigarettes, and driving. (Why I always tell this story with driving being the last thing I mention is still oddly funny to me.)

With Mike belted into the passenger seat, I eased the car onto the Sagtikos Parkway, one of those little snake-thin north-south corridors all over Long Island that were designed before the concept of traffic. Mike was terrified and mesmerized.

"You stop and go with that stick?" he commented.

"I control the wheel with the hand spinner," I explained, trying to point out all the different functions on my control. It was fun to explain to someone who had never seen this sort of equipment in operation before, and Michael couldn't have been more impressed. I could do turns in that car that I can't do today using *two* hands. He truly was fascinated with my driving. But what blew him away even more was everything else I did while driving.

"You smoke while you drive," he said more than once in awe. "How do you do that?" He then proceeded to grab a cigarette from my box of Marlboros, which was sliding from side to side on the dashboard. "How do you drink coffee, smoke, and drive at the same time?" To which I answered, "Same as you, carefully!"

Michael was a wonderful boss and a great man (still is). He started defending me from some of my soon-to-be-coworkers before I even started, saying their jobs were on the line if they had a problem with my stature. The firm was a big medical device distributor that received orders from big umbrella home health care agencies like Gentiva, which served tens of thousands of homebound patients a day as well as many of the hospitals across the country. We'd supply things such as home infusion supplies, tubing, needles and syringes, medication and infusion pumps—anything ordered by the supervising agency. When I started out, I was a sales rep for the south. Specifically, I was responsible for all alternate care (home) infusion companies throughout Alabama, Georgia, and northern Florida. Most of my days were spent speaking with pharmacy owners, pharmacists, and purchasing managers about their business needs, products, and the services we offered. I would ask for orders and help expedite requests when patients were being discharged to my clients' care. They would rely on me to save them from service failures (an inability to care for the patient). I was good at what I did, too. I grew revenue in that territory by double digits in just months. I was moved to another struggling region, the Midwest, including Wisconsin, Michigan, Ohio, Illinois, Indiana, and parts of Missouri, Nebraska, and Iowa. There, I really did well. After six months in the territory, I had signed major contracts with big home infusion pharmacies and grew the revenue and profitability by 200 percent.

Thanks to my motivation and execution, the growth in my territories afforded me promotions two or three times within a couple of years. First I became a regional sales manager and then a director of sales, which was the job Michael had when he hired me. He was doing well, too, enjoying a couple of promotions of his own—first vice president and then president of the division.

It was a good, healthy firm, and a lot of fun to work for. But with the world of home care exploding and changing as fast as it was, mergers and acquisitions were the next logical progression for our company. My company soon merged with a few other corporations to make one larger organization that had a diverse range of products and services, manufacturing, and distribution. That company conglomerate of nonsynergistic divisions was soon broken apart and sold to other companies. Two of the divisions went in a different direction, and the two home care divisions (of which I was still a part) were sold to a New Jersey–based company. The acquiring company had been on the acquisition trail for years, and we were the final purchase before the fall. We should have seen it coming. The integration of our business, a mere $60 million in revenue, into this company of a quarter billion was done terribly. After thirty days, we saw our revenues trending at 50 percent of what they once were. Then the news came down that the parent company was filing for bankruptcy, which meant *we* were filing for bankruptcy, too.

When we emerged from bankruptcy six months later, my team, which included Mike, took over the parent company. Since we had filed for bankruptcy, and the bank technically owned the company, we had to sell. We broke it back into two pieces and sold the main corporation to one firm and our division to another.

For the smaller sale, I was part of the deal team, which made me some money. I did well enough to buy a house, an eighteen-hundred-square foot ranch in Port Jefferson with a lovely outdoor deck and pool, which was perfect for summer nights. It needed a little updating, but I was handy and could do a lot of the work myself. My friends and I tackled some of the electrical, plumbing, and cosmetic stuff. When it got crazy, I let my paycheck do the work and hired professionals for the bathroom revisions, hardwood flooring, and replacement of the oil burner.

My increased compensation finally afforded me the ability to purchase some custom-made suits. Buying clothes, especially suits, had always been a challenge. My dimensions are not exactly "off the rack." My chest at its widest is forty inches, and my waist (at its narrowest), twenty-four inches. I have a waist, one that has been ever expanding and contracting over the years, but I am more like a big barrel in the chest. Combine that with my height, and a suit coat has no choice but to drape on me.

The first place I used to go to buy suits was Macy's. They had a decent selection, so I'd pick one or two in the men's department and have them altered. The tailoring was where I spent an arm and a leg, not the suit itself. Sometimes the pants were too baggy, or the crotch was too low. Or the jacket was cut so short that the pockets were barely over the hem, and the jacket looked as if I had gotten it caught on something. If I raised my arm, the sleeve would pull all the way up the elbow. For dress shirts, I'd buy a dress shirt with a seventeen-and-a-half-inch or eighteen-inch neck and the shortest sleeves possible for a guy with an eighteen-inch neck. Normally a 30/31 was the shortest I could find. To make sure the cuff was correct, the tailor would have to cut away six to ten inches of sleeve, and when they reattached the cuff, it was sewn onto a much wider part of the sleeve, up toward the bicep and shoulder. The "poofy" arms looked like something a pirate would wear. Sometimes, the person altering would want to shorten the sleeve at the end closest to the shoulder, thereby leaving the cuff intact, but this made for awfully narrow sleeves.

Once I had a little money, I started going to Giliberto Designs, Inc., in the garment district of Manhattan. The clothes were fully custom, with nothing off the rack. Giliberto dressed President George W. Bush for his first inauguration, so to say he had distinguished clients was an understatement. He dressed many players for the New York Giants, Knicks, Yankees, Mets, and Jets—all the guys who don't fit into a "regular" suit and want top quality.

In his shop, photos of famous people wearing their Giliberto suits covered the walls. I was starstruck that I was buying suits from the same tailor as Bill Parcells and President Bush. One day years later I looked up, and by gosh, Bill Klein was hanging on that wall, wearing blue pinstripes, looking only slightly more subdued than a hit man.

Giliberto made a template for me on my first visit. This template, completely unique and specific for me, wasn't just a pre-existing pattern he altered for me—it was *my* template, for Bill Klein and only Bill Klein. The suits were two thousand dollars, and that was ten years ago, but worth every penny.

I'm not going to lie—I've become accustomed to getting only custom fits. When I first started to be able to afford it, I would buy everything custom. My shirts were from the Custom Shop. When their business consolidated and closed all of the locations in the tristate area, I'd drive the six hours to Washington, D.C., their only location in the mid-Atlantic/Northeast, to get my shirts. I'd get to town and stay in a hotel overnight. In the morning, I'd get measured, order five or six shirts, have lunch, and drive the six hours home. Once, I decided to take my friend Andria with me, which was great, as I loved the company. She thought I was a bit crazy to go to such lengths for some shirts, but considering my options, she understood. My assortment of shirts was usually ready in three to four weeks.

More recently, I discovered a place in Beverly Hills called Jimmy Au's For Men 5'8" & Under. Jimmy sells to all the height-challenged stars—Tom Cruise, Jason Alexander, Danny DeVito. He also has dress and casual shirts that are made specifically for people who are short (which, incidentally, seems to include much of Hollywood—even the big guys are topping out at six feet), and he can get them to me in three to four days. I was concerned that the price in Beverly Hills was going to scare me away. But in the end, Jimmy's clothing is made small enough that normal tailoring is all that is required to take an off-the-rack shirt and make it fit perfectly. This was a great find, and like Jennifer, once I find a brand that works, I don't let it go.

Getting nice clothes as a Little Person has become easier in the past twenty years, thanks to children's clothes becoming a lot more stylish. When I was growing up, the only shoes that fit me, men's or boys, looked like Keds. When I reached adult age, the last thing I wanted to buy was kids' dress shoes, with rubber soles and big, ugly stitching. They had no arch support—and they were just embarrassing to wear. So I used to buy Allen Edmonds shoes in size six, because that was the smallest adult size—$225 a pop. My true size was four and a half, wide, but at least I wasn't in "big kids" shoes. My ostrich leather shoes were my favorites—so very nice. I'd suck it up in the wrong size, even if it meant tripping on the carpet from time to time.

BACK TO BUSINESS. Once the divestiture of the companies was complete, Michael elected to move on. I stayed behind and did the wind-down of the Deer Park office. Upon closing the office in June 2005,

I left the company, too. That July, I was back in business, with Michael as my partner. Together, we opened our own lead generation and business-consulting firm that catered to companies in the health care industry. The model was fairly simple. Our clients were medical device manufacturers, distributors, and providers. We would offer a variety of services, including lead generation, whereby we would contact our clients' target customer base and identify those with an interest and need to do business with our client, and forward the key contact and prospect information to the client for follow-up. We would also work with clients to develop their internal sales teams, help with product and sales training, and consult with executive management on direction and vision of companies, operational efficiencies, and adoption of technology. Our clients included Fortune 500 companies in the health-care sector, as well as start-up companies with innovative products. We had our first sale the very first month we were in business.

We had our ups and downs, but we did pretty well. Like many start-ups, we started our business out of my house. Within months, our business was doing pretty well. We had nine employees working out of the home office—an odd-shaped twelve-by-twenty-five-foot room that I had turned into two twelve-by-twelve shared offices with desks, computers, and phones in every corner. The commute was great for me, but I knew it was time to find a commercial space when I found one of our employees on *my* living room sofa, watching *my* television, and enjoying some cheese he had found in *my* refrigerator during his lunch break.

CHAPTER THIRTEEN

Jen

MEDICAL SCHOOL

MEDICAL SCHOOL TRIED MY intellect and stamina more than anything I have ever done before. Going to Johns Hopkins was a dream, but nothing worth working hard for is easy. My first days of freshman orientation included lots of bonding with my classmates. The first two years, all two hundred of us spent eight to twelve hours a day together in lectures, labs, and small group discussions.

My least favorite class was immunology, but my favorite was gross anatomy. Gross anatomy is what most people think about when they envision what medical school must be like. It is a defining step in becoming a doctor. For gross anatomy, we were grouped into teams of four students and we each were assigned a cadaver. Our cadaver was a seventy-year-old woman. We were instructed to have the utmost respect for our cadavers, who had been willing to donate their bodies so future doctors could learn. For the next nine weeks, these were our "persons." Their real identities were never given to us, so many groups named their cadaver. At the end of the course, we had a memorial for our "persons," and then their bodies were returned to their families for funerals and/or burials.

We spent hours dissecting everything from skin and bones to delicate nerves and veins. The whole lab smelled like formaldehyde, and so did we. Because the protective gowns we had to wear were so big, I bought my own smaller aprons, which then meant that I had to transport them back to my room to wash every week—that was not pleasant—and at some point my room began to smell like formaldehyde. I also brought my own step stool—the same one I ended up later using on the wards—but given the number of "messy things" (subcutaneous tissue and fat) that end up on the floor during gross anatomy, the school eventually made me a more sturdy one to prevent a potential fall. What I didn't expect was that the further along we got in the class, the deeper the dissection got into the body—and the deeper in I got as well. While my teammates might have been up to their elbows dissecting, I was up to my shoulders.

Gross anatomy can be pretty . . . well, gross. However, I was never unduly grossed out by anatomy. In fact I loved it. But I didn't like entering the lab late in the evening to cram for an exam when not many other people were around. I tried not to do that too much. It is a little creepy to be in a room with fifty cadavers by yourself!

After the first year and a half of basic sciences, we got to enter the wards, but not before the traditional White Coat Ceremony. This event celebrates your transition from the basic sciences to clinical medicine. During the ceremony, each student receives his or her first "white coat" with the Johns Hopkins insignia and his or her name embroidered on it. At Johns Hopkins, this is a short white coat, more like a blazer. Of course, mine had to be specially made, but I was very proud of it.

My first year, I lived on campus in the Lowell J. Reed Medical Residence Hall, a ten-story red brick building on McElderry Street designated for all first-year med students. Reed Hall had two wings with vastly different accommodations connected by a communal lobby area. Fortunately, I was in the east wing, the nicer of the two, so our suites had semiprivate bathrooms and small kitchenettes. I had three suite mates, Tracy, Asma, and Carmen, and we each had our own bedroom with shared kitchen, bathroom, and living room. The west wing was basic dormitory singles and doubles with communal bathrooms on all the floors. The building was really old, but at least recent renovations had given it central air, wall-to-wall carpet, and 24/7 security. Everyone living there loved that it was so close to the medical school classrooms and the library, even if we didn't love the accommodations. Besides, we were hardly in our rooms anyway, not with the amount of work, labs, and studying we had to do. Everybody at Hopkins was fairly driven and had been a top student at whatever undergraduate school they had come from, so there was pressure and a lot of competition. I studied hard and spent hours upon hours studying everywhere and anywhere, from the undergraduate campus library (as it was much prettier and more comfortable than the one in the medical school), to our favorite local coffee house, to hospital cafeterias.

As a student at Hopkins, I did get to spend more time (albeit not a lot due to the rigorous academics) with my close childhood friends from Baltimore. I got to see Donna, my former primary nurse, and Diane, Dr. Kopits's nurse practitioner, on a regular basis.

At least once every few months, I talked to Dr. Kopits. I didn't have any family in Baltimore, so he was my go-to person for an emergency. Obviously, he was a very busy man, so I didn't call him for small things, but we stayed close. Every once in a while he would invite me over to dinner or we would meet for lunch. Because I had already started to feel the pains of early osteoarthritis associated with my skeletal dysplasia, Dr. Kopits gave me special permission to use the specialized heated pool at St. Joseph's to help keep my joints in shape and limber.

The summer between your first and second years of medical school, you're strongly encouraged to work in a research lab. I wanted to be able to spend some time closer to home and also catch up with my close friends in Miami, who were now also in medical school. My good friend Brian helped me find a mentor at the University of Miami School of Medicine, and I spent six weeks doing research with him there. After that, I spent the rest of the summer at home with my parents in Orlando. I bought my first car, a Kia Sportage, and my family taught me how to drive in less than four weeks. I was going to need a car in the fall, as the apartment I would be moving to was no longer on campus, and public transportation was not an option. Although I failed my first road test, I passed on my second try.

I still hold a grudge over failing my first test. My evaluator requested I make a left-hand turn on a single-lane road during rush hour where the oncoming traffic was backed up for twenty cars. I watched three green lights go by and couldn't make the left due to oncoming traffic. There was a growing pile of cars building behind me. At the fourth green light, a car in the opposite lane flashed his lights, honked his horn, and waved me on so I could make the left. I felt very stressed because everyone behind me was freaking out, so I made the left. I failed the exam because you should never make a left with oncoming traffic regardless of whether they wave you on. Apparently, you're supposed to just wait, even if it means waiting for rush hour to end. Needless to say, when I went to take my test the second time, it was not during rush hour.

That fall, I was going to be moving into a high-rise apartment in a building across the street from the George Peabody Library, the exquisite library for the whole university, not the Welch Medical Library, which was for medical students on the hospital campus. My roommate was one of my medical school classmates, Aruna, whom I had become good friends with. My father drove back to Maryland with me, and we pretty much split the time behind the wheel on the trip. I didn't mind the highway stretches as much as I thought I would, and at least I wasn't alone in case I panicked. What a relief it was for me to be driving to Johns Hopkins to be on the opposite side of the "knife!" It was kind of funny that my first long haul in my new car with my newly gained license was to Johns Hopkins Hospital.

It was no surprise, given the short time that I had to learn to drive, that within two weeks of getting back to Baltimore I got into my first car accident. I was with my friend Eileen, who had actually gone to St. Charles and Bishop Moore with me. Now she was in Baltimore getting a master's in nursing at Johns Hopkins, and we had reconnected. The day of the accident, I was dropping her off at her condo after a day of fun bopping around the city. I was just pulling up to the front of her building when a parked car suddenly pulled out and hit me on the passenger side, where Eileen was sitting. I probably wasn't road smart enough yet to notice that the car was about to move. The driver did not have her blinker on, which she was supposed to when leaving the curb. Nevertheless, she sideswiped us and caused significant damage to my car. Although I was pretty shaken up and that sound of metal on metal was etched in my mind, fortunately, everybody was okay. It was a very low-velocity accident.

It was a Sunday afternoon, and we were stuck without transportation while my car was being towed. Donna lived pretty far outside of town, so I called Dr. Kopits to see if he could help. I trusted him and knew if he was available, he'd be there. He was there within half an hour and found us quite shaken up, but otherwise fine. He was very calm about it all, and to my great relief, he even agreed to call my mother. "Judy, Judy," I could hear him say into his cell phone in his very thick Hungarian accent, "everything is okay." He told her he would arrange for the car to be towed and take me home. Thank God for Dr. Kopits!

I had a couple more fender-benders after that. One time, I side-swiped the concrete block inside the parking garage trying to back out of my space. I hate to make excuses for myself, but in all seriousness, having a fused neck that prevented me from rotating my head at all might have played a part in that particular bender.

Another time, I was late getting to the hospital for one of my rotations and forgot that I was in reverse and slammed into a car behind me. I had just backed up a tiny bit in order to reach the button for the gate to the parking garage at the hospital, but then I forgot to put the car into drive before I stepped on the gas pedal, so I backed into the car behind me. What made this accident particularly bad was that the other driver was a pediatrician, which was the field I wanted to pursue. I was mortified. Even though I didn't know this pediatrician well, I knew he would never forget *me*.

At Johns Hopkins, I continued the passion for being involved in student government that I had developed at University of Miami. I became secretary and later vice president of my class during medical school. Along with three other class officers, I was responsible for academic affairs, activities, and planning social events. It took some time, but I developed some great friends in medical school—Aimee, Michelle, Tony, and my roommates, to name a few. I got along with everyone in my class, though. Given the amount of time and stress we all went through together, it was hard not to feel close to your medical school classmates.

We planned one social event, the Fall Ball, that I will never forget. Because I lived so close to the Peabody Library, where we were holding the event, I offered to drop off the two-thousand-dollar deposit check at the office of the events coordinator. This part of town was not the safest, and I was not the speediest person on the block, but at four o'clock in the afternoon with the library directly across the street from my apartment, it didn't make sense to drive across the street only to struggle to find parking.

As I was moving down the sidewalk toward the library, a seedy-looking character walked right up to me out of nowhere, as if he were going to bump right into me. "Hey, I know you," he said, "I've seen you in the ER." I smiled and realized by his tone I was not getting by without speaking with him. I didn't know who he was, but he said he was just in the ER and proceeded to lift up his pant leg to show me his recent gunshot wounds. He must have seen me while I was on my ER rotation, but of course I didn't remember. I was concerned about the two-thousand-dollar check in my pocket, but I was more worried about my safety. Although we were on the sidewalk in broad daylight, a large semi truck was parked on the side of the street, so we were unfortunately sandwiched between the brick wall of my apartment complex and the truck. No one driving on the street or walking on the other side of the sidewalk could really see us. I just kept thinking to myself, maybe someone else will turn the corner and walk by, so he will leave me alone.

"You are not walking away without talking to me," he said, moving along the sidewalk to reach me again. He then asked me for some spare change for the bus. I gave him a couple of dollars, but he still didn't back off. "Hey, you are really cute. Do you have a boyfriend?" he asked.

I should have said yes and continued walking, but hindsight is always 20/20. This guy had caught me completely off-guard, and I stupidly blurted out that I didn't. This was his opening to be my "friend."

"You are not going away without giving me your number," he declared. I was afraid that if I continued walking and didn't pay attention to him, he might get angry and do something aggressive. So I gave him a phone number—a made-up one, of course—and finally, he let me by. I walked as quickly as I could to the Peabody, delivered my check, and ran home.

Some people may think I was a little paranoid, but at three feet tall, you can never be too careful. Fortunately, the anecdote ends there, with this creepy-looking person going his way and me going mine. The nicest part of the story was that the Fall Ball was one of the most successful events of the year. I even got to rotate in as one of the "bartenders" for a while. That was amusing, since I didn't even know how to make a screwdriver at the time!

During medical school, I also became more involved with the organization Little People of America, only this time on a national level. Little People of America is primarily a support network, with activities and social events taking place at all its branches. However, one of the greatest things about LPA is the access it gave us to the most up-to-date medical information and specialists in the world. The Medical Advisory Board consists of a wide range of medical specialists, and many attend the LPA convention every year. The medical specialists represented in many fields, not just orthopedics. They come to the conference to see patients and consult and network with each other. At the convention, many doctors not only give seminars, but they set up a "clinic" in hotel rooms to see patients. Their schedules usually book up nine months in advance, but it's a great opportunity to see multiple specialists from all over the country or the world at one time.

When I was younger, I had done a few things with the local LPA chapters in Florida, but I had never participated at the national levels. Now, I really wanted to go to a national convention, and this year it was in Atlanta, Georgia.

In Atlanta, I shared a room with a Little Person named Angel, who was ten years older but whom I had known from our local chapter in Orlando. She was absolutely fantastic and helped me understand what a national convention is all about. The conference includes social, medical, and general networking meetings. Primarily, nationals are an opportunity for thousands of Little People and their families from all over the world to meet and socialize.

At this first national meeting, I met Martha for the first time. Martha is my age, and she took me to parties and outings where I met more LPs from all over the world. I remember one party at which drinking, socializing, and hooking up was the theme—probably a good example of why my parents never wanted me to attend a national conference! Martha had her video camera out at the party and was documenting all the fun. She tells me to this day how ironic it was to capture me with a look of shock and awe as I took in all the partying, dancing, and drinking in the room. Because I didn't know anyone other than Martha—and the famous Vern Troyer, Mini-Me from *Austin Powers*—I refrained from going crazy. I had a lot of fun at the Atlanta convention and made great friends that I kept in touch with for years, and I knew that I definitely wanted to come to another one soon.

The LPA national convention moves to a different city each year, but always ends up in a destination known to be popular with tourists. But medical school and my first year of pediatric residency were so time-consuming and overwhelming that I didn't go again for five years. With thirty approaching, and no prospect of finding true love, I finally decided to make it a priority to find time to start attending the national conventions. In my second year of pediatric residency at Children's Hospital of Pittsburgh, I attended the LPA national in Salt Lake City. There, I befriended four ladies from New York and a woman named Melody, whom I am still good friends with.

After the 2002 Salt Lake City convention came Boston. When I later met Bill in 2006, he said he had been planning on going to that one, which would have been his first national LPA conference, but work got in the way. He even had his ticket and his hotel room booked, and his mission in Boston was going to be to find a woman. But his company was in the midst of being sold, and his CEO called him back. So our chance encounter in Boston was not to be.

The next LPA convention was in San Francisco. There I met my first long-term boyfriend, Jeff. He was a New Yorker, an international stock trader who did well. He lived in Manhattan and we completely hit it off at first. He seemed to really like me, but I think he just wasn't ready to love someone long term. Although we had a whirlwind relationship for about six months, he broke it off after he said it was too hard not being able to see each other more easily. You see, I was in the middle of my neonatal-perinatal fellowship, working up to one hundred plus hours a week. He said he wanted to remain friends, and even invited me to go to Africa with him on a safari after we broke up. It took some time for me to realize it, but I had to ultimately break ties with him or I would continue to have my heart broken if we kept in touch as friends. I later came to realize, of course, that Jeff and I were not meant to be and my true love was still out there looking for me.

Nevertheless, after four long years of medical school, I was ready to graduate. There had been enough study sessions, labs, and all-nighters to kill a moose. I had seen classmates break under the pressure, but remarkably few dropped out. I had taken a series of licensing exams that were required to take my study to the next level. I had worked in all areas of the hospital, from pediatric orthopedic surgery, to obstetrics and gynecology, to ophthalmology, to adult oncological surgery, to internal medicine, to pediatrics, and more. I had the privilege of taking care of patients and observing surgeries, and had finally decided on a specialty for residency—pediatrics.

This final year had not been without family struggles. My mom had been diagnosed with a benign, but growing, brain tumor, a meningioma. She had gone through gamma knife radiation the previous year, but had suffered a severe complication, cerebral edema, from the treatment. For months she suffered from outrageous headaches and had to take high-dose steroids. She ultimately had to have brain surgery in the fall of my last year of medical school to have the tumor removed. Because it was my last year, I was able to take an "away" elective rotation at the children's hospital in Orlando to be home for her surgery.

By the spring of that year, things were looking up, and March 16, 2000, a few days after my birthday, was match day. That is the day when medical students all over the country find out where they will be spending the next three or more years in residency training. After students have applied, interviewed, and then ranked their top choices for residency through the National Resident Matching Program (NRMP), the NRMP pairs students with the needs of hospital residency programs based on both parties' rank lists. This is another big milestone during medical school.

At this event, I had a lot of support. My very good friend from college, Suketu, had driven from Pittsburgh, where he was an OB/GYN physician resident, to visit for the event, and my dad flew in. The genetics coordinator at the skeletal dysplasia center at Hopkins, Dee, came, and Donna also showed up to support me. At the ceremony, they distribute the envelopes to all the students, and then, in an almost drum roll fashion, everyone opens them at the same time! I was matched to Children's Hospital of Pittsburgh at the University of Pittsburgh Medical Center. I was thrilled, because Suketu was already an OB/GYN resident there, so I would have an instant friend and colleague. I later found out my best friend from college, Lakshmi, who stayed at our alma mater for medical school, also matched to Pittsburgh that same day for family medicine. I had loved my interview at Pittsburgh, and ultimately I loved my three years of pediatric residency at Children's so much I decided to stay an additional three years for my neonatal-perinatal fellowship. I couldn't have been more thrilled with my match!

After the match celebrations came spring break, and I had plans to take a last-hurrah road trip with my good friend in medical school, Michelle. We drove from Baltimore to Orlando and finally Miami for some fun in the sun! Those were good times, and by that point I was, fortunately, a much better driver! We called it our "Bad Girls, Good Road Trip."

My medical school graduation took place on Thursday afternoon, May 25, at the Meyerhoff Symphony Hall, one of the premier music venues in Baltimore. My dear friend Aimee Nielson gave our class's graduation speech and the former surgeon general, Antonia C. Novello, was our guest commencement speaker. It is tradition at graduation to be able to invite either a family member who is a physician or, sometimes, your favorite faculty member or mentor from the school to "hood" you—or place a colorful hood over your graduation gown. Different degrees get different-colored hoods, and for medicine, it is green. Since I didn't have a physician in the family and Dr. Kopits could not hood me because he no longer worked at Johns Hopkins, Dr. Victor McKusick, who had diagnosed me as an infant, offered to hood me at graduation. His brief bio in the program read: *University Professor of Medical Genetics, Institute of Genetic Medicine, Johns Hopkins School of Medicine. One of the founding fathers of medical genetic research, he has been a member of the Johns Hopkins University faculty since July 1, 1947.* It was extraordinary—on the faculty of Johns Hopkins for more than *fifty years.* I was incredibly proud to be receiving my diploma in his presence.

Dr. Kopits had planned to be at my graduation ceremony as well, just as he had been at my college graduation. He was my biggest supporter. He said he wouldn't miss my graduation for all the world. However, he was delayed because of a patient issue—not surprising given his dedication to his patients—and missed the ceremony. That was Dr. Kopits, all right—the patient's needs *always* came first. How could I forget how he had blasted out of a dinner ceremony honoring him in Buenos Aires when he heard I was in crisis?

He had a strained relationship with Johns Hopkins at this point, having opened his specialized pediatric orthopedic unit at a different hospital, but fortunately nobody was worrying about the politics on this glorious day.

When I crossed the stage, Dr. McKusick was standing there in the middle to place my doctoral hood around my neck. I was smiling so hard, I wasn't sure I could hold it together. It had been a rough four years, and I couldn't believe I had made it. He draped the colorful hood around my shoulders, beaming just as much as I was, and the dean of the medical school handed me my diploma.

As I walked off the stage, I waved my diploma in the air, smiling, and the entire audience cheered. I don't really know what got into me at that moment, but I think I couldn't hold back my pure excitement at that point! I was getting a standing ovation from the crowd! It was one of the highlights of my life, a memory I will cherish forever. As I walked back to my seat, my dad popped out into the aisle and gave me a big hug—my parents were very proud!

The dinner afterward was pretty awesome as well. Besides my family, I was with so many of my heroes: Dr. Kopits, who fortunately at least made that event; Donna, my hero nurse and always my friend; Diane, another great caretaker throughout my surgeries and recoveries who had a proclivity for matchmaking; and Dr. McKusick, medical geneticist extraordinaire. They were all at my table rallying for me. I couldn't believe that these were the same people who had held my hand and promised me everything would be all right when I was only two years old in the hospital. It was beyond—absolutely beyond—special.

Sadly, Dr. Kopits was with us for only another two years after my graduation. The master healer for everyone he touched became terminally ill himself. Brain cancer, a gliobastoma multiforme, was his undoing, much too soon. He was only sixty-five when he died on June 2, 2002. There is not a day that goes by that I don't think of him and the wonderful out-of-this-world things he did for Little People. I was in my second year of pediatric residency when he passed away. My mother and I went to his funeral at the Cathedral of Mary Our Queen in Baltimore, as did almost five hundred Little People he had cared for. At the end of the service, they carried his casket down the aisle, at which time—without any announcement or planning—all his patients came into the aisle and held hands, sobbing as we saw him off. He was a miracle worker to thousands, truly thousands. There are countless LPs who could not walk until they met Dr. Kopits, or who had been disabled because of botched surgeries by other surgeons who did not understand the nuances and complications of skeletal dysplasias. He healed them with love and dedication as well as with surgery. Doctors like him, with surgical dexterity, brilliant inventiveness, and a bedside manner too kind for words to describe, are nearly impossible to find. I work with many wonderful doctors every day, but have never met anyone like him. There will never be another doctor in the world like Dr. Kopits. If anyone is up in heaven with the saints and angels, I know Dr. Kopits is!

CHAPTER FOURTEEN

Bill

DaTeaLITTLe

IF JENNIFER HAD MET me when I was twenty, there would have been no way she would have dated me, let alone married me, and if by some mistake she had, she certainly wouldn't still be with me now. I mean, most people aren't very adult when they are twenty. They make mistakes, think they know everything, and do some downright dumb things. Ideally, by the time thirty-one comes around, they have grown out of that reckless or self-indulgent behavior.

I used some of this wisdom that comes with age and reflecting on my parents' divorce. I could see how things in their lives changed, how their circumstances changed, and how their behavior changed after they got married. Even what was important to them had changed. I was disappointed about the divorce for a long time, but I don't hold a grudge against my dad. He has been married to his second wife since 1987, close to thirty years. Debbie, my stepmother, was a part of my upbringing, and my stepbrothers have been my brothers for a long time. When any one of us is discussing a "brother," we have to wonder which of the four others he is referring to. Regardless of how the circumstances had changed between Mom and Dad, Dad always kept the interests of his children front and center. Looking back, I am sure some of my bad behavior toward my father and Debbie was an attempt to aggravate them simply because of my frustration that things had changed, that things were different and stressful. I saw my mother in so much grief, and I was hypersensitive about protecting the woman who had created me and taken care of me every day of my life.

My initial contact with Jen was like the modern-day version of the way my parents made contact. They had been pen pals, but strangers, learning they liked each other through their communication. Jen and I first started "corresponding" on a site called DateALittle.com, an online dating site for single Little People.

I had been a member of the site for only a short time when I came across Jennifer's profile (circa December 2005). I recognized her as the girl that Diane, Dr. Kopits's nurse practitioner, had been so enthusiastic about ten years earlier. Since then, I had heard updates on her progress, from when she was at U of Miami throughout Johns Hopkins medical school and beyond. She was kind of a celebrity in the Little People community because she was one of the very few who became practicing physicians. I loved her profile portrait. She was very pretty, with long blond hair combed perfectly straight and funky, pointy cat's-eye glasses. I wrote to her immediately, but she didn't write back. I shrugged it off, thinking that she was seeing somebody, or that I did not interest her. I couldn't dwell on it, so I moved on and "talked" to other people instead.

About a month and a half later, a "New Message" arrived in my

Inbox. It was from Jen, who had sent me a lame note. "Have we met at a Little People of America convention? You look familiar." I chuckled, because I hadn't been to a convention in twenty years! So this was Jen's corny, innocuous pick-up line. Of course, I had to write back. "No, probably not," was the way I started my reply. I didn't elaborate too much on the subject, quickly moving toward a more formal introduction, a bit of background about myself, and a barrage of questions that I had, hoping to learn more about her. She never mentioned my earlier message to her, and I didn't ask, although she later claimed she never received a communication from me, and that if she had, she hadn't seen it. She also talked about some property in the Everglades she wanted to sell to me!

I also later learned why she had written that goofy pick-up line. She and her best friend Lakshmi were in their early thirties and despairing that they didn't have social lives and never had dates, being too busy with all their medical training. Jen was living in Pittsburgh, Pennsylvania, and working in excess of one hundred hours a week at the hospital where she was doing her fellowship. Over a glass of wine one night, the two had decided they were each going to join a dating website and write to one person to see what happened. Jen chose DateALittle.com and out of all the profile pictures she saw, she picked mine. I think she liked that I was wearing little round eyeglasses and was driving a speedboat in my "mug shot." Lakshmi was not a Little Person, so her candidate came from the average-size-people dating site, Match.com. Unfortunately for Lakshmi, her initial efforts with Match.com didn't produce anything long-term, although there was a happy ending for her when she found her husband-to-be not long after Jen and I started dating. They are now married with two boys!

Jen's "have we met before" introduction soon turned to "let's exchange phone numbers." We talked on the phone almost daily for over a month until we finally decided it was time to meet. I love to tell the story of that first face-to-face encounter, so Jen is letting me have the honors. It was a dark and stormy night in Pittsburgh. HA! Actually, it was a damp, cold day, Friday, March 10, 2006, in the 'burgh on the day of our first meeting. Although we had been talking on the phone since late January and knew we were ready for a relationship, it took only one face-to-face for me to be smitten. It seemed to be the case with her, as well.

It was unbelievable and totally romantic. I flew into Pittsburgh for the date, as Jen's schedule was too hectic for her to come to Long Island and she wasn't a big fan of air travel. I got a hotel room in the Courtyard by Marriott, not too far from the Children's Hospital, because I didn't want to presume anything, I didn't want to blow it, and I didn't want to awkwardly end up sleeping on her couch.

Jen said she would pick me up after work, and I was really nervous. Because I was freaking out, I went to the hotel bar first and grabbed a quick beer. I'm not a big drinker these days, but a beer and some barkeeper's small talk seemed to keep my nerves under control. Jen, who was coming off a thirty-hours-straight work marathon, said she'd pick me up outside. So, there I was standing on the street in front of the hotel, and she pulled up in a very dirty and scarred white 1996 Kia Sportage. Jen let me know this was her first car. She was so proud of it and thought it was cute. From anyone else's point of view, it was about ten years old but looked about twenty. It sounded like either a Sherman tank coming across the battlefield, or a '73 Plymouth with a bad muffler, although Jen told me she must have changed the muffler ten times already.

"Oh, no," I said to myself, "this can't be her." I assessed each vehicle that arrived at the Courtyard by Marriott in this manner.

"Oh, no, it *is* her!" There was my date behind the wheel! My butterflies went crazy. She was in hospital scrubs, and I knew pretty much then and there that I was in love. This was my girl. I loved everything about her—except the car, but that was replaceable! What really captured me were her wide smile and the blue of her eyes, popping through her glasses. I had really liked her when we'd talked before, but at that moment, my heart melted. I knew I was headed to the altar.

The huge grin on Jen's face made me very happy when she stopped the car and idled in front of me. First off, she could have just kept driving when she spotted me, but she didn't. She told me later that she thought I was very handsome, and she knew that she liked me, having loved everything about me from our phone conversations. But she was a little more hesitant than me, because she had already been burned a few times. So she liked me, and I was in love with her. "Well, I was in love with the idea of you," Jen reiterated with her big grin when we reviewed our first impressions of each other years later.

I opened the passenger door, climbed in, gave her a hug and a peck on the cheek, and we went to Starbucks to enjoy what would turn out to be the first thing we had in common—our LOVE of coffee. I don't remember what we were talking about, but it was two hours over coffee and refills, just talking. I remember Jen telling me she was nervous that I was going to judge her by her car. I confirmed that I had judged—and decided that she was the coolest person on the planet—and that her car needed to be replaced as soon as humanly possible! It was just one of those weird connections, where we were totally in sync with each other at first glance.

After coffee, Jen dropped me off at my hotel and we made a plan to meet later on that night. She drove home, where she was supposed to get some sleep, but that didn't happen, as she had to fight off a migraine. She also had to figure out what to wear. Jen is so stylish, always looking good and put together. That night was no exception. She was all dressed up when she came to pick me up, even though she was not feeling her best.

Jen asked me what I wanted for dinner. Sushi restaurants were the new "in" thing in the early 2000s, and as I had acquired a taste for it, I suggested sushi. It turned out Jen didn't like sushi at all, except the wimpy kind like California rolls and tempura. But she agreed. I have since learned that because Jen is always making big, life-saving decisions at work, she likes to be indecisive and dependent on others with small decisions, such as dinner plans. She also didn't tell me how carefully she had thought out her backup plan in case this date went awry. In case there was trouble with me, and I tried to kill her, she would page her best friend, who was on standby. Wow! I had no such backup plan! I could have been thrown from one of the many bridges into the countless tributaries and rivers around the city!

At the restaurant, the staff hooked Jen up with some linens folded over so she could sit down and we could be eye to eye. I sat across from her at our table for two. We ordered an amazing amount of food. We had all these dishes on the table, but we just kept talking. They brought all the food and they took it all away. We didn't touch any of it, including the edamame, which Jen said she loved. We were just so wrapped up in the conversation and elated to be with each other that we didn't even have time to eat or think of eating. When we got up to pay, the sushi chef actually came over, seemingly insulted or concerned, and asked what was wrong with the food. He accepted my explanation that it was our first date, the conversation was too good, and his rolls looked great enough to have us return some other time.

After dinner, Jen took me for a little tour of the city. Eventually, we headed up to Mt. Washington, Pittsburgh's "the Point," where there was a great view of the Pittsburgh skyline across the Monongahela River. The climb wasn't super high, maybe two hundred feet, but it was steep. We went up the windy road in Jen's crash derby reject car, and I wasn't sure we would make it. I was amazed we made it to the top. The view was amazing. There were several spots from which to view the city; one of them being a concrete sidewalk perched high above the river below.

This was, of course, where I had a chance to put on my smooth moves. My first attempt was quite benign, just a little peck. Once it was apparent my peck was welcomed and I wasn't going to be shoved over the rail to my doom, we actually had a "grown-up" kiss. What I remember most about that night was when I enveloped her in my coat because she was so cold. The overcoat I had made a couple of years earlier was loose on me, since I had lost weight, and it was big enough for me to fit Jen in there with me. Cold Pittsburgh night, clear skies, twinkling lights, and Jen warmly snuggled in my overcoat with me—it didn't get better than this.

Because the weekend I went to visit Jen was her birthday weekend, there were some planned activities already on the schedule for Saturday, specifically a birthday party for her that evening. So, we did a few things during the day—brunch, sightseeing around the historic Squirrel Hill neighborhood, and of course lots of coffee. Then I dropped her off at Lakshmi's, who was the hostess for the evening birthday event and got a ride back to the hotel to get dressed. A couple of hours later, Jen, looking stunning as usual, picked me up.

The party was great. There were forty to fifty people crammed into the apartment, mostly doctors. At first, I felt a little intimidated. I only knew Jen, and she was the person of the hour, so her attention was divided between me and the many guests who had come to wish her a happy birthday. After a short time, I began to settle in, cracking some jokes and finding out more about Jen's "crew." She had a lot of great friends in Pittsburgh, and soon I considered them my friends, too.

Jen drove me to the airport for my flight home the next morning. "Can I see you next week?" I asked her. "I want to come back and see you next weekend." She was on call, which meant I would only get to see her for one night, but it was worth it to me. So I flew back the next weekend, barely able to endure the days in between. Her friend Lakshmi loved me, which was a huge bonus in helping Jen see my charm through my idiosyncrasies. For the next year and a half, I flew back and forth to Pittsburgh every weekend that I could.

In May 2006, two months after we had met, Jen let me know she was already entertaining the idea of moving closer to me. "Doctors have to apply a year in advance for positions in hospitals," she informed me. "So I have started my search, and it just so happens that Stony Brook University Hospital has a good reputation and is currently hiring neonatologists."

"Oh, that's great," I think I said. The hospital was only five miles from my house, and I had already fallen for her. There wasn't a doubt in my mind that if Jen wanted to move closer, I would welcome her with open arms.

She had already applied to the hospital and had been offered an in-person interview. Some guys might have been upset that she was moving too fast, but I couldn't have been happier. For me, the prospect of being closer to each other was very exciting. Long-distance relationships can be tough. Inclement weather and flight delays would often cut the trips short, if not cut them out entirely. And when you know you love someone, you want the rest of your life to be together, not just weekends, and it can't happen fast enough.

FOR THE INTERVIEW, Jen flew on JetBlue to JFK, where I picked her up and brought her back to my house in Port Jefferson. It was a great little house, perfect for me in every way. The previous owners didn't have exactly the same taste as me, but they had kept it in good shape. I had turned it into a bachelor pad, complete with microfiber forest green couches in the living room; a simple guest bedroom in case a friend stayed overnight; and a universal gym in the third bedroom because I didn't have any more furniture to put in there. There were no pictures, knick-knacks, or art on the walls. I had repainted all the walls and installed hardwood floors in all of the common areas, replaced all the light switches and fixtures, and put in a sliding glass door in the master bedroom to provide easy access to the deck. The deck and pool in the backyard meant lots of friends in the summer. Parties and casual get-togethers were a regular occurrence.

The trash cans outside still had the name "Arnold" on them, as the previous owner's last name was Arnold. When Jen and I got back to the house, that was the first thing she noticed. She didn't know that the previous owner's last name had been Arnold, a bizarre coincidence. When she saw the trash pails with her name on them, she was baffled.

"What the heck is this all about?" she wanted to know. She worried I was a stalker who trolled the Internet for victims, and then after a successful murder, ground them up and deposited them in garbage pails with their names on them. It would have made for a good season of *Dexter*, imagine me as the "Long Island Garbage Man." Fortunately, she accepted my explanation!

That night, I took Jen out for a nice dinner at Pace's Steak House. Pace's and I had quite a history by now. This was where Michael had taken me to celebrate my first job. Over the years, any time there was a celebration, Pace's was the place. We hosted many corporate holiday parties there, family birthday parties, retirement parties, you get the picture. I was such a regular, I would have had a table with my name on it if they'd had a custom like that there!

When Jimmy Pace, the owner, found out I was bringing a possible love interest named Jennifer, he had everybody in the place treat us like royalty. When we got there, the maître d', Tommy, said, "Good evening, Mr. Klein, your table is ready." I pretty much knew all the patrons in the restaurant as we headed to our table, but this night was too important to stop for a tableside chat. I kept it to the casual wave of acknowledgment instead. I was with the most beautiful girl in the world and had to make the most of our time!

The maître d' hooked Jen up with a set of pillows so she would be comfortable at the table. The dinner was amazing. The appetizers were delicious; the main course was off the menu and prepared especially for us; and the wine was a great bottle of Groth cabernet. Jen and I talked about how great it was going to be when she moved to Long Island while we drank our wine and feasted on stuffed lobster, the first lobster being stuffed with more lobster. She was truly blown away by the whole thing, as was I. All I could think was, *This is what it could be like every day (if I owned a lobster farm).*

Jen and I went back to the house, where we stayed up talking and laughing until late into the night. I told her that in the morning we would go shopping for the last few things she needed for her outfit for the interview at Stony Brook. She needed a scarf for her neck. She wanted to present herself perfectly. She put a lot of pressure on herself, but that was Jen. I didn't think she was going to have much of a problem and would sail through the interview, but she tended not to give herself that much credit.

The next day, we hopped in the car and drove over to Smith Haven Mall, the only big shopping mall in that part of Long Island. Jen was all excited to go, as one of her favorite things to do is shop. Unlike Jen, I don't like shopping. In fact, my old friend Andria and I used to go to the mall as teenagers. We would be no more than one hundred feet in the door and my eyes would start watering as I began to sneeze. Andria was convinced I was actually allergic to shopping in the mall.

Jen and I arrived at the Smith Haven Mall in my new little Infiniti G37 coupe (I'm an autophile, so I talk about cars whenever possible), and I was feeling quite proud to be in this moment—with the gal I loved at first sight, shopping for something to help her prep for the interview that would start her career as an attending physician, which would be only five miles from my front door . . . excuse me, our front door! We got out of the car near the food court entrance, and I could see a bunch of young teens, skateboarders, hanging out to the left. I had become quite attuned to anticipating issues with people before they developed, and these guys popped up on my radar a bit. I heard someone mumble out of the corner of his mouth, "Blah, blah, blah, midget . . ." It definitely bothered me a little bit, because Jen heard the comment, too.

From the instant Jen had told me she was flying into Kennedy, I had wanted to put my best foot forward and make sure she got to see the best of Long Island. I wanted her to absolutely love it here and see no other future for herself than sharing my home and my home turf with me.

Jen and I had even talked about this very subject, how the population on Long Island treated Little People. I had told her that for me, it had been great. I belonged to the local chapter of the Little People of America. There were about fifty members, maybe thirty Little People and twenty others who were family members. When I had been growing up, the group was mostly adults and very few kids. By the time I became an adult, the group was mostly kids and very few adults. However, I'd found great support in the group, and my local community had always been very cordial and supportive.

In general, although I had suffered more than my share of being bullied, I had encountered very little outright prejudice. I had had some issues with trying to get a job, but that was more like discrimination than mean-spirited bigotry. Anyway, I blew it off, and Jen did the same. We walked around the mall a little until Jen finally found the perfect scarf, and, of course, I started to sneeze—that mall air! We walked out to the car, where Jen noticed something on my windshield.

She said, curious what it could be, "What is that?" I told her it was a mystery to me, too, and chivalrously opened her door. I closed her door, walked around to the windshield, and grabbed the piece of paper from underneath the wiper. It was a Post-it size piece of paper with a message that read, *"Die midget die."*

I was stunned. I stood by my car holding the note looking around the parking lot in complete disbelief. I wanted Jen to love Long Island like it was a dream come true, and now someone was taking the rude but benign comments to a new level with a real threat. When I didn't see anyone, I realized it was probably one of those skateboarders, who had since disappeared from the mall entrance. The safety of my girlfriend was at the forefront of my mind, and I quickly surveyed the immediate space around me to see if any of the hoodlums were still skulking around, looking to pick a fight or worse.

Jen was waiting patiently in the car. "Well, what was it?" she asked me when I finally slid into the driver's seat. "Wow, that is totally messed up," she said when I reluctantly showed the note to her. Jen was horrified. She was actually terrified. She had heard insults before, but this was among the worst she had ever experienced. It actually made her very nervous. "Do you think they could follow us back to the house?" She wasn't sure if the threat was random or truly personal. I told her that was crazy; they were just a bunch of kids.

I presented myself as calm, but I was absolutely boiling inside. I was trying to make it seem that it hadn't upset me as much as it had, but I was livid. The "die" was the part that upset me the most. They took ignorance and escalated it to a threat by saying, "Die midget." This was not the first time I had been threatened. But this was the first time I had been threatened with Jen.

I drove home at a thousand miles an hour, smoke pouring out of my ears. I was processing thoughts that shouldn't even have been occurring. *Maybe we should move someplace else . . . maybe I should sell my freaking house . . . maybe Jen is done with me and Long Island both . . . maybe I should have stayed outside the mall and called the police. Maybe I should go back to the mall and look for retribution.*

I just hated everything about the three words on the note. I understood that our size was different from that of the majority of people. Little People walking into the Smith Haven Mall probably happened rather infrequently. However, the timing of the note, in the middle of my trying to showcase my Island, couldn't have been more horrible. A bunch of cowardly bullies, as ignorant as the day is long, were trying to intimidate us and make us feel uncomfortable, even threatened.

It bothered me more than it bothered Jen. Well, in truth, it really bothered both of us. The reality was, it was everywhere. Any place you go, there will be a bully or two, despicably mean, ignorant loud-mouths who hide behind notes or other places cowards hide. They don't single out Little People or different races or religions, or fat or thin, young or old. They are not discriminatory in their prejudice.

Basically, they are so insecure, they will bully anyone who doesn't look like them and who maybe won't fight back. I mean, to leave such a note on my car window? Come up to me and say that to my face, and I will give you a wonderful story to take home to your buddies about how you got your ass kicked for being hyperignorant to the wrong person.

To Little People, the word "midget" is completely derogatory. Aside from using the word to lump together anyone short in stature, people used to use the term for proportionately "correct" little people as opposed to those with unmistakably shorter limbs. When P. T. Barnum made Tom Thumb a feature act in his circus, the term started to be used a lot everywhere. His sideshows in the "Greatest Show On Earth" had more Little People on display for the amusement of others, and the signs above the circus cars read "Midgets and Freaks" or "Strange People of the World." The "M" word has nothing to do with a medical condition. No one who has employed the word in my presence has said it with good intentions. At best, their use of it can be chalked up to a lack of education or a legacy passed down from a previous generation. At worst, it is used to specifically taunt, insult, and enrage the person it is directed toward. In my opinion, often times, it is both.

Nonetheless, there was no one to challenge in the mall parking lot. The skateboarders had disappeared into their bully holes, probably snickering about their low degree of intimidation. Back home, Jen and I had a nice dinner and put this rogue group of nasty cowards behind us. Moving forward was what we did best.

At her interview, Jen pretty much got the position on the spot. She called me up afterward, very excited. The division head who had interviewed her was fantastic; she had some friends there; she thought Stony Brook University Hospital would be a great fit, and it had the convenience of being close to her one true love, me. It didn't hurt that a Starbucks was literally the first building on the right once she left the neighborhood on the way to work, either. Talk about kismet.

For the most part, her interview weekend was action-packed. She met my mother and stepfather, Chuck, when they came over to the house. Mom was very excited, as was Jennifer. Correction, Mom was over the moon with excitement. Based on how I described Jen and the love we had for each other, Mom knew this was the girl I would be with for the rest of my life. They got along great. I knew they would. They say that you look for characteristics you've become fond of or accustomed to from your parents when you are in search of your perfect mate. Jen and Mom are alike in a bunch of ways, the most noticeable being the kindness they have toward others. Anyway, my mother led the conversation, asking Jen all sorts of questions. Jen must have felt like she had more than one interview that weekend! Mom is one of those bubbly, personable types, so there was never an awkward silence.

Mom was my biggest fan, and while she felt I was handsome, smart, and deserving of a wife of the same caliber, she wasn't sure I would ever get married. When she met Jen, she knew I had found the right girl, someone whom I would put in front of everything else, including work, which Mom knew spoke volumes about where my heart was. She thought Jen was very sweet, which made me very happy. She knew that when I told her months earlier, "Mom, I think this is the one," that I was right.

Jen also had the chance to meet my brother Joe. Joe lived in Port Jeff, too, and had heard a lot about my new love, as I had told everybody I could get to listen. Joe and Jen hit it off, too. I would have loved for Jen to meet everybody, but my stepbrother James was in Charleston, South Carolina, where he had lived since college; my stepbrother Jonathan was living in Cincinnati, Ohio; and my brother Tom and my father and stepmother, Debbie, had all moved to Florida.

Jen had one other interview in New York City, at Albert Einstein College of Medicine in the Bronx. She got that job, as well, but she accepted the job at Stony Brook, which meant she was moving to Long Island! Unfortunately, as doctors apply one year in advance, she had a fellowship in Pittsburgh to finish and wouldn't be moving in for a year.

We kept up our long-distance romance into the fall, and I finally proposed to her on November 3, 2006. Two weeks earlier, I had gone to the Diamond District in New York City. One jeweler helped me pick out the diamond and another one helped me pick out the setting and a third helped me get it all together in a wooden box. I took that ring with me everywhere, never leaving it behind. In September, Jen and I flew to Florida to see her parents for a mini-vacation. It was my chance to pop the big question . . . not to Jen, but to her parents. As an old-school New Yorker, respect for elders and my future in-laws was at the top of my list, so I wanted to ask the Arnolds for permission to marry their daughter.

I took Jen's mom and dad out onto their back porch and told them my intention was to ask Jen to marry me. I asked for their permission and their blessing. "It would be an honor," her mom said, smiling. "You love Jennifer, she loves you, treat her well." They both gave me a hug, and Judy started talking about how excited she was to be able to give Jen the family pearls to wear on her wedding day.

With permission granted, I started scheming. I booked a flight to Pittsburgh for Friday evening, November 3, even though I actually intended to fly in in the morning. I sent my phony evening itinerary to throw her off the scent. The first thing I did when I got to town Friday morning was stop at the florist, where I picked up an order I had placed for seven dozen roses and a few bags of rose petals. Then, I went to Jen's apartment, where her super let me in. I put roses and candles everywhere—rose petals on the bed, on the doors, on the floor, and a single rose that I set aside to give to Jen when she walked in the door. I dressed in a tuxedo and put on some cheesy Frank Sinatra music that I had burned on a CD. The biggest problem was how to get Jen back to her apartment, as she thought she was picking me up at the airport after work.

I had a great idea. I called her and told her there was something very important I had mailed to the house, and that she needed to get it before she got me. I also told her my flight was delayed, so she couldn't argue that there wouldn't be enough time to do that. So she finally said, "Okay, I will go home and stop really fast, and then come pick you up."

I knew she was home when I heard the keys in the door. She poked her head in and saw me in the tux, the roses, the candles, the whole thing.

"Is this really happening?" she wanted to know.

I got down on one knee, opened the little box with the ring, and asked her to marry me. She quivered for a moment, then said yes! That was it, we were engaged.

In fifteen seconds, she was already on the phone with her mom and Lakshmi, planning the wedding. We hadn't even had dinner yet. Finally, I coaxed her off the phone and we went out to Morton's Steakhouse to celebrate.

Jen moved in with me in July 2007, and I really did start showing her the best of Long Island. I took her to the Hamptons, Quogue, Southampton, East Hampton, and Amagansett, specifically, to show her the ocean and the estates. There was also great shopping out there, as there wasn't a New York designer who didn't have a store in one Hamptons town or another. There were lots of people around, but this was before the summer season really kicked in, so we didn't have to fight the crowds. This was Jen's first time to the Hamptons, and she was duly impressed. I also took her to wineries, the farm stands, and the bakeries on the North Fork. I wined her and dined her at all my favorite restaurants. In the summer, we rented a house four blocks from the ocean, had a few of Jen's best friends from the 'burgh make the trip, and enjoyed a week on the beach. We were in love.

CHAPTER FIFTEEN

Jen

GOING TO THE CHAPEL

AFTER GRADUATING FROM MEDICAL school, I moved to Pittsburgh for my pediatric residency training and then stayed for my fellowship in neonatology at Children's Hospital of Pittsburgh and the University of Pittsburgh Medical Center (UPMC). My years in Pittsburgh were probably some of the most tiring and amazing years thus far. I worked hard as a resident at Children's, overnight calls, sometimes thirty to thirty-four hours straight in the hospital. That was before they had work-hour restrictions limiting medical trainees from working more than eighty hours in a week. I fell in love with medical education and neonatology. I realized that I loved the adrenaline of intensive care, but never wanted a critically ill patient to be bigger than me.

Neonatology seemed to offer the best of both worlds. I decided to stay in Pittsburgh for my fellowship in neonatology because I finally felt at home there. I had developed strong roots. I had also developed close friendships and two of my very closest friends from college were also there for their training: Lakshmi was doing her family medicine residency at UPMC and Suketu was doing obstetrics and gynecology. The city of Pittsburgh was not only easy to live in but the people were all very nice. It had a small-town feel without actually being a small town. During my fellowship I pursued a master of science in medical education and fell in love with health-care simulation as a powerful teaching tool. I knew early on that no matter how much I loved clinical care, there was the distinct and likely possibility that my body would not allow me to practice medicine forever. Intensive care is just that, intensive. As much as I loved it, I knew that I needed a plan B in case my body wore out before my mind did. Education as an emphasis in my career made so much sense. I loved it and found out over time I was not too bad at it, either!

I feel as though my years in Pittsburgh were the years I truly became happy with the life I had created for myself. I loved where I was living, had a robust social life, and loved my career and where I was working. The only thing that had been missing was true love. I finally found it in March 2006 when I met Bill, a little over a year before finishing my fellowship, and by 2008 we were getting married!

I was getting married! My dad told me I was a lucky person to have met Bill, and my mother was almost as happy I was. From the day I started fantasizing about getting married, I knew I wanted to be with someone who truly loved me. My future husband needed to be intelligent, funny, handsome, and kind—*and* of course treat me like a princess! Not too much to ask! Now I had found my prince charming, Bill!

When I first met Bill, he mentioned that he was always a gentleman, but he was far more than a man who opened doors for me. He'd go out of his way for me in every way he could. When he was living in New York and I lived in Pittsburgh, I'd get chocolates or flowers delivered to my door almost every week. Before we got married, he even bought me a new car. While I think some of that had to do with his embarrassment at being in my cute but slightly dilapidated Kia Sportage, the larger concern was my safety. My Kia had died on the side of the road on snowy days in Pittsburgh one too many times for his liking, so he bought me a car—not any car, but a dark blue Audi A4. I went from a Kia to an Audi; he started spoiling me early on in our relationship.

Bill and I initially struggled over a wedding date. He proposed on November 3, 2006. This was during the second year of my fellowship, about nine months after we had officially met. Because I wanted plenty of time to plan our wedding, we decided to wait to get married until after I graduated from my fellowship, which would be in June 2007.

The hardest part about choosing a date was that after I graduated I would need to take my neonatal-perinatal board exam, and I really didn't want to have to spend the last few months of wedding planning studying for my boards. Because there is only one date every two years that this board exam is given, I had to guess, based on the last cycle, when the next one would be. The last exam had been in the fall of 2006, so I reasoned that if we planned a springtime wedding after I graduated, it would be far enough from my boards for me to be able to enjoy those last four to six months of wedding planning. We choose April 12, 2008. It seemed to be the best day for us, as we knew we might have the wedding in Florida, and not only is April in Florida beautiful, but it is after the craziness of spring break and before the summer thunderstorm and hurricane season. It was also my dad's birthday, which I thought would make it even more special.

But just to be sure, Bill and I immediately asked my father if he would mind sharing his birthday with our special day, and his response was, "How lucky is that, to be able to share my birthday with my daughter's wedding day?" So, that was that! April 12, 2008, was going to be the big day.

It probably should not have surprised me, given the frequent ironies of my life, that after we'd finally picked a date and secured the church and reception location, the American Board of Pediatrics decided to move the board exam for the first time ever from the fall to, yes, you got it, the spring. And the date they picked was exactly five days before our wedding date. Of course, it wasn't announced until we had already booked and announced the wedding date and venue. Being the typical crazy person that I am, I thought to myself, *I can handle it—what's a little more stress to add to the year?* That year I was graduating from my fellowship, moving to New York from Pittsburgh, starting a new job as an attending neonatologist, planning my wedding in another state—Florida—and oh, by the way, taking my boards! Another example of how good I am at piling it on.

The second decision Bill and I had to make was where we would get married. Because I was moving from Pittsburgh to Long Island to be with Bill after graduation from fellowship, just deciding which state to hold the wedding in was challenging. I had strong roots in Pittsburgh after having lived there for seven years. However, I would soon be living in New York, which is where Bill grew up and where much of his family still was. But I was originally from Florida, almost my entire family was there, and even some of Bill's family now lived in Florida.

I had always envisioned a beach wedding—not necessarily barefoot on the sand in front of the setting sun, but at the beach. So Pittsburgh was out. Long Island had beautiful beaches out in the Hamptons and Montauk. We toured quite a few wedding venues there, and the benefit would be that we didn't have to travel far. Although we liked the idea of the beaches of Long Island, we found the venues very expensive and ultimately realized the beaches did not have as much sentimental value to us as the ones in Florida.

One weekend, Bill and I flew to St. Petersburg Beach, the beach I had grown up on, to try to make a decision. We met my parents and my aunt Barbara and uncle Jack. We both stayed at the Don Cesar Hotel and fell in love with it. I felt that if I was going to plan a wedding remotely, this was the best place, since my mom and Aunt Barbara were there. Bill was in full agreement. He fell in love with the beach I already loved so much.

I wanted to check out the Don Cesar Hotel for the reception not only because it was a beautiful, old-Florida-style beachfront hotel built in the 1920s, but also because I knew it had sentimental value to my family. It had been abandoned for many years in the 1960s, and my mom and her sisters used to play in it. What an amazing playhouse!

Now it was refurbished and beautiful. It was built during the height of the Art Deco era and exuded sleek elegance, with really cool architectural embellishments. It was affectionately known as "the big pink hotel" to the locals, because the entire exterior was almost a Pepto-Bismol pink. If you were driving along the beach in St. Pete, you could not miss it. Many people had their weddings/receptions there, because it offered every kind of option possible, from formal soaring indoor ballrooms to pavilions on the beach.

Because we had such a large invitation list, we choose the grand ballroom for the reception. With magnificent chandeliers and floor-to-ceiling arched windows looking right out at the Gulf of Mexico, the views were truly breathtaking. The room had two tiers connected by curved staircases. The dance floor was on the lower tier. Although many people elected to get married at the hotel or on the Gulf of Mexico right out in front, we decided to have a traditional Catholic wedding, which meant having the wedding in a church. We toured many churches in the area, and ultimately chose St. Mary Our Lady of Grace Catholic Church in downtown St. Petersburg. This meant guests would have to take the bridge from St. Pete Beach to downtown and back.

Bill was very excited to plan the cocktail hour. Since he had given me free rein in almost everything else, I wanted him to choose all aspects of it. He picked a selection of sushi, seafood towers, and cheese platters, as well as an open bar with unlimited Glenlivet Scotch for the guys, Veuve Clicquot champagne, and the signature "starfish fruit" cocktails as the featured drink. For the dinner, the guests could pick from a filet mignon, chicken, fish, or a fancy vegetarian chef's special. Bill and I had done some of the tasting before we committed to a menu, and we both picked a favorite.

Planning a wedding, there were so many details to address—so many whats, wheres, whens, hows—fortunately, at least I knew the "who." I also knew the one aspect of the wedding that I wanted—a starfish theme. I love everything about the ocean, and one of my favorite stories is *The Starfish Story*, a lovely parable about an old man who walks the beach trying to rescue the starfish that have become beached. A young man who sees what he is doing questions his motivation, "You can't possibly save them all, you can't even save one-tenth of them. What you're doing isn't going to make a difference." At which point, the old man picks up another starfish, throws it back into the ocean, and replies, "It made a difference to that one." It was the perfect theme for our wedding, and fortunately Bill was willing to go with it, too!

My mom was truly our wedding planner and organized the whole process from start to finish, although we did hire a day-of wedding planner to take some of the pressure off the big day. With her attention to detail and interior decorating skills, I knew she would not let me make any mistakes in planning my dream wedding.

One detail that we had to take care of, the one that I think all brides get excited about, was picking out my dress and dresses for our bridesmaids. I had been searching the Internet for styles I liked for about a month before I went home to Florida on a long weekend and decided to start shopping with my mom. We went to a local wedding boutique, The Collection, in my favorite shopping area near Orlando, Park Avenue in Winter Park. I brought printouts of all the dresses I had liked online.

At the shop, I couldn't believe it—they had one of my top three dress choices on sale, 75 percent off, in a size eight. I, of course, had to try it on. Their bridal tailor helped me pin it all up using large clasps that look like chip clips on steroids, and the dress went from a size eight adult to size eight my size—it was amazing. The tailor said she could completely break down the entire dress for me and make it a perfect fit.

After trying on many other dresses, I kept thinking about the first one I tried on that had caught my eye from my Internet search. Because the alterations were going to cost as much as the dress, I realized that getting a dress at 75 percent off might be the only way we could afford one that I wanted. So I decided to buy my wedding dress off the rack. I never thought in a million years that would happen. After many fittings, my amazing tailor created basically a brand-new dress that fit me perfectly! It was fantastic!

We didn't want too large a bridal party, since we were getting married in our thirties. However, it was our first wedding, and, we hoped, our only, of course. We decided on five attendants for each side. My bridal party included my closest friends, Lakshmi, my maid of honor, Chetna, my matron of honor, and three other bridesmaids who were close friends from Pittsburgh, Manju, Nickie, and Danelle. Bill's groomsmen included all of our brothers: his two brothers and two stepbrothers and my brother, David. Bill had a crazy insane fondness for his little brothers. Tom, six-foot-four, was a professional firefighter, paramedic, and lieutenant in the Brevard County Fire Department. Joe, a slightly shorter six feet, was a banker and had plans to go to law school, which he later did.

According to Bill, Tom was a man of bravery and selflessness, and Joe, the more buttoned down of the three, was smart as a whip and an enthusiastic get-things-done type. Bill's pride in "these two clowns" was beyond brotherly, and he loved that he had helped them buy their first cars and find their first jobs. Bill was equally proud of his step-brothers, Jonathan and James. Jon was very similar to Bill, both academically and professionally. They both loved sciences and had gotten bachelor's degrees in biology. James had elected to stay in South Carolina, where he had gone to college, and made quite a home for himself, with the sun and sand nearby. He was the last of the five boys to get married, six years after our wedding day.

We asked Bill's younger cousins from New York, Paige and Patrick, to be our flower girl and ring bearer. We would have asked our only niece, Maddie, to also be a flower girl, but she was still too young.

All the other details slowly fell into place. We picked French blue and silver for the colors. I picked out a designer, Carolina Herrera, and the color for the bridesmaids' dresses, an almost Tiffany blue, but allowed them to pick out the style dress that they liked, so the dresses went together but each was different.

My mom started gathering all the decorations for the reception in an elegant beach theme with starfish embellishments. My mom and I were back and forth on the phone and sharing pictures of decorating ideas via email almost weekly. We designed our wedding invitations with the help of Bill's youngest brother Joe's girlfriend, Karen. He had recently started dating Karen, who would later become his wife. He proposed to her the day after our wedding in Florida. Bill and I even took a few dance lessons. Neither of us has rhythm, unfortunately, but we had a blast doing it.

When our wedding weekend finally came, I had just taken my boards and was so ready for some fun. We flew to Florida and spent a few days staying at my parents' house in Orlando. We did a few last-minute preparations—final dress fitting, nails (even Bill got a manicure), and looking over all the beautiful decorations my mom had put together. My mom had her close friends she worked with at Walt Disney World helping us, too! Our florist was also a friend and the florist at the Grand Floridian Hotel. My mom's best friends Gloria and Lulu, both of whom I had grown up with, were going to be there, and although they were supposed to only be guests, they were my mom's right-hand women, making sure all went well that day. My mom has great friends.

The day before the wedding, we checked into the Don Cesar Hotel. We had a rehearsal at the church, which was when the first bout of drama occurred. As my dad was driving Bill and me into the church parking lot, another car hit us on the passenger side! Fortunately, it was a small fender-bender, but, of course, it shook us up a bit. We had a fabulous wedding rehearsal dinner with all of our immediate family, out-of-town family, and the bridal party, which was hosted by Bill's dad and stepmom at a local Italian restaurant. Quite a few people made speeches, including Chetna, my matron of honor, and Joe, Bill's youngest brother.

Bill and I formally thanked all our family for their support and for coming from near and far. We gave out gifts to the bridal party and did all the traditional things you are supposed to do at a rehearsal dinner. After that, we organized a cocktail hour in the Don Cesar lobby for all our guests who were in town and available to get together. Although I was very tired, I was very glad we had added this event to the evening before the wedding, because it gave us much-needed relaxed quality time with all our out-of-town family and friends.

We had about 225 people accept our invitation. There was my family, scattered all over from Florida to L.A., Bill's family from everywhere, and our friends, mostly from Pittsburgh, New York, Chicago, and Maryland. No one objected to our destination wedding, especially at such a beautiful place.

The wedding day, Saturday, April 12, 2008, began with a Continental bridal breakfast and mimosas for the ladies of the wedding party, but as is typical, it was interrupted by the groom's party raiding the room and stealing a few muffins and coffees. The wedding itself took place at St. Mary Our Lady of Grace Catholic Church in downtown St. Petersburg. The priest who married us, Father Tom Hartman, was very close to Bill's mom and had baptized Bill when he was a baby. He was now a monsignor and quite famous for a television broadcast he shared with a New York rabbi, Rabbi Marc Gellman. Together, they called themselves the God Squad, and they were very respectful of each other's faith as they addressed issues of spirituality and religion on a Sunday morning television show.

We flew Father Tom and his assistant down from Long Island and put them up in the hotel so Father Tom could preside over the wedding mass. He had Parkinson's disease, but he wanted to marry us, and we couldn't have been more appreciative.

For the wedding day, my parents had rented a limousine to get everybody in the wedding party staying at the Don Cesar to the church and back. The guys would go first, and then the limo would come back for my bridesmaids and me. Of course, there was another moment of drama—another car accident. This time it was a major accident that resulted in the bridge from the Beach, where we were all staying, to the mainland, where the church was, closing.

The men, who had gone to the church first and had seen the accident happen en route to the church, didn't think it was going to affect traffic. But the limo could not get back to St. Pete Beach by way of that bridge, so it had to drive all the way back to St. Petersburg, over to Tampa, and across Tampa Bay, which took an extra hour. There was no way the women (the bridal party—including the moms and sisters) could possibly get to the church on time, nor could most of the guests. Everybody was stuck in traffic.

On the morning of the wedding, we ladies were all enjoying ourselves getting hair and makeup done in the salon and getting dressed. Trying to help me relax, my bridesmaids confiscated my cell phone. After we were all dressed and ready to head downstairs, I began to wonder why no one seemed eager to get to the church. I kept asking, "What time is it?" "Don't we need to get moving?"

All the bridesmaids and the moms kept saying that the limo wasn't ready for us yet. Finally, after time kept passing, I demanded to know what was going on. My mom and my bridesmaids were trying to protect me from any stress on my wedding day with vague responses. Finally, after more questioning, they told me there had been a bad accident on the bridge, and they couldn't get ahold of the limo.

Of course, my heart stopped and I said, "Has anyone heard from Bill?" My mind immediately went to the worst possible thing that could possibly happen on my wedding day. *Had Bill been in the accident? Was he okay?*

I demanded to have my phone back and started texting him. Fortunately, he responded. He was fine, waiting for me at the church, and was so glad to hear from me and that I was not standing him up. He told me that no one in the wedding had been involved in the accident. I was so relieved to hear that he was all right that at that point I didn't care when or where we got married. At one point, we were joking via text that if the church canceled our wedding because we were too late, we would just elope to Bora Bora, our honeymoon destination.

Fortunately, the church let us proceed with the ceremony two hours behind schedule. As I was standing in the back with my dad, waiting to walk down the aisle, I started to tear up. He looked as if he was about to cry, too. I will never forget the conversation I had with my dad at that moment. He didn't want me to cry, even though they were happy tears, so he tried to make me laugh by saying, "Just think of dying kittens!"

"What?" I replied. "That isn't funny at all." But we both began to smile again at each other! As "Here comes the bride" started playing, and we took our first steps down the aisle, I am pretty sure my dad and I were not the only ones crying. In fact, I later heard that there was not a dry eye in the church.

The ceremony itself was a traditional Catholic wedding with a mass included. We wanted to include the people who were closest to us who had either supported us or brought us together. Our parents gave the readings, and Diane, who had been the first person to have a try at being our matchmaker back when we each did our summer internship with Dr. Kopits, sang "Ave Maria" during the ceremony. I was thankful she could be there, and I knew Dr. Kopits was there, too, watching over us from above.

As Bill and I were exchanging vows, I had one crazy thought flash through my mind, one of those "what a long strange trip it's been" thoughts. I thought about the chaos of getting to the church—the closed bridge, the circuitous detour, the things that were out of our control, and the way we managed to still get to the church. I thought about the stress we'd experienced, the release from stress I was feeling at this very moment, and how I was staring into Bill's eyes and knowing we were committing to each other forever. The two hours it had taken to get to this point were like a metaphor for Bill's and my lives. We had had so many bridges that were difficult to cross, so many detours to get to places the long way, so many stressors we couldn't control, and so much happiness and fulfillment in the end. I was the happiest bride there ever was.

I probably shouldn't even mention the third occurrence of drama. We almost didn't get married, after all! We inadvertently forgot our marriage license at the hotel, so when the ceremony was over and we were supposed to sign our official decree of marriage with the priest, we couldn't prove we were legally married! Lakshmi's new husband, Nikhil, saved the day and rushed back to the hotel to retrieve the license for us.

By the time the ceremony was over and we had all our official documents signed, the accident on the St. Pete Beach bridge had been cleared, and we all made it back to the Don Cesar without further delay. Bill and I had taken our dance lessons well in advance of the wedding, so we were ready to kick off our shoes, boogie down, and celebrate our new life with the people we loved.

We started off with a nice slow song by Van Morrison, "Someone Like You." As we started dancing, all I could think about as I looked into Bill's eyes and saw all of our friends and family I loved so much around us was how lucky we were. Almost everyone who loved us and supported us was in that ballroom at the same time. At that very moment I knew I needed to burn the memory into my brain, because I doubted there would be another one like it where I felt so much love all around us. I was with my true love I had been seeking my entire life, with everyone else we loved watching us have our first dance together as husband and wife. His family—the Kleins, Croners, and Diecidues—had known him through all the tribulations of his life, as my family, the Arnolds and the Shipmans, had known me. Now, all of these people who had birthed, nurtured, encouraged, and launched us were supporting our union. These were the people who had told us never to let our size hold us back, and here they were, cheering for us now. It was a pretty awesome moment.

Of course, we couldn't stay too sappy for too long. Halfway through the song, Billy Idol's "White Wedding" cut in, and that was it, the party was officially started. We motioned for the wedding party, who had been in a circle around us, to start dancing, and before you knew it, everyone was on the dance floor. Time for some fun!

The reception went on for four hours, heated up by the live music of the Land Sharks, who play Jimmy Buffet–style songs and who rarely stopped playing, even for a break. All the guests loved everything—the food was delicious; the cake, Tiffany blue and embellished with starfish from top to bottom, was spectacular; and like all brides, I don't remember a thing. The headwaiter built plates of food for Bill and me, knowing we'd never sit down, but we never got to those, either. Between visiting every table to say "hi" and thanking each person for coming and the dancing and socializing, the time flew by, and our dinners went uneaten.

There were so many family members and friends to see that there was never enough time, but I tried to spend time with everyone. My aunt Chrissy and aunt Barbara and uncle Jack were there. I had not seen my uncle Jack and aunt Barbara ever have so much fun before!

Uncle Jack is a slightly eclectic vegetarian with long blond hair who loves the sixties, listens to classic rock, watches World War II documentaries, and wears T-shirts and jeans every day. He owns his own carpet-cleaning business on St. Pete Beach, so dress wear is not part of his daily attire. I think my wedding day might have been the first and only time I have ever seen Jack wear a suit, and he looked great in it!

Chrissy unfortunately had not been doing so well emotionally, but she was there for me, smiling every time I saw her. She suffered from major depression, and I knew big family events were very stressful for her. Sadly, that was one of the last times I saw her happy. It would be less than a year from that day that she committed suicide. I wish now I had had more time with her that day. I wish I had known life would soon never be the same. The pain of losing Chrissy, especially that way, is something I still struggle with every day. I'd rather have a million surgeries than to have lost my best friend that way. But on this day, my entire family was happy, and nothing can ever take that away.

Of course, my parents were both elated! They had been back together for years and everyone was healthy and happy. I even saw them dancing a few times. Bill and I made a special recognition of my mother and presented her with flowers for all she had done to make my dream wedding come true. We even had a cake for my father, and had the whole room sing "Happy Birthday" to him. After all, it was his birthday, too!

Family members I had not seen in years joined in our celebration that day, among them my uncle Ray, who is my godfather, my half-aunt Sandee, and my cousin Tish, who had even made the trip from California.

Sandee was actually my mom's half-sister. My papa had a daughter with another woman before he met and married my grandma. Times were different back then, and I don't think anyone talked about his prior relationship. Although I think my mom and her siblings knew of Sandee, they had met her for the first time only ten years earlier. My aunt Chrissy had actually found Sandee via the Internet, and our families had reconnected!

My brother, David, and his longtime girlfriend, Lisa, who is now his wife, both looked great, and I was happy to see them having such a good time. They were the youngest of all of the sibling couples, with David being a year younger than Bill's brother Joey. As I saw David escort Chetna down the aisle in the wedding party, I thought it might have been nostalgic for the two of them. I had matched them up in the bridal party line since they had known each other from our childhood. I know Chetna remembers the days of us having sleepovers when we were younger, and David crashing our parties! I never asked David if they talked about some of those memories.

One of the more fun aspects of the wedding was watching Bill's family getting to know my family! Bill's mother was with his stepfather, Chuck. They were fairly "newlywed" themselves, having gotten married in 2000, although they had been together for more than a decade. His mother was wearing a beautiful dress she had tailored for the special occasion. She looked fantastic and glowing because she was so happy. I thought about the first time I met her—the day after Mother's Day, as a matter of fact. We hit it off instantly. She loved telling me she thought Bill would likely be a bachelor, loving work above anything else, but hoped he would find true love some day. Well, I hoped today was that day!

Bill's father and Debbie, his stepmother, were really rocking it, too. Debbie, who was also dressed in a tailored gown, looked wonderful. On the dance floor, they were really cutting a rug. Bill and I may have been the ones who took dance lessons, but they looked as if they had, too!

Last, all of our friends, who had been some of our biggest supporters through some of the roughest times, had traveled from far and wide to be there. I couldn't believe the Pittsburgh contingent that made it to Florida!

Lakshmi, my maid of honor, had just gotten married herself. We had been best of friends since college, having studied for boards together, traveled for residency interviews together, and shared weekly dinners together during residency and fellowship in Pittsburgh. I have her to thank for ultimately bringing Bill and me together. If it wasn't for our commiserating over a bottle of wine one night at my apartment about being single at thirty-two, I might never have logged on to DateALittle and never would have emailed Bill.

At the reception, Lakshmi and Tom, our best man, both gave heartwarming toasts. They had me laughing and in tears. My dad made the initial toast, welcoming everyone, and Diane even made a toast. She told the crowd about how I had called her after I found Bill online to get a "background check." I did do that, and in fact, that's how I found out Bill had been the same guy she and Dr. Kopits had wanted to set me up with way back in college. Diane spoke of Dr. Kopits and how he was there with us. Imitating his thick Hungarian accent, she ended her toast with something he said often, "BEAUTIFUL!" There was not a dry eye in the room again.

After the official reception was over, everybody went down to the beach bar to keep the party going. Meanwhile, my bridesmaids had set up Bill's and my hotel room with tons of candles and rose petals scattered everywhere, and a bottle of Scotch for Bill and a bottle of champagne for me. However, we were having so much fun at the after party that retiring for the evening was not popping to mind. Finally, my bridesmaids insisted we go to the room to be sure we blew out the candles before the hundred-year-old historic hotel burned to the ground!

The next morning, we woke up as a happily married couple—extraordinarily exhausted, but happy and married. We had reserved half of a restaurant down the block from the hotel for a brunch so that our guests could come and enjoy some greasy eggs and coffee as they shook off the cobwebs from the party. The breakfast place I had picked out, the Pelican, was a place on the water that I loved to go to with my aunts Barbara and Chrissy before a long day at the beach. While planning the wedding, I found out that my brother's soon-to-be-wife Lisa's uncle actually was the owner. I had been going there for years, long before my brother met Lisa in college. It is a small world!

After the brunch, Bill and I went back to Long Island, took a day to pack for the honeymoon, and left for Bora Bora—so far, so good. But things don't always go the way you plan in life. Are you sensing a theme here?

Bill and I had come to expect that things did not always go perfectly. We left for our honeymoon on Tuesday morning, right on schedule. American Airlines, New York to Los Angeles. We arrived at LAX and had to migrate to the international terminal, with all five pieces of our luggage in tow. We probably overpacked—we *definitely* overpacked. We had dress clothes for dinners out, shorts and tees, bathing suits, socks, undies, toiletries, shoes, sandals, flip-flops, snorkel gear, some electronics in case we got bored on the plane, books, and so on. So Bill stacked all of our luggage onto one Smart-Cart, we moved to the international terminal, and checked in for our 11:00 p.m. flight to Tahiti by way of Air Tahiti Nui.

At the gate, we were informed that the flight would be delayed a bit, and the three hundred plus passengers for this fully booked flight began to moan . . . and sweat . . . and grow cranky. Then midnight came. Over the loudspeaker, the gate manager announced that the pilots had gone on strike as of midnight, and the flight had been canceled! Now, three hundred people bolted to the customer service desk, but the news was the same.

"We are sorry, but we don't have any information about when the strike will end," was the blanket statement from the representative. "We will gladly put you in a hotel for the night and update you tomorrow with the status of the flight." I could see Bill was getting frustrated, because we were now losing a day of our trip and potentially the entire honeymoon. Our travel insurance was now useless, as we had already "begun" our trip, so we decided to wait it out.

We went to the first hotel via shuttle, but it was sold out. We got back on the bus and went to the second—also sold out. Because everyone else doing the same thing as us (and our five bags) was quicker, they got to these places faster. The third and fourth hotels were also totally booked. Finally, we got a room at the La Hacienda near LAX, where a negative star rating would have been appropriate. It was totally gross. In fact, it was so bad, Bill and I didn't even take off our socks.

The next day, we went back to the airport early. The customer service person at Air Tahiti offered to put us on a Korean Airways flight, but that meant going to Korea first! Since I wasn't as avid a flyer back then, I insisted we decline that generous but insane offer to be in the air an extra eleven hours. We waited for another few hours and, miraculously, by that evening the strike was over, and we were moved to the eleven o'clock flight that night.

We arrived in Tahiti at 4:00 a.m. Tahiti time, completely exhausted. The airline put us up in a hotel called the Intercontinental, which was very pretty and clean. There, we showered and slept for a few hours before the shuttle bus back to the airport for the final leg of the trip. A smaller jet was needed to get from Tahiti to Bora Bora, so we boarded that island jumper and headed to our final destination only a day and a half late.

The wait was worth it. At the airport, we were greeted by a few native Tahitians who were armed with leis and fruity drinks. We also met the captain of the small boat that would take us to our hotel, Le Meridien, which was located on the Motu, an outer band of islands surrounding the main island. There, our luggage was finally handled by someone else, and our honeymoon felt like it was finally beginning. Our room was an over-water hut that was beautiful inside but had a thatched roof to give it that "Island" feel. It had air-conditioning, cable TV, a sound system, a big comfy bed, a deck with loungers to sit out on, and a ladder leading down to the crystal clear lagoon below. It even had a glass floor through which we could see fish, sea turtles, and rays swimming under the hut any hour of the day or night. I was in heaven!

I think our experience in Bora Bora was probably unique. The staff treated us as if we were royalty. At first we thought it was because we were honeymooners, but after a few days we realized it may have been something else. It turns out people with skeletal dysplasia do not end up in Bora Bora very often. In fact, the local news had heard of our arrival and came knocking on the door of our hut the day after we arrived! Mind you, this was before our television show existed, so it wasn't because of that.

Again, being Little People, we were not completely surprised that we stood out to others, but of course never expected the news to show up. We were nice to the reporter, I think mostly because we were still in shock about what was happening. She followed us on our boat ride to the main island for dinner and then kindly we asked her to leave us alone—we were on our honeymoon.

The treatment we received on our honeymoon went beyond anything we could have expected. Our breakfasts were very special. Every morning, the restaurant's team would make a special seating arrangement for the two of us. They would adorn our chairs with dozens of flowers, while the other guests ate from the buffet and served themselves. The staff wouldn't allow us to do that, even when we tried. They would, instead, create a small buffet table in front of us, and then ask us to select from the private buffet they had created—eggs, omelettes, and meats, croissants and pastries, fresh fruits and veggies, cereals and beverages, French press coffee and cappuccinos. It was an amazing spread, every day. And when we had our fill, they would make new plates of fresh fruits and chocolate croissants (my favorite) and place them in our room for us in case we wanted a snack later that morning.

One of the other guests, a regular at that resort, had asked us what we had done to receive this sort of treatment. He went on to say that in the years he had been coming to this resort in Bora Bora, he had never seen any other couple treated with this amount of personal attention. So Bill and I invited him and his wife to come eat with us the next day. It was only fair to share the experience.

Our royal treatment didn't end with breakfast. The head of guest relations offered to take us for a tour of Bora Bora. We accepted the generous offer and one day sailed over to the mainland and hopped in his car. First stop, his house! We were introduced to his entire family and extended family, all twenty plus people! We next traversed the entire island—winding roads, local hangouts, even the place where, six hundred years ago, ritualistic sacrifices by fire of godlike people, such as those who were short in stature, had been performed! I joked to Bill, softly, "I hope we are not next!" Fortunately, we had an agenda that kept us from "rekindling" old flames. By the time we returned to the hotel, I had been the recipient of more than fifty handmade necklaces made of shells, pearls, and other ornaments only found on the island. The women of the main town, Vaitape, just wouldn't let me leave without making me look like the Mr. T of seashell necklaces. It was an island shopping spree!

The whole trip was fantastic. We were "swimming" with black tip sharks and stingrays, dining on the water, and lying out on the beach. Even though our ten-day trip had become nine, thanks to some disgruntled pilots, it didn't get better than a tiny island in the South Pacific with the love of your life. Every day was bliss!

CHAPTER SIXTEEN

Bill

BECOMING "THE LITTLE COUPLE"

AFTER THE CRAZINESS OF our wedding and honeymoon, we settled into our lives back in New York. Jen liked Long Island and Port Jefferson, but after almost a year at Stony Brook Hospital, she was a little discouraged with her job. It was not as challenging as she had hoped, and while she really liked her coworkers, Jen's true hunger was for education through simulation, something she had been doing in her fellowship. As an educator, Jen is looking for new and innovative ways to help educate physicians and medical staff. She is a true believer in simulation, because she feels the value of being able to create realistic scenarios in a safe-to-learn environment is the future. Thus, when the person at the hospital who had hired her accepted a job elsewhere, Jen was ready to make a move herself. "I'm ready for a new challenge," Jen told me one evening. "Is it okay if I look around at other hospitals?"

I was nervous, as I wasn't quite sure what Jen had in mind. This would potentially be a major change in many aspects of our life together. I was comfortable on Long Island. I had a business I had established there, so of course, I was concerned about the business. I had my house, which I had really fixed up to my liking. And while she was a little concerned that she had just gotten the job at Stony Brook, we both came to the realization that change is good.

She had taken her position in order to be with me. If it wasn't as satisfying as she had hoped, I wasn't going to be the one to hold her back from pursuing her career. Because I owned my business, I had more control over what I could do. Still, I knew that a job change for Jen would likely mean a major upheaval in our lives.

The trouble was that neonatology is a subspecialty that isn't present in every hospital. Usually, one hospital with an NICU will serve many hospitals in a certain geographical area. Therefore, there weren't that many choices for neonatologists. On Long Island, we had more than forty hospitals, but there were only two fully equipped, state-of-the-art, "level 3" NICUs, Stony Brook and Long Island Jewish. Even though New York City had a handful, Jen was specifically interested in an institution with a simulation center, and none of the nearby openings had both a simulation center and a neonatology position available. This newly emerging field of medical simulation was fascinating to Jen on many levels. The simulation centers were pioneering new techniques for testing systems, teams, and response time to improve overall patient outcomes in real life by allowing people to learn from mistakes in a simulated environment. In simulation training, doctors can develop such new procedures, processes, techniques, and communication without ever putting a patient at risk, because they are working on a high-fidelity mannequin, not a living patient. Jen felt that this was an important new field that could lead to immense patient care breakthroughs, and in many ways this field was at the forefront of medical innovation. In traditional medicine, innovation has historically come at a hefty price of trial and error on real people. But in a simulation center, mothers of preemie newborns could learn how to respond to a breathing crisis using a Sim Baby mannequin, so that they would be prepared should their own baby have a breathing crisis. Teams can go through common emergencies and train on how to better communicate with one another. And they can take all of their simulated experiences back to a room, where they can discuss errors and omissions in a "safe place."

This field was compelling to Jen, and her goal was to be a part of leading simulation efforts at a major institution, and she had focused a lot of her academic efforts toward this field. She had studied at University of Pittsburgh's WISER Institute, WISER being the acronym for the Peter M. Winter Institute for Simulation, Education, and Research. It was a world-class training and research facility renowned for its simulation training. I had become most familiar with Jen's participation in simulation when she invited me to attend one of her training presentations, which she had conducted for more than thirty physicians from the tristate area. It was truly impressive to see her in action. She was like the conductor of an orchestra as she managed myriad simulated crises. The participants were shouting, doctors were sweating and unsure of themselves, and Sim babies were dying. If anyone in the room felt simulation was "too fake" to give it respect at the beginning, he or she certainly left with a different opinion. So I encouraged Jen to take the leap and explore other opportunities.

Jen, as it turned out, was in high demand. When the people at Children's Hospital–Pittsburgh heard she was considering options, they immediately contacted her and offered her more money to come back there, where she had done her residency and fellowship. She liked the idea of going back to Pittsburgh and returning to work with her fantastic colleagues there. Even though Pittsburgh could get exceptionally cold in the winter, I had started to really enjoy the city, too. Pittsburgh was a great city, and aside from the Steelers games I would undoubtedly have to sit through (no one was going to the Pirates games at that time), I would have moved there willingly. We could both imagine what our lives would be like there, and there was some comfort in that, again, Steelers games aside, of course.

While Jen was considering this offer, though, she was approached by her former boss at Stony Brook, who was now at Children's Hospital of Philadelphia. She received an offer to work there, and Philadelphia would still have us fairly close to Long Island. I was even more torn about this offer. The upsides were that I would be three to four hours away from my office, which meant I could go to work two or three days a week and work from home on the other days. I would also be close enough to Mom to be there in a pinch without much trouble. On the downside, it's Philly, home of the Dirty Birds, and I am a die-hard Giants fan. So Philly was a less likely candidate. As Jen was deciding between these offers, an esteemed person at Texas Children's Hospital in Houston contacted her unexpectedly about a position that seemed quite ideal. He was interested in hiring someone to *run* the new simulation center at Texas Children's Hospital and provide clinical care in his neonatal intensive care unit. It was the perfect opportunity. I couldn't even believe it when the words came out of my mouth, "Go for it, Jen. I'll move to Texas." She was nervous heading to Houston for the interviews, but as usual, she nailed it and received an offer before the four-interview process was even half-over.

Jen gladly accepted the offer, triggering a new chapter for both of us in uncharted territory. Now, we were really moving all the way to Houston, Texas. We packed our stuff into a fifty-three-foot trailer, leaving behind a queen-size mattress, a nineteen-inch TV, an old dresser, my Infiniti coupe (and Jen's ugly Kia Sportage, which some-how had survived the trip from Pittsburgh), and a few things for the kitchen. We were keeping the house, so I could go back and forth be-tween Houston and Long Island during the week for my business. We wanted to sell it, but it was a slow housing market, so we were going to take our time.

The hardest part was leaving Mom. She came over on the day of our flight to say good-bye. She had always had one of her sons liv-ing close by, so this would be the first time that all three of her boys would be at least a thousand miles away. I felt comforted knowing she wouldn't be totally alone. She had been married to Chuck since 2000, and her brother also lived in the area. As for me, I would be back fre-quently for business, and I promised to make sure to see her every time I returned to Port Jefferson. Still, it was hard to say good-bye. Mom had sacrificed so much for me throughout her life, and I was devoted to her.

After long hugs, they left, and Jen and I watched the truck pull away from our very first home. We then went to the airport, got on a plane for Houston, and moved right into our new apartment. I had no regrets. I was looking forward to our life together in a part of the world that neither of us had connections to. I loved that she was pur-suing her career, and I had a feeling that Texas was going to work out.

JEN FELT RIGHT at home at Texas Children's Hospital (TCH), one of the largest children's hospitals with the largest NICU in the country. She was grateful to have found such a wonderful fit—she loved them, and they loved her. She arrived at TCH to blueprints and a construc-tion hat. Texas Children's hadn't yet built the simulation center. The build-out was part of a larger project, adding multiple floors on the top of the building where Jennifer's office now resides. Jennifer started as construction began. One of her responsibilities from the very outset of the new job was overseeing the construction of the simulation center, which included placement of cameras, observation and control rooms, and debriefing rooms in the Sim Center. She needed to assist in figuring out how rooms were to be configured, including things like placement of electrical outlets and ports for gas, where beds and incubators would go, location and access to supplies and equipment. All of that needed to be done in a way that mimicked a working hospital room to help facilitate effective simulation. Jen needed to do this while anticipating growth and expansion from the then-current applications to potential future uses of simulation to educate teams of people. She had a lot of work ahead of her. Her job was anything but simple. She was the new medical director of the Simulation Center. She also carried the title of assistant professor of neonatology, Department of Pediatrics. If her titles were big, the work ahead of her was even bigger.

As for me, Michael—my business partner and mentor—and I had agreed to do our best to continue our work relationship and further the business, even though I had moved. Unfortunately, as time went on, it became apparent that a long-distance business relationship wouldn't work out. My decision to pull out coincided with a down period in the business, which compounded my anxiety about the move to Houston. Then there was Mike, who felt abandoned and read my move to Texas as my not caring. But that wasn't true. It was just too difficult to start up a life in Houston and still commute to Long Island for work.

For a while, I didn't take a paycheck, because I wanted him to do so. When we had first started out together, he made sure that I was taken care of. But I owed my start in sales to Michael, and I was grateful, so when I had a chance to reciprocate by forgoing a paycheck to make sure the business continued, I didn't hesitate to do so. In the end, we decided to part ways but preserve our friendship.

As for myself, I knew eventually I'd return to a business venture, but for now I'd just feel out the landscape and take time to think about what I wanted to do. Sometimes—as with Jen's job offer to run the simulation center in Houston—a development comes along that can change your own expectations about what may be possible.

The story about how we got our show on TLC is an interesting one. It began when we were still living in Port Jefferson, and *Good Morning America* (*GMA*) reached out to Little People of America in hopes of finding two women who were both short in stature and leading professional careers. LPA referred them to Jennifer and one other woman who had a career in entertainment. *GMA* then did a joint interview, asking both women about their careers and how they had gotten to where they were in their respective fields. *GMA* also showed a short video about each of their lives.

At the very end of Jen's segment, there was a scene with Jen and me at the kitchen table. The scene was supposed to have an interview with both Jen and me, but after it was edited, all that was left of me was a shot of me serving coffee at the table. Ha ha, *GMA*. The viewer could hear the reporter commenting to the anchorperson that Jen was getting married the following April to the attractive man serving her coffee (me). After the segment aired, Jen and I never thought any more about it. We never dreamed it would turn into something else.

It wasn't until a couple of months later that we received a call from LMNO Productions, Inc., a leading producer of network and cable reality shows. An executive producer there wanted to explore whether we would be interested in allowing them to follow our wedding story, from dress design and tux fittings all the way to the magical day. We turned them down, as we didn't aspire to be on a television show. But they persevered, and a month or two later, the production company called us again and asked us if we would be willing to at least listen to their pitches. They thought our story, Jen's and mine individually and now together as a couple, might make for an intriguing television program with a positive message.

In a television world where so much reality TV is full of negative personal drama and extreme conflict, they wanted to produce an upbeat and true-to-life story. We laughed, thinking how absurd it was that they had such interest in us. Their vision for the show was inspiring, and we agreed to think about it some more. They kept calling us from time to time, with different pitches about how they would shoot a television show about our lives.

For a long time, we resisted any serious consideration of a television show. Then something changed, and quite surprisingly, Jen and I both reached the same conclusion at approximately the same time. Jen had experienced a moment while shopping that gave her confidence that making this program might be the right thing to do. As she walked past a mother with two children in the cereal aisle of the grocery store, she overheard the youngest daughter make a comment about her. "Look, Mommy, that's a Little Person like on *Little People Big World*." *Little People Big World* was a reality TV show featuring a family of six—a little couple and their four children, one little and three average-size. Two boys were twins, and after they were done growing, one was almost six feet, the other four-foot-four. The show about the family and their life on an Oregon farm had been on the air since 2006.

At the moment Jen heard the little girl "recognize" her, she realized *Little People Big World* had been doing a great job of breaking down barriers and educating people about vernacular and proper etiquette related to people with skeletal dysplasias. The child had an understanding of Jen's condition as well as respect for Jen, because of the child's exposure to skeletal dysplasia on the show.

As for me, about that same time, my decision to participate in a television show came about entirely because of Jen. As I watched her doing all the wonderful things she does at work and proving to so many people that despite her stature, anything is possible, I reconsidered the show more seriously. If doing the show would in some small way highlight the achievements and sometimes failures of two people who were trying their best to succeed despite challenges, well, maybe that was worthwhile. After seeing Jen on *Good Morning America* and working in the simulation center, I began realizing how truly impressive her achievements were.

What she does is incredible to me, and I felt that it might be worth taking a chance and seeing where this adventure would take us. We had defied many expectations before. Signing up for a television pilot that could highlight Jen as she inspires, educates, and saves lives, and does it with humility, competence, and compassion? I was in. A television show without me—just Jen—would be great, too, but I could provide my sexy mug as eye candy between serious situations.

So after about a year of negotiating back and forth with the people at LMNO, we agreed on a vision for the show, how the story would be told, and the time that we could afford to set aside to produce the program. All of these questions were important, and we wanted our story to be authentic and real. We eventually signed a contract for a pilot episode.

Of course, show biz is odd, and everything was new to us. We were recruited to tell our tale and share it with the world, and then we were told that we would be extremely lucky if the show ever made it past the pilot. With this kind of ambiguity and the great odds stacked against the show's being on the air at all—let alone seeing any kind of success—we were shocked when the first season's order came in.

When it was picked up for the first season, we were told 99 percent of shows don't make it to the second season. Yet, season after season has followed, defying everything that we were told was even remotely possible. We certainly never envisioned that the show would last as long as it has.

I think it's fair to say that for the most part, it's been a very enjoyable experience, and we are thankful for all of the people we've worked with and encountered along the way. It holds great meaning for us to receive emails daily from viewers who love our story. We also really like meeting people who watch the show and enjoy it when they share their own stories with us.

Doing the show has its ups and downs. There are personalities, technical aspects, notes, contracts, deadlines, questions, scheduling, and other challenges to deal with.

While we strive for times when we can relax and we love a good beach vacation (well, Jen does, so I do, too, now), since the show began, our lives have been filled with unexpected left turns, challenges, and out-of-the-blue situations that give us insight. It turns out the drama that naturally occurs in our lives has made for years of inspiring, relatable, joyful, and sometimes tearful television. Just what the television doctor ordered.

Even though Jen and I were doing the show, I still wanted to go into business for myself. Ever since selling off my interest in the consulting firm, I had needed to find something new to challenge me. I missed having my own business and was looking to do something interesting that I had never done before. I decided to step into the world of retail sales—specifically, pet products retail. I opened a twenty-three-hundred-square-foot brick and mortar pet store. Our niche was that we sold a lot of products not commonly found in the big-box stores. We would carry organic foods, high-quality apparel, and one of the largest collar and leash collections in all of Houston. It was in the heart of Rice Village, next to Rice University, and I chose to name it Rocky and Maggie's, after our two dogs, Rocky the Chihuahua, and Maggie the terrier-mutt rescue. Since Jen was the professional shopper, I often looked to her for opinions relating to the store's style, our products, and everything else. I brought my mother-in-law, Judy, on board, too, as she and my father-in-law had moved to Houston to be near us. Judy helped me to open the shop and staff it. She became the store manager and took on the day-to-day management of the shop while I handled the sexy jobs like accounting, purchasing, product development exploration, and marketing. I was pleasantly surprised to see how well the shop did. We opened our doors on February 3, 2012, and grew the business every month. Today, we serve many dog and cat owners and are continuing to grow and expand.

We also decided to build our dream house. We found the perfect location in the city limits, not too far from the medical center. We hired a builder and worked with him and his architect to start drawing up our plans for a customized home. We started by taking down the existing house. Since many of the existing houses in the neighborhood were more than sixty years old, it was common to tear down an old house and build a new one in its place. We wanted to build a home that had enough room for us, a future family of one or two children, space in the garage for a car or two, and maybe even a den to watch movies in. And, just as important, we wanted to incorporate some changes that would make things easier for us to reach. For thirty-five-plus years, Jen and I had scaled counters, climbed on stools, and used grabbers to reach things that were otherwise out of reach. This was our chance to make things easier, at least at home.

This was exhilarating, but at the same time quite overwhelming when we really got into the process. With Jen's job demanding a lot of her time and my new business just getting off the ground, it was sometimes very stressful. But as things began to take shape, it seemed worth the stress and aggravation. The coastal craftsman-style home was right up Jen's alley. Since Jen couldn't work on the beach, we brought the beach to Jen. Inside the house, the kitchen and bath featured a lot of customization to make life a bit easier. The kitchen counters in the work area were lowered, as were the cupboards. Whereas before Jennifer had to climb up onto a counter to get a glass, now she could reach the glassware without a stool. The dining island in the kitchen was a standard height to accommodate guests, while the stovetop and sink were lowered to a safer and more comfortable level for us to cook and clean up afterward. In one of the two bathrooms we lowered sinks to make hand washing a simple task. The other was left at average height for guests. And our windows were installed on the lower side of average so we could actually enjoy looking out of them.

The house took nearly two years to be completed, and our move-in day couldn't come soon enough. Literally. We had been in a rental most of the time, but as a favor to the neighbor, we terminated our lease just in time for their cousins, who were moving into town, to move right in. We had expected to move weeks, if not a month or two, earlier than this lease expiration date, but that wound up not being the case. Delays prevented us from moving into the house on time, and since we didn't want to go back on our commitment to make the rental house available, we vacated the rental without a new home to go to.

We moved all of our possessions into the garage of our still-under-construction home, covered everything in plastic, packed up Jen's SUV with only the essentials, and went to Galveston for what we thought would only be a short-term rental. We found a place on the beach, and instead of getting angry that our house was taking so long, we made this tough time into a vacation. We contacted Jen's parents and invited them to join us in Galveston. Four days later, they arrived at the beach, and our beach vacation was in full swing.

Two weeks in Galveston still wasn't long enough for the house to be ready, as delays pushed it back another month, but when we finally moved in, we had our perfect home to live in as a family.

A house is not a home without kids, and Jen and I were both hoping to start filling it with children before our new home was completed. We started with the "let's get pregnant" route, so Jen scheduled a lung function test and an OB exam, the things she would need for clearance to start trying. However, the recommendation came back that she not try to get pregnant. A pregnancy would be potentially life-threatening to her, due to her restrictive lung disease. If she were to carry a baby, that baby would push on her diaphragm, further complicating her breathing and putting her life at risk. It was not impossible—people with her exact type of dysplasia had delivered successfully—but it was considered very high risk in her case.

I couldn't bear the possibility of losing Jen by trying to have a child. We decided we were going to go the surrogacy route, instead. Jen and I would provide the fertilized egg, which would then be implanted into a surrogate, who would carry the baby to term.

First, we had to find a surrogacy center. We found one in Encino, California. In fact, quite unbelievably, the center was even in the same building as LMNO Productions. We learned about it from the executive producer of our show. Jen and I vetted the center and liked what we learned. It had a stellar reputation and an excellent track record in successful births. It also handled high-profile clients and was great with confidentiality, which was important to us.

Jen and I went to California to begin the process of selecting our surrogate. The first step was looking through a dozen or so profiles, hoping to find the right match. For us, it was very simple and straightforward, as we were providing the fertilized eggs. Our criteria were that the woman be nice, understanding, healthy, and share the same philosophical and religious beliefs as us. After we went through the resumes, we made several phone calls to our top candidates and finally set up a meeting with a woman named Cindy.

Right off the bat, Cindy seemed like the right choice. She and her husband, James, were both on board and were wonderful people. They had two children and weren't looking to have any more, and Cindy was around our age. We contracted with her and the implant took place a few months later. We were ecstatic when we heard the news that Cindy was pregnant, but our joy was short-lived when she miscarried at about eight weeks.

While she was very depressed about it, Jen still woke up the next morning and said, "We are going to do it again." As devastated as she was, she thought it would be worse to give up after just one try. That is Jen, and I love her for it. She seeks out happiness and doesn't ever give up the search.

It wasn't too long before Cindy was pregnant again, and we were overjoyed. This time, she carried the baby for just ten days before she miscarried. She had what was called a "chemical pregnancy," which meant there wasn't a truly viable embryo developing, just a rising beta HCG. This miscarriage was harder for us to handle. It was Christmas, and our families, who were in town and staying at our house, were there when we got the bad news. We were hoping dinner would be punctuated by an announcement that we were on our way to having a baby, but instead we had to live through an awkwardly somber afternoon. Fortunately, we were surrounded with our families' love, support, and encouragement, even though it was still really hard.

I was disappointed, but I was even more concerned about how Jennifer would handle the loss. I didn't want her to take on any blame for these unsuccessful pregnancies. We were told it was commonplace for expectant moms to feel that way. After a bit of time passed, she was able to rebound, and we once again began the process of retrieving more eggs.

The process of stimulating eggs and the retrieval procedures were intense, painful, and potentially dangerous, but Jen felt it was worth it. And if she felt it was worth it, I was going to support her. We had been trying to get pregnant for almost two years. The miscarriages were disappointing, but they weren't the reason we eventually stopped trying. It came to something much simpler. At some point, you realize the way you create a family isn't as important as having one. And while we had discussed adoption as a definite part of how we would grow our family eventually, we now wanted to refocus all of our efforts on that. We didn't want to wait any longer to begin a life with kids in it.

We had talked about adoption shortly after we had gotten married, nearly four years earlier. LPA had formed an adoption committee, which helped facilitate adoptions of children with dwarfism. Their goal was to make themselves known to adoption agencies and health-care providers who knew of children with skeletal dysplasia needing a loving home. They would help connect those agencies to families within LPA that expressed an interest in adoption.

When we put our names on the register, we were told there were *thirty-two* other couples ahead of us, which meant it would probably take years for us to be considered. But not long after we registered with LPA, Colleen, the adoption coordinator from the organization, posted a profile of a girl, about four or five years old, who was available for adoption. However, she had already been adopted once. It had been an international adoption and unfortunately, her adoptive parents, who were average in size, hadn't known of her particular disability until after the adoption had been completed. They subsequently realized that the added strain of dealing with the medical issues associated with her skeletal dysplasia was more than they could handle.

Jennifer followed up with Colleen to explore the possibility of adopting this wonderful girl. But because of her unique and fragile situation, the placement needed to happen quickly. Since we hadn't completed our home study yet and knew we were months away from being ready for initial consideration, we weren't able to pursue adopting her.

Home studies need to be redone every six to twelve months, so when we refocused our efforts to have a family, an international home study was a logical first step. The home study consisted of exhaustive paperwork and interviews with a caseworker. The agency wanted to know everything—family background, references, education and employment, relationships and social life, daily life routines, parenting experiences, details about our home and neighborhood, readiness, and reasons for why we wanted to adopt. There were two home visits during this process, although the real time-consuming aspect was the paperwork. In the end, we were approved and officially ready. Now, all we had to do was wait for the call.

In addition to LPA, we also listed ourselves with RainbowKids Adoption and Welfare Advocacy Group, the Internet's largest adoption website for international adoptions of children with special needs. We were looking for a child with a particular type of disability, one with skeletal dysplasia. We had been on these two lists even before we tried the surrogacy route, but now our mission was clearly set to adoption. Based on what we had been told, we braced ourselves for a very long wait until a possible adoption match came about. Fortunately, and quite unexpectedly, the wait wasn't very long.

In March 2012, just three months after the second miscarriage and weeks after we decided to stop egg retrievals, we received a call from the head of the organization, a woman named Martha, who wanted to pay us a visit. When we were all settled at the kitchen table, she told us why she was so excited to meet us. "I have a child who is available for international adoption," she told us.

Martha opened a file folder and pushed it toward us. "Here are some pictures," she exclaimed with delight. Our excitement was hard to contain, because we couldn't believe she was at our kitchen table presenting us with photos of a little boy who could possibly be our child. We fell in love with him that very moment. He was a little Mongolian boy, almost two years old, who had skeletal dysplasia. He had been born in Hohhot, the capital of Inner Mongolia. For the first ten months of his life, he had been living in Hohhot in a state-run orphanage, but he had been transferred to Beijing for medical care when he spiked a high fever and it was feared that he had contracted meningitis.

Martha showed us several more photos of Ri Jin—the little boy's given name—that had been taken at various ages. One was of him as an infant and showed a little boy, all head and torso, with short arms and legs (just like his soon-to-be daddy). He was adorable. In another, in which he was closer to his then-current age of two, he had clearly grown. He had a huge smile and his hair was cut very short.

Martha told us that he was not in the best of health when he had arrived in Beijing for treatment. He was so malnourished that his eyes were bulging, his skin was taut, and the seams in his skull were still quite visible. After seeing his detailed medical records, Jennifer suspected that he hadn't had meningitis. But his high fever and transfer out of Hohhot turned out to be very fortunate. After receiving treatment in Beijing, he was placed in a foster facility there for children with special needs, which was a far more appropriate facility than the one he had been in. From that point forward, Ri Jin had begun to thrive, as evidenced by what we saw in his photos.

Jen and I were surprised to learn that the Beijing foster facility was run by a couple from New York who had first gone to China in the late 1980s on business and went back to open the center. The facility was Christian faith–based and subsidized by the state, but it also received private funding. Ri Jin was one of the fortunate ones, as not all of the children with special needs who were waiting to be adopted ever left the many subpar orphanages.

I wasn't the only one who felt this little boy was a part of our family the moment we saw his picture. Jen was just as in love, and we told Martha to begin the process. Smiling broadly, she gave us the contacts at the adoption agency that was handling his case, Children's Hope International (CHI). Tina, one of the senior people there, helped us navigate the process, from the paperwork to what we would need to plan for when it came time to make the actual trip to China. Since I was the paperwork guru, I got our dossier together, and it was sent off to China for consideration.

By June 2012, three months after we first sat down with Martha, the initial approvals were issued, and we were told it would likely be another six to twelve months before we would be able to travel to Beijing to get our son, whom we would name William, after me. We would keep his given name, Ri Jin, which means "Golden Sun," as his middle name, as is common with many families that adopt children from other countries.

With Will's paperwork under way, Jen and I were starting to get excited. It was late June when, unsurprisingly, Jennifer and I were in the drive-in line at our local Starbucks. We were catching up on some of the progress that we had made recently regarding William's adoption process and talking about how eager we were to meet our son. I forget which one of us started talking about how many kids we want to have, but half-kidding, I proposed, "Wouldn't it be awesome if now we could just find a little girl in India?" knowing Jen's love of Indian culture through her many Indian friends. "We would be all set!"

"Yes," she said and smiled. We went on to fantasize about traveling to China and India in the years to come, visiting our children's homelands and enjoying the experience, culture, and being with our family. It was only a "what if," a supposition, a "wouldn't it be cool" kind of thing. I was joking.

Two days later Jen received a call from Colleen at Little People of America informing her that our name had come up (after nearly five years), and there was a child available. Colleen explained that she knew we still hadn't even brought our son home, but if we were interested, there was *a little girl from India* available for adoption.

Jen was speechless. A second child! She wrote down the essentials Colleen gave her about the child and called me immediately. "You are not going to believe this," she blurted out. "That daughter from India we were wishing for a few days ago? Well . . ." she said softly.

I could barely wrap my own head around the news. At first, I thought she was messing with me. It was as if someone had been in the car with us that day at Starbucks and had overheard our conversation. Jen described Nidhi to me, an eight-month-old girl with some form of dwarfism, medium complexion, and huge brown eyes. She said she was utterly beautiful.

And while it certainly wasn't the timing we had envisioned, we knew this wasn't a little girl we should let pass us by. Of course, we

wanted the confidence of being competent parents of one child before we considered a second. But I had more confidence in our being
decent parents than I did in Nidhi's being in a good, safe, forever
home if we weren't her new family. We never intended for our son to
be an only child and did indeed wish to expand our family. So we decided to move forward and work toward welcoming this little girl into
our family, too.

That very day, Jen got on the phone with the adoption agency
handling the little girl's case. She expressed our interest and excitement to move forward. She was told we needed to get the paperwork
in right away. The Indian laws regarding international adoptions were
changing at the time. We were told that if we submitted our paperwork too late, there was a chance the child's file might become un-
available, and we would be unable to adopt this little girl at all. They
also sent us a photo of her. Everyone we shared the picture with made
the same comment: "What beautiful eyes!"

Now, for some odd reason, I had made two copies of every document needed for Will's adoption. It wasn't something Will's agency
had told us was necessary, just something I did inexplicably. It turns
out there was a reason for it, I just didn't know it at the time. Where
the documentation took weeks upon weeks to accumulate for the
dossier we submitted to China, we were able to turn around the bulk
of our dossier for India in just three days.

In January 2012, we had been reeling from our second miscarriage and unsure of how we would proceed with our family plan. By
the Fourth of July of that year, we were waiting for the Chinese and
Indian governments to allow us to come pick up our children.

CHAPTER SEVENTEEN

Jen

NOW a FamILY

THE TRIP TO CHINA to meet our son after what felt like an eternity of waiting took seventeen hours. We went through San Francisco, then hopped on a flight to Beijing. Packing for our trip had taken us almost as long. I had been researching blogs of what to bring when adopting your child from China. There were things I didn't even think of. I learned they only have diapers there, and not pull-ups. We debated bringing our own car seat or buying one there. The list of items we needed for Will was long. Not only were we first-time parents of a toddler, but we would be in a foreign country where running up to the local Target might not be an option. We were so excited to meet our son for the first time that we didn't even go to sleep the night before.

We landed in Beijing having not slept in twenty-four hours. Because we had the television crew in tow, things at the airport were a little more complicated than usual. The place was monstrous and unbelievably crowded. We had to take little airport trains just to get to the baggage area. Just like in the movies, everybody was pushing and shoving in order to pack as many people as possible into the train cars.

At last, we got to the baggage claim area, where we met the government minder who had been assigned specifically to us. She told the crew about the restrictions that they had to honor, such as no videotaping of anything that might besmirch the People's Republic of China. She wasn't just a government enforcer; she had lots of power as well. It turned out that she could get us around security checkpoints or other obstacles. Being accompanied by a government minder gave us a kind of VIP status, although at the same time we were keenly aware of just how much we were being watched.

This was our first trip to Asia, and it was very special. Bill had always wanted to visit China and Japan. Ironically, one of my dreams has always been to go to India, because I had so many friends who are Indian and I had grown to love the culture. How amazing that the reason a trip to India was in the stars was that our soon-to-be daughter was waiting for us there.

Beijing has about forty million people, so it is overwhelmingly large. Most of the people didn't seem particularly friendly or happy, but busy and focused.

The adoption process in China actually requires prospective parents to take some time sightseeing before meeting their child so that we can have a better appreciation for the country and culture that the child is from. On our first night in Beijing we met with our local adoption agency guide, named Amy (which was the "English" name she used when meeting with adoptive parents from the U.S.). She gave us our schedule, told us the dos and don'ts for the adoption process, and even taught us a few vital phrases in Mandarin such as how to order food or find the bathroom. She would be our best friend while we were in Beijing, but we would have guides in each of the cities we would be traveling to.

Because Beijing is the capital, I could feel the presence of "Big Brother" more than in any other city we visited. We were told to expect that at any point government officials might look through your belongings and download any media that they felt suspicious of. For that reason, we didn't bring our cell phones, but got a new one without any personal information just for the trip, and we cleaned out our laptops. Good thing, because after dinner one night it was obvious to me someone had been through my suitcase. Nothing was missing, but things were rearranged.

We were only in Beijing for a few days, but we got to see some amazing and historic landmarks. Bill and I loved being able to tour Tiananmen Square, so rich in Chinese history. We were able to sidestep the crowds because our government minder got us around the security. The next day we made the journey to the Great Wall of China. That was amazing, and as we walked up the steps, all I kept thinking was how much I wished Will was already with us! The Great Wall historically was the divider between China and Mongolia—now, of course, Inner Mongolia, on the other side, is part of China. Knowing that Will was from Inner Mongolia, I wished I could explain to him the history of where he was from. I guessed we would just have to make another trip when he was officially ours! Practically speaking, however, it was probably a good thing he wasn't with us, because it was absolutely freezing on the Wall. We didn't last up there very long.

As much as we enjoyed seeing the highlights of Beijing, all we really wanted to do was get to Will! His foster facility in Beijing was a bit far from Tiananmen Square in one of the outer rings. The government minder explained to us about the rings of Beijing. The city was developed in a ring structure, with every few miles having a ring of traffic. These rings also established socioeconomic boundaries, with the rings farther from the center of the city being the most impoverished.

Will's foster facility was out in the sixth and outermost ring. On our third day in China, we were finally able to visit it to see Will, and we drove with Amy and our government minder to New Day Foster Home. It was fascinating to see how the city changed as we went from the inner rings to the sixth ring. It went from a busy and bustling metropolis almost akin to Manhattan to farmland with small houses and buildings spread out among larger areas of grassland and trees.

New Day Foster Home is a privately run facility that was started by a family from the U.S. They saw a need to help orphans in China who needed complex or specialty medical care, which is difficult if not impossible to get in a government orphanage. This family started New Day with the goal of taking in children who had medical needs and who would otherwise die in a government orphanage. Will was clearly a very lucky little boy to have found his way there.

The facility itself was like a commune of buildings, with an office building, a building for the recreational facilities, a building for housing for younger kids, and another for housing the older ones. The children ranged in age from newborn to school age. Nothing about the complex was visually interesting, but inside, it was clean and well maintained, and the children appeared well cared for. As was customary in Asia, everyone was asked to remove his or her shoes at the door before entering to keep the quarters clean. We got to see Will's room. It was about six feet by ten feet, with two cribs in it. Each child shared a room. Will's roommate was an infant, but we were told he liked it because he preferred spending time with the grown-ups or caring for the babies rather than being with kids his own age. He has always been a caretaker!

Now, the moment we had been waiting for was upon us. When we walked into the room where Will was waiting, he immediately recognized us. "Mama! Baba!" he squealed. It was as if in this moment, halfway around the world, the three of us recognized and "found" one another as a family. Our instant connection felt timeless and unlike anything either Bill or I had ever experienced before. To see the wonder and joy in Will's eyes when he recognized us as his Mama and Baba moved us to our core. Bill and I had tears of joy at the sight of him. It was a unique, wonderful experience. Even though Will spoke very little, we didn't need to speak at all, as our body language spoke volumes.

We got to spend almost a whole day at New Day. We were able to have lunch with Will, play in the modest playroom, tour the facility, and meet with many of the staff. Both Bill and I were very impressed with what we saw and learned. We met the founders from New York, Byron and Karen Brenneman. They welcomed us with Chinese hospitality and told us that Will was not only a favorite in the foster home, but would be greatly missed.

Will had two primary nannies who cared for him on a daily basis. We got to meet with them and learn about Will's likes and dislikes, his mannerisms and personality. You could tell that they loved him and were tearful but happy to see him adopted. The foster facility had a pediatrician who came weekly, a speech therapist, a physical therapist, and teachers for school. We learned about Will's daily routine, medical issues, and everything in between. I audio recorded the whole meeting with his caregivers, so I wouldn't forget any details that I might need later.

Unfortunately, we were not able to take Will home with us that day, as this was just a lucky visit we were able to have with him before the official adoption process in Hohhot. We would have to go to his birthplace in Inner Mongolia to actually complete the adoption process and take custody of Will. Leaving him at New Day was one of the hardest things we had to do, but of course we knew in two days all this waiting would finally be over.

Before we left, Will's nannies gave us all of Will's belongings in case during the official adoption process his government liaison failed to pass them along. One of the precious items we got back was actually the photo album we had sent to him a few months earlier. We had been told after our adoption application was accepted that we could send him photos of us, our home, and family for him to start to get to know us. Someone from the staff had actually laminated some of the photos onto one page, so that Will could carry the page everywhere without getting the photos damaged. We were told he would show it to all the other kids and say, "This is my mama and baba." Additionally, we were allowed to send him one small gift. We got him his own "Flying Lion" to keep him safe until we were able to bring him home!

The next day, all of us left for Hohhot, where Will's birth records were located. We didn't travel together. Bill and I flew, but Will and his travel companion, Gon Lu, took the overnight train, as Will wasn't allowed to fly with us, not being officially ours yet. Gon Lu, a young woman who served as New Day's photographer, was truly his best friend, and had volunteered to travel with Will because she loved him so much and wanted to be there for him as he made this transition. She had been with him for two years, ever since he had arrived in Beijing.

Amy actually traveled with us, but she would only be staying a few days, so we met another guide, Sondra, in Hohhot as well. On our first day in Hohhot, Amy and Sondra took us shopping at a local mall to get a few items for Will. We bought a stroller, a car seat (which is not commonly used in China, but the pediatrician in me would not allow me to put Will in a car without one), and of course, a few presents for him for our official first "Gotcha Day."

The mall reminded me of an indoor flea market. It was a very large warehouse type of space with individually run "shops" that were divided by partitions, different from our malls in the U.S. Although Hohhot is small by China's standards, a mere five million people, it was actually very crowded, and with the camera crew capturing the trip, we drew lots of attention.

The official meeting to finalize the adoption took place at our hotel the day Will and Gon Lu arrived in Hohhot. Before Will's entrance, Amy brought us to a small, nondescript hotel conference room that had been set up with a table draped in a tablecloth for ceremonial purposes. There, we met the people who ran Will's state-run orphanage. The officials took their places at the table—two women sitting on either side of an authoritative-looking man. We went through all kinds of official paperwork, signing official documents such as the adoption decrees and certifications, paid the money still due the state for the processing fees, and signed off on the adoption. When it was over, we were officially in full custody of Will. He was legally our true son!

Next, Amy brought Will and Gon Lu into the room. We both knelt on the floor to hug Will. He was finally, officially ours! Will started to cry as Gon Lu said her good-byes to him. Gon Lu tried her best not to upset Will, but she was still crying. Two years was a long time to be with him, and they had grown really close. But, she was also happy for him, especially knowing that he was going to be so well cared for. Will cried for a little while, and we let him have his space, as we both knew he must have been completely overwhelmed and confused. We thanked Gon Lu profusely for caring for and watching over our amazing son over the last two years, and we promised to keep in touch!

After everybody else left, Bill, Will, and I were together and on our own for our very first time. We left the conference room together, and Will started exploring the hotel, running around with a new burst of energy. The traffic outside the window seemed to excite him. "Beep beeps," he exclaimed, looking at the mobs of cars and buses driving floors below. We were having so much fun just watching him explore everything around him, but eventually, we had to take him upstairs to our hotel room for our first diaper change. While I changed diapers in the neonatal unit once in a while, this was our first diaper change as parents, and of course, it was a number two!

After we got Will cleaned up, his demeanor changed completely. All of a sudden, he went from being sad to see Gon Lu leave to seeming happy to be with us. It was as if he all at once recognized that we were his parents, his forever parents, and he liked that, so he relaxed. He explored the hotel room and found all the presents Bill had spread around the room at his level on purpose for him to find.

Our first outing as a family took place that afternoon when we went for a walk in a park right outside the hotel. Will was pretty happy on the walk, but it was fairly cold, so we made it a short one. On our way back into the lobby, Will started pointing down the hall and screaming "Beep beep." Our hotel was connected to a very high-end mall, not at all like the one we went shopping in the day before. Near the entrance to the mall on the other side of the lobby were two very high-end cars on display, a Ferrari and a Maserati. Bill and I couldn't believe he even saw them so far away, but he did, and he was freaking out! We took him over, and he immediately ran up to the Ferrari, apparently his car of choice, and literally started to hug it! Bill, being the car aficionado that he is, said, "Now I know he was meant to be my son." Clearly, Will loved cars as much as his baba. The representative watching the cars was so moved by Will's enthusiasm, he unlocked the doors and let Will climb into the driver's seat. Will had the biggest grin on his face as he started to move the steering wheel back and forth. Boy, will we be in trouble when he turns sixteen!

During our first family dinner that evening in the hotel restaurant, we witnessed Will's voracious appetite for the first time. He was thrilled with his meal. The hotel had an amazing buffet. This being his first dinner with us, and knowing that he likely had had limited and very structured meals, we of course gave him anything he wanted. We were told by our adoption agency that due to limited access to food, kids may hoard food or eat a lot at first. Well, he never became a hoarder of food, but that night it appeared that he had an endless appetite. We literally sat at the table for two hours while Will kept eating. Obviously, we tempered our eating after that night.

After settling in our room for the night, we got Will in his pajamas and got ready for bed. Bill had his first alone time with him when I left to take a bath, something I like to do when my tired bones are hurting after a long day. They sat on the bed and watched *Rio*, a 3D computer-animated film about a blue macaw named Blu who traveled to Rio de Janeiro to mate with a feisty female macaw named Jewel. They watched the entire movie together, and Will seemed to really enjoy it. I came out of the bathroom to find them head to head in bed watching. After that, we looked at a book, cuddling in bed together.

Not knowing what kind of a sleeper Will was, I thought it safer to put him in the crib for sleeping. I didn't want him to wake up and get into something unsafe while we were sleeping or have him fall out of bed and hit his head. It was then that we discovered he likely had significant sleep apnea, when we noticed he snored very loudly, at times worked hard to breathe, using his accessory muscles, and had long pauses that appeared as if he had stopped breathing. Because I knew children with achondroplasia were at high risk for this, it didn't surprise me. Of course, it made me more anxious seeing it and not knowing if this level of difficulty breathing was the norm for him, but there was not much we could do. If he had lived for the last three years without a sleep study and CPAP, he should be fine for another week until we get home, I tried to reassure Bill and myself. We would just have to keep an eye on him and get him evaluated after we got back to Houston.

The next morning, Will woke up smiling. He was standing up in the crib with his hands over the railing, ready to have something to eat, and that was it. He was totally part of the family and ready to go. That day, when Will was up, dressed, and comfortable, Bill and I went with Sondra to the State Department to finish the paperwork for Will's Chinese passport, and we were told it would take exactly three days, no more, no less. With the bureaucratic part of the trip out of the way with unexpected ease, we now had the time to do some sightseeing in Will's birth city.

The Old City of Hohhot is incredible, with architecture from thousands of years ago and ancient Buddhist temples. Many people didn't wear traditional Mongolian garb, but tourists like us did. There were people outside the temples with all different sizes of traditional Mongolian outfits, most notably "deels," which were very large, colorful overcoats, often held tight by silk belts and ornate buckles. They used them for tourist photos. They dress you up and then take your picture as a memento. Of course, we did it! It was actually a lot of fun, and Will looked absolutely adorable in his outfit!

We also went to the Inner Mongolian Museum, where there were thousands of artifacts from all of Mongolian history. I loved the Genghis Khan statue. He was one of the most deeply feared personalities of all time. He created the largest contiguous land empire in human history, and being there, where he had been, was pretty amazing.

We enjoyed our three days in our son's birthplace, but when we received Will's passport we were ready for our final stop on our journey. We needed to travel to Guangzhou, the third-largest city in China, to obtain medical clearance and secure a visa for Will's trip home to the United States with us. Guangzhou, the capital of Guangdong Province, is a port city about twenty-five hundred miles south of Hohhot. The three-and-a-half-hour flight would be Will's first time on an airplane, and we worried how he would do. He surprised us both—he was calm, happy, and enjoyed watching a movie on the iPad! I hoped this was a glimpse of how he would be on the long seventeen-hour trip home to Houston.

Guangzhou was very interesting. The climate was considerably warmer than Hohhot, where the temps never really reached above freezing, and the city itself was much more Americanized, with Western favorites like McDonald's and Starbucks. Will picked out his first pair of sunglasses during a shopping trip to the mall, and he looked very cool.

We were now in a hotel with many people from all over the United States who were also in China to adopt a child. We met two other families who were also adopting with our agency. Our adoption guide here, Sam, took all three families out sightseeing and to lunch. He organized all our medical appointments on the same day so we could travel together. Once Will's medical clearance was granted, we needed to secure him a visa for travel to the United States. Again, we were told that would take five days, no more, no less. The process was very structured and organized in China. On the day we received his visa, we had a little celebration in the room and gave Will a mini American flag. As soon as we landed on U.S. soil, he would become an official citizen of the United States.

Bill and I were hopeful that he would be a pretty good flyer as he had been so well-behaved on the flight from Hohhot to Guangzhou. It was a long trip back home and we had heard that likely there would be other adoptive families on the plane, so if he wasn't, not to worry— we wouldn't be alone.

Our journey home was another seventeen plus hours. First, we had a small flight from Guangzhou to Beijing. We had a layover in Beijing, and then it was Beijing to San Francisco, and then Houston.

We had a little customs issue trying to get out of Beijing, due to the camera crew's camera battery, as it was flagged as suspicious. For some reason, they wouldn't let us proceed to the gate, and we feared at first it had something to do with Will's adoption. A small part of me couldn't rest until I knew we were on U.S. soil with our son. Security let Will and me go, but not Bill. The production company had asked Bill if he would mind having one of their bags put under his name to help defray the cost. His generosity, however, made him part of the group of production people that now couldn't leave the country without getting the battery issue resolved. So, Bill told me to go ahead just in case he didn't make the flight. I, of course, had no intention of getting on a plane without him, but to keep things calm, I agreed.

Fortunately, Bill and our cameraman figured out and solved the battery problem and, literally as they were closing the doors, they made it to the plane.

The flight from Beijing to San Francisco was the longest leg. I thought if Will could handle that flight, we would be fine! To our pleasant surprise, we found out Will was a natural flier, as if he had been flying his entire life. He was the perfect gentleman, sitting in his seat as the flight attendant served him lunch on his little tray. We had given him an iPad to play with, and he had loved that, too, wearing his headphones like an old pro. We watched *Finding Nemo* on the plane, and to this day that movie is a favorite in our house.

On the jet in San Francisco, Will finally started getting irritable, and then he let loose. I really couldn't blame him; I was ready to have a meltdown by that point, too. He screamed for the first forty minutes of the flight. We felt bad for all the other passengers, and I kept apologizing as we tried to walk him down the aisle to calm him down. Being a new parent, I felt terrible. Now, however, I have more perspective and realize that all parents have been there at some point.

We made it, finally. The last leg seemed interminably long, as you can imagine. To say it was great to be home was an understatement. I couldn't wait to get in the door, as we were all exhausted. Will and I had slept a little bit on one flight or another, but Bill hadn't, so he could barely stand. We were both really glad that my mom and dad met us at the airport. They were thrilled to pieces to meet Will! They had a surprise party prepared at our house with balloons, presents, and a cake for a "birthday party" for Will's welcome home. Will had just turned three a couple of weeks earlier, and we finally got to celebrate his birthday as a family!

When we opened the door, Will saw all the decorations and his excitement was uncontrollable, despite how tired he was. One look at the cake, and he was all in. He loved his Thomas the Tank Engine scooter, as well. As for Bill, suffice it to say that he was passed out cold on the couch fifteen minutes later.

Bill and I give Will all the credit in the world. What a trouper he turned out to be. I think he was numb for a while, completely dumbfounded that he was in this new life with this house full of toys and balloons. After our little party, Bill and I took him up to his new room and showed him his bed and his stuff. We stayed in there with him the first night. We put him in his bed, and then we slept on the trundle that went underneath it.

For his first night, we were all in there with him, and it was just the greatest feeling new parents could have. We were together as a family and we were home.

ALTHOUGH IT SEEMED destined to be, adopting a child from India wasn't easy. Will's adoption process had taken just under a year from start to finish, so we hoped for a similar experience with our daughter. Unfortunately, different countries work at different paces. And the delays we experienced with the U.S. Customs and Immigration Department and the Indian government, which were very common, pushed back our trip to India to get our daughter. In the end, we left for India after sixteen months of waiting.

As our travel date approached, we received one of our very infrequent updates about little Nidhi. She was very small. Even for a Little Person, she was small, and I was becoming more and more alarmed that she might be severely malnourished. At two years old, she measured only twenty-three and three-quarter inches in length and weighed just fifteen pounds. She was well under the third percentile from a "failure to thrive" perspective, which meant that she was in the lowest 3 percent of the population in terms of growth.

It could have been a combination of genetics and her dwarfism that exacerbated her diminutive stature. My Indian friends tell me it is typical of girls from India to be extremely petite, but I also was concerned that being in an orphanage with limited resources, malnourishment might have been a large component. She had been brought to the orphanage when she was only a week old, we knew very little of her environment or orphanage, and we had been warned that often infants and children in orphanages have very poor nutrition, which can contribute to growth delays. In fact, the rule of thumb for international adoption is to expect developmental and growth delays. Of course, multiple factors other than nutrition can influence this, but in any case, time was of the essence.

Will was going with us. He had arrived on March 14, 2013, seven months earlier, and he was now a seasoned traveler. So, on October 12, Bill, Will, our nanny, Kate, five members of our television crew, and I boarded a flight for Mumbai via Newark International Airport.

We landed in Mumbai the night before Bill's birthday, Sunday, October 13. He was about to receive his gift, a brand-new daughter. We had been in Guangzhou, China, for my birthday, and now we were in India for Bill's birthday. Birthday gifts didn't get better than this. Unfortunately, we couldn't actually see our daughter until Monday, as visitation was not allowed over the weekend. On that Sunday, we did just a bit of sightseeing, including a trip to Juhu Beach, a popular tourist spot about twelve miles north of Mumbai on the shores of the Arabian Sea, and had dinner at the hotel the night before our big day. We went to bed exhausted from our trip, but Monday couldn't come fast enough.

Monday morning found us boarding the large van we had hired with room for everyone who was going with us. We had two cameramen, two executive producers, a field producer for the filming, and three people we had hired in Mumbai—a driver and two security personnel. Bill and I decided Will would stay behind at the hotel with Kate when we went to get Nidhi. He would have his own private meeting as soon as we had his sister with us.

The trip to the orphanage took over an hour, even though it was only seven miles from our hotel. No sooner had we crossed our first bridge, which was almost in sight of the hotel, than we had to pay money to people with guns who wouldn't let us pass unless we gave them something. The traffic and driving conditions in Mumbai were horrific. Imagine thousands of cars and no traffic rules, and drivers who had little regard for each other, pedestrians, or the livestock that meandered through the streets. Cows received some respect, but everything else was fair game, to be bumped, nudged, scraped, or cut off.

We didn't spend the entire hour worrying about all the accidents we saw, but we easily could have, as there were so many. We were both nervous and excited about meeting our daughter, whom we would name Zoey Nidhi. We chose the name Zoey as it was one that I loved and was the name that my mother had wanted to give me. Even though that was what I was supposed to be named, my grandma had thought it wasn't a proper name and insisted my mother name me Jennifer Lynn. Just like with Will, we kept Zoey's Indian first name as her middle name.

I was more worried about what condition we would find her in. Was she well nourished? Would she be too sick to travel home with us for any reason? Was she walking and talking? How well was she achieving her developmental milestones? She had just had her second birthday a few weeks before we got there. But she had been in this orphanage for quite a long time, and we didn't know what kind of care she had received. The long months of waiting that we had to endure before this trip weighed on my mind. All I wanted was to get her and take care of her.

The orphanage was on Jail Road, which was no coincidence. The place had been a prison and was still surrounded by the eighteen-foot walls that had protected it then. It was probably in the worst part of town. There was stinky, rotting garbage piled up all along Jail Road. The homelessness was beyond anything I had ever imagined. On the sidewalks right near the orphanage, babies were lying on bedsheets spread right on the sidewalk. Probably every two feet, there was another man, woman, or child, seemingly with nowhere to go.

When we finally got to the orphanage, the van backed into a designated spot. No one but Bill and I got out, thinking the best way to meet the folks at the orphanage, including the head of the facility, was privately. Oddly, the staff there wanted to know where the film crew was! It seemed the adoption agency in the United States might have purposely disclosed that we had a television show, hoping it would motivate the Indian government and the local management of the orphanage to be as diligent as possible with our case, and perhaps hoping, moreover, that the documentary-style filming of our adoption story would benefit other families in the midst of their adoption story if we shined a positive light on the hard-working people within the Indian government helping children find their forever families. So, with the orphanage's encouragement and approval, we brought some of the crew inside.

The orphanage housed about 150 kids, about two-thirds under the age of seven. For those over the age of seven, the facility served as a rescue home for girls and women who came from situations of abuse. For those seven and under, the facility was a co-ed orphanage. Kids could arrive there within days of being born.

We went into a meeting room where we were introduced to most of the senior staff at the orphanage. It wasn't long before Zoey was brought in. It was a moment that we will never forget. She was beautiful and much tinier than we had imagined, even though we knew her measurements. This little meeting was supposed to be a first chance to say hello and hold her, but as it turned out, it was pretty high drama. No sooner had she gotten into the room than she started screaming furiously! We took some time trying to soothe her, but nothing was working. I knew this was expected, but it was still so hard to meet our daughter for the first time and feel that there was nothing we could do to comfort her.

Zoey's caregiver quickly scooped her up and took her to get cleaned up and dressed for her departure, while we went on a tour of the facility, which had its own surprises. It was a compound of old prison buildings, and most of the buildings didn't even have windows. The buildings had an oppressive and dank feel. The walls were actually moist due to the humidity and no air-conditioning. The facility was understaffed and poorly funded, and it was a miracle that the staff managed to do what they did with the limited resources they had. All the staff except for the teachers were volunteers with Asha Sadan, the women's charity that started the orphanage. The play yard seemed okay, and the few rooms for arts and crafts had some supplies. The older kids made handbags here that were sold to visitors to raise money for the orphanage.

We were disappointed to find that because Zoey was so small, she was lumped in with all the infants even though she was two. Her nursery had twenty or so cribs and was overseen by three rotating caregivers. Zoey was still being treated like a baby, probably bottle fed and then put back into her crib. Because she was in with this age group, she didn't get to participate in any toddler activities, such as running around playing with the children her age. She just wasn't being engaged with in the same way that the other two-year-olds were, due to her small size.

In a way, Bill and I recognized this was probably safer for her, seeing she was so small and underweight, but it was still extremely sad.

In Will's foster facility, he had been with a much smaller group of people. He had also been with other children with special needs, so the level of care had been a lot better. They had a staff physician who addressed issues in the foster facility that didn't demand emergent care. He had even gotten speech therapy in Mandarin.

We tried to find out as much as we could about Zoey's health, personality, and background from the staff who had been caring for her for so long. They gave us her medical records, but not a whole lot of other details. We longed for any information about her that would help us to understand and know this lovely little girl, but we were able to find out very little. The staff was very nice, though. All the female caregivers were called "Auntie" by the children. They were responsible for everything: the food, the cleaning, the education, and the general care.

While we were doing the paperwork, we were treated to little sweet dessert balls and a cup of tea. We finished signing the last of the logbooks and left the orphanage with Zoey in Bill's arms to climb into the van. She yelled all the way to the van, where things actually got worse. We didn't think she could actually scream any louder, but she proved us wrong. Once inside the vehicle, she got so upset that first she tried to bite Bill, then tried to bite me. Her rage was so intense that she was soaked with sweat. We were happy to be bringing her home with us and at the same time extremely worried about her. Luckily, she finally calmed down and slept the last couple of miles back to the hotel.

When we got back to the hotel suite, we wanted to get Zoey ready to meet Will, but before that, we wanted to give her a quick bath, a change of clothes, and a bedbug inspection. We had had a bedbug scare when we brought Will home from China and didn't want to make that mistake again. It was a "do not pass go, go straight to the

bath" process. Her cries were finally quelled as I became a bit familiar to her. By the time we finished giving her a bath, she was rather attached to me, and she wouldn't let me put her down.

Next, we brought her into the living area where Will and Kate
were playing and waiting for us to return. Will was sitting at the coffee table playing with a toy, ready to meet his sister. At first, he kept
a bit of distance so as not to crowd her too quickly. Zoey looked
like a deer in headlights, but who wouldn't? She was surrounded by
strangers and had been taken from all she knew. Will hopped off the
couch and crouched below her. He leaned in and kissed her foot as
he said, "Hi, Ozoy," his pronunciation of Zoey. It was one of the most
endearing things I had ever seen, and in that instant, I knew that
our new family was complete. Will was obviously ready to be a big
brother!

DURING ALL THE joy and excitement of bringing a new daughter into
our family, I started having a frightening medical issue. I was experiencing very heavy vaginal bleeding. I assumed it was related to a medical procedure I had undergone the previous month, a dilatation &
curettage (D&C) for a molar pregnancy, a nonviable pregnancy, which
needed medical intervention. A molar pregnancy begins the way a
normal pregnancy does, but instead of a fetus forming in the uterus,
a ball of cells begins to grow. It was the first time we had ever gotten pregnant, but it wasn't viable, it wasn't expected, and it required a
medical intervention in the form of a D&C.

After the D&C, I was told by the doctors that they *believed* they
had removed all the tissue, and I was good to go. After the pathology
report came back as a complete molar pregnancy, we were informed
that I would still need to be monitored to make sure my hormones re-

turned to normal levels, and by the time we left for India, I seemed to be problem free and my hormone levels were coming down nicely. Now, with this bleeding, I wasn't sure what was going on, but obviously I was concerned. It started slowly and then while we were in Mumbai would increase, then decrease, making it difficult to make a decision about whether I should be really alarmed. Given my short stature, any significant loss of blood can affect me greatly.

When I told Bill about it, he was quite upset and worried about me. I tried to put his mind at ease, but the truth was that I was frightened. The bleeding was increasing, and we were in a remote city with poor health-care access should something more serious develop. I knew better than anyone that the last thing any of us wanted was for me to get a blood transfusion in India, where the screening process is not as extensive as it is in the United States. We were only in Mumbai a few days when this all began.

During our flight to New Delhi to complete the adoption process for Zoey, I really started to feel as if I was hemorrhaging. It was almost as if moving around more caused the bleeding to get worse. We were already overwhelmed with the process of meeting Zoey and getting her settled, as well as traversing this new country to get her documents. It seemed almost unreal that I might have a real health crisis on top of everything else that was going on. And yet the bleeding persisted and then started to get more serious.

The two-hour flight was Zoey's first airplane ride, and amazingly she did great. She didn't want to be in anybody's lap, she just wanted to be alone in her seat. I was still bleeding, starting to feel more lightheaded and nauseated. Coincidentally, my boss, Dr. Stephen Welty, the head of neonatology at Texas Children's Hospital, happened to be in New Delhi at this very same time on a two-week trip for medical work he was doing with a local governmental hospital. We were supposed to meet for fun when we got to New Delhi, but instead I ended up calling him for a recommendation on an OB/GYN he might be working with at the hospital whom I could see. He was unbelievably helpful and connected me with a gynecologist, who gave me something to stop the bleeding. It was a clotting agent that slowed the bleeding down, but it didn't arrest it completely.

I got in touch with my gynecologist in Houston, who told me to get home immediately. When I explained that I needed to stay and finish Zoey's adoption and then return home, she insisted that it was urgent for me to return to Houston on the next possible flight. We estimated that my blood loss was already significant. Of course, my brain went to the worst-case scenario at this point, and I became worried that if for some reason I became unconscious due to more blood loss and shock, the people treating me would not know how to care for me—providing medications and fluids, and more important, securing an airway and intubating me, because I have a truly difficult airway due to my cervical spine structural issues and anatomy.

This couldn't be happening, and yet it was. For the last few days, I had been managing to convince myself that the bleeding would be fine during the times when it slowed down, but then out of nowhere, it would pick back up again. But it was after I spoke to my doctor in the States that the serious nature of the situation really hit me.

The juxtaposition of a major health scare and a joyful bonding experience with Zoey was making my head spin. The thought of leaving my newly united little family to head home without them was heartbreaking and almost unimaginable. Because it was so uncertain what was going on and whether the bleeding would continue, I really struggled with the decision. I truly couldn't imagine leaving them on the other side of the world. Bill couldn't leave, as Zoey still had to finish up her adoption and secure her visa. If I left, I wanted to take Will with me so that Bill would only need to concentrate on one child, but again, he pointed out that, heaven forbid, if something happened to me en route back to the U.S., who would take care of Will? He was right. So, after much deliberation, we agreed I needed to go home and seek medical attention.

I gave Bill my power of attorney, so he could finish up Zoey's adoption, and arranged my flight home as soon as possible, trying to keep my panic level in check.

Meanwhile, that same Wednesday, Bill took Zoey for her medical clearance exam, which was required by the U.S. government for entrance into the United States. Everything was good, but final clearance would still take another two days, the amount of time it took for the TB test results.

Saying good-bye to Will, Zoey, and Bill was not at all easy. I felt some ease knowing Bill had our nanny, Kate, with him to help out and also the support of the film crew. At the airport in New Delhi, it was a difficult good-bye, but we both knew it was time to get into survival mode and get through this. We had to for our children and for each other.

The whole situation was nothing I had expected to be dealing with, and was almost surreal. I was leaving my husband and two kids, one of whom I had only had for two days, in a third world country for a medical emergency. But, I think both of us knew there was nothing we could do to change the situation, and now we had to focus all our energy on getting through this as quickly as possible.

I was very appreciative that at least I wasn't traveling completely alone. Because we were filming this trip, we had two security personnel with us, and one of them accompanied me back to the U.S. We discussed a plan for him to carry out if indeed the worst happened, and I lost consciousness during the flight. I actually had a note in my pocket, telling the flight crew what to do to secure my airway and prevent further injury to my spine, as my neck fusion made things more complicated.

Bill told me months later that he had tracked my entire journey on his phone, never sleeping the entire night and making sure any plane I was on was not diverted, which could mean a medical emergency for me. It still brings tears to my eyes when I think of him in India with our children, staying up all night to track my flights to be sure I wasn't in danger. I can't exactly explain in words what his love means to me. It is actions like these, gestures that I might not even know about at the time, that make Bill the incredible partner that he is, and I love him for it.

The fourteen-hour flight to Newark was uneventful, thank goodness. I was uncomfortable for much of the trip, so I was really relieved when we landed. Between connections, I called Bill to let him know I was okay, and he told me he was making out just fine with Zoey and Will, although everybody missed me.

Unfortunately, our flight from Newark to Houston was delayed. But fortunately, my bleeding had stabilized somewhat. When I finally got to Houston, my parents picked me up at the airport and took me to see my doctor, where I immediately had a CAT scan, an MRI, and some other tests. I was relieved to be back in the United States and was hoping for reassuring news to pass along to Bill overseas.

The news was not good, though. I had a malignancy in my uterine wall, the direct result of the molar pregnancy. It was this tumor that was causing the bleeding. But the news was far worse than that. The problem was that the cancer had already spread to my lungs, and I needed to start aggressive treatment right away.

Again, there was no time to waste on self-pity or misery, but rather it was time to intensify the survival mode I had already been in. For a few seconds, I did wonder how this could be happening to me. I felt like I was in the middle of a very bad dream, but all I could do was keep moving forward. It seemed crazy to me that I had been in India two days ago, having just adopted our daughter, and now I was home without my family and diagnosed with a stage 3 cancer that required intensive treatments immediately. My gynecologist immediately referred me to a gynecological oncologist, and I met Dr. Concepcion Diaz-Arrastia, who has turned out to be not only a talented oncologist and surgeon but a dear friend.

When I told Bill, he took the news as well as he could. I think it was still unbelievable to both of us in different ways. Life had turned upside down on what felt like every front in a matter of a few days.

Somehow Bill managed to complete the rest of Zoey's adoption in three days, possibly the fastest international adoption ever. He had a little hangup getting her visa, as they weren't able to get to the U.S. embassy in New Delhi until Friday afternoon. The embassy told him they would probably not be able issue the visa until Monday. Bill wasn't willing to accept that, explaining how urgent it was that he get back to the United States and that he was willing to wait all day for the visa. His stubbornness paid off. Even though the embassy was officially closed, with the monitors turned off and the lights out, he left there with Zoey's visa.

There was also a little trouble at the airport. Someone from the Indian army stopped Bill as he was going through customs, wondering why he had a little Indian girl with him. Apparently, there was concern that Bill might have been trying to smuggle Zoey out of the country. Even though Bill pulled out a document that showed Zoey was his daughter, they unzipped all his bags and detained him, while both kids were crying and screaming. I know it wasn't easy for him. Finally, a supervisor walked over to see what was happening, examined Bill's documents, and concluded he was legitimate. It wasn't surprising that this happened to Bill, as there are not many international adoptions out of India. Bill was extremely grateful when he was finally aboard the flight to the U.S. I was certainly glad to have him and the kids home.

DECIDING ON THE hospital where I would be cared for put me in a bit of a quandary. The hospital where I worked, Texas Children's Hospital, had recently opened the Pavilion for Women, a comprehensive women's care hospital within our children's hospital. My oncologist, Dr. Arrastia, was the chief of gynecological oncology there, but also continued to care for patients at the other adult hospitals in the area. Although my oncologist worked at Texas Children's Hospital's Pavilion for Women (my hospital), they were not yet equipped to administer chemotherapy to adults, so I was supposed to have all my treatments—both inpatient and outpatient—at Methodist Hospital down the street. However, Dr. Arrastia talked with the executives at Texas Children's, and they ultimately made an exception to care for me at my own hospital because of my size and airway issues. Methodist only had adult-sized surgical and airway equipment, and Texas Children's was also much more adept at managing my difficult airway for surgery. My greatest relief was that my anesthesiologist was someone I worked with all the time and knew well.

Because initially the chemotherapy wasn't stopping my tumor's growth, we decided I needed to have surgery, a total abdominal hysterectomy, which took place on October 30 at my hospital, Texas Children's Hospital. I was more nervous about surgery than the chemotherapy or the cancer. I knew I had a difficult airway, and I had not been intubated since my hip replacements during pediatric residency more than ten years earlier.

Fortunately, the surgery went well. My anesthesiologist was able to intubate me without complication, and Dr. Arrastia felt the removal of my uterus was very straightforward, no surprises. I was in the hospital a few days and then my chemo regimen began almost immediately, as I still needed to treat the nodules in my lungs. The hormone levels in my blood that tumors secrete had been so high that we knew my cancer was aggressive.

I was back to going to the hospital weekly for chemo, with alternating levels of treatment. One week would be on an outpatient basis, in which I would be hooked up to an IV for four to six hours. The following week, I would stay overnight at the hospital for my treatment.

Because before and after surgery, the beta HCG numbers—the hormone markers used to test for pregnancy and my type of cancer—weren't going down at the rate we were hoping for, and I wasn't initially experiencing as many side effects as I should have, Bill had an epiphany, and it had to do with the dosing of my chemotherapy. To his way of thinking, I wasn't getting the proper dosage, because even though I was a Little Person, I had close-to-average-size organs for adult maturity, specifically my liver. My organs just happened to be packed into a tighter space. I was getting dosed, though, based on my weight and height, which is typical for chemotherapy dosing. The risk of arbitrarily increasing the dose too much is that chemotherapy is toxic and that could be life threatening to me.

Bill and Dr. Arrastia discussed the theory, and they agreed that I should be getting a higher dose than was normal for someone of my height and weight. Instead, Dr. Arrastia based the calculation on my liver size. His theory turned out to be correct. As Dr. Arrastia increased my dosage, my hair started falling out and my numbers went down, after a little over three months eventually reaching zero!

To add to the stress during all of this, Bill and I had given our nanny some time off to aid us in the bonding process with Zoey. Even before my medical emergency, we had decided we would give her a four- to six-week hiatus when we got home from India with Zoey, just as we had done when we brought Will home from China. When you adopt any child older than an infant, it's important to minimize the number of people in the household those first weeks to keep the child from becoming confused. When children grow up in an orphanage, they are accustomed to caregivers coming in and out in shifts, so we needed both Will and Zoey to understand that we were their parents, not caretakers, and we were never going anywhere. This helps them to develop a secure and loving bond with their new parents. The process had worked beautifully with Will, and we wanted to do the same with Zoey, despite the medical whirlwind of treatments that I was experiencing. We kept the camera crew away, and we even limited the amount of time the grandparents could visit. Even though the relatives thought we were crazy, everybody respected our decision.

Given the fact that I was undergoing weekly chemotherapy and recovering from major surgery, the decision to give Kate time off was no longer as easy as originally planned, but we were also fully committed to bonding as a family unit during this crucial time of transition for Zoey. To say it was overwhelming would be an understatement! Bill became super dad and super husband!

Bill and I, as a result, were beyond exhausted. Bill was bringing me back and forth to the hospital for treatment, all the while taking care of Zoey and Will. My parents helped out a lot, and when we felt it was appropriate to bring Kate back into the fold, we felt some relief. However, Bill, who was and always is the rock of our family, was at the same time enduring a herniated disc in his back—the result of a combination of scoliosis and an injury he had sustained while working out at the gym—that would eventually require surgery.

I would be horribly sick for five or six days after a chemo session, but I still had the strength to hug the kids, tuck them in, and tell them how much I loved them. We even moved them both downstairs to the master bedroom so it would be easier for us to care for them or mobilize them if I needed to urgently go to the ER. I'm not sure exactly how, but in the end we made it through my post-op complications, weekly chemotherapy, and the challenges in bonding with Zoey.

I officially went into remission on January 16, 2014, the date I was declared cancer free. My prognosis was excellent. I had a 10 to 15 percent chance of the cancer coming back in the first year, and if it didn't, the chances of it coming back were only 3 percent.

All in all, the year was an unbelievable one for Bill and me. We adopted two incredible children, Will and Zoey, and I beat cancer. At the time of this writing, February 2015, I am thirteen months cancer free, putting me in the 3 percent category.

While we began 2013 as a couple, we ended 2013 as a family of four, gathered together from far-reaching countries and now home. The journey to get here was unlike anything we could have predicted. We couldn't possibly have known what was ahead, both good and bad, and we wouldn't trade any of our experiences for the world. We look ahead with this same mindset, ready to embrace and appreciate all that life has in store.

EPILOGUE

Bill and Jen

SINCE RETURNING HOME FROM China and India with Will and Zoey, our hearts are full. Every day we see them grow and change, and in them we see boundless enthusiasm. In a lot of ways, they remind us of us and exemplify the lesson we learned from our parents—there is nothing we can't achieve.

So much has changed in just two short years. Zoey started off with us as a very frightened little girl. She was failing to thrive in her environment. Now, she is happy, bright-eyed, and well-adjusted. She is growing both in size and in character. Her personality is starting to shine through the shell she had developed out of necessity during her first two years of life in the orphanage. She has always been the quiet observer in the room. She soaks it all in, but don't let her silence fool you, she is paying close attention to everything. At three, she is making great strides to make up for lost time.

Will has always been pretty well-behaved. While no child is perfectly mannered, Will is the kind of boy who says "please" and "thank you" without being prompted. He is considerate of others and has an emotional IQ far beyond his age. He loves being around people, young and old. Most recently, during a parent-teacher school night, Will introduced me to each of his classmates by name. I didn't see any of the other twenty-eight students doing the same. There is just something about him that goes beyond average. His heart is gigantic. He cares for his sister in ways only an older brother can understand. If he has a cookie, she gets half. If she is scared, he holds her tight. For a boy of four, he continues to impress.

Both kids are now in preschool. They are making huge strides developmentally, leaving the past behind them and happily accelerating into their brighter future. We are both very proud of them.

Since both Will and Zoey were diagnosed with achondroplasia, the likelihood they will require corrective surgery similar to the kind Jen and I had is slim, fortunately. Of course, there is a chance surgery will be in their future. And if that day comes, we will be there for them, watchful and worried, as our parents were for us.

In terms of our recent medical issues, the last couple of years have been challenging to us both. Jen's battle with cancer was downright scary. And while the doctors seemed confident it was always beatable, we are so very thankful it worked out that way. For Bill, his surgeries in November 2008 for the right hip and January 2009 for the left were far overdue. Since his time on crutches in high school, Bill had been walking around on a dislocated and partially dislocated hip. His pain was reduced dramatically and his happiness increased by a similar measure with the surgery. In 2014, he required surgical repair for a vertebral disc he had herniated while at the gym back in late 2012. That surgery took place at the Hospital for Special Surgery in New York, only nine months after Jen completed her chemotherapy.

Bill's decision to delay his back surgery until things at home had quieted down had him enduring significant pain for months on end. The back surgery was actually scarier than the skeletal surgeries of our childhood. There was always the risk that things could end up worse than before the surgery, and there was so much at stake. Recovery was a lot more difficult than we had anticipated and progress was slow, made harder by the fact that we have two energetic young children at home who love to be active with us.

Bill is really not supposed to do any lifting, which is both frustrating and disappointing, as one of the best parts of being a parent to young children is lifting them up and snuggling with them. Things are getting better, though. Bill has recently been cleared to start physical therapy, which means he will gain more strength with every day. Jen, being cancer free, is also getting physically stronger and able to do much more.

Going through these difficult times together has made us both realize just how much we were meant to be together. Bill has said that he doesn't know if he would have done so well during and after his surgery if he hadn't had Jen, and Jen is thankful for the incredible support that Bill has shown her.

The truth of the matter is we are very grateful for every part of who we are, what we are, and how we were raised. We continue to seek inspiration from others whose stories of triumph over adversity help give us the strength to rise to the many challenges we face every day. In our younger years, we had to prove to everyone else that size didn't matter. Now, we only need to convince two people of that.

We wouldn't change anything about our lives, not one thing. Had either of us not been born with skeletal dysplasia, we probably would have never met. It was in the stars that we be together, and from the moment we fell in love, our blessings have multiplied beyond our dreams. Thank you everyone for embracing us just the way we are.

As we enter the latest chapter of our lives—being parents—we put all our energy into being a family unit and enjoying every minute we can spend together. We make every effort to look out for the best interests of our two amazing children, as do all parents. We both believe that Will and Zoey have had a remarkable few short years on this planet, but that the most exciting part of their story has yet to be written.

Our lives have been a fantastic journey thus far. So much has happened in such a short period of time. Just eight years ago, we were single, living in different parts of the country, and didn't know what we wanted out of life. Fast-forward to today, and the most amazing turn of events has occurred. We are parents of the two most amazing children in the world. Uncertainty and joy, which no doubt lie ahead, make life exciting. There are challenges we will need to meet in our future, some that we know about, and some beyond the unexpected vistas of possibility. We are learning so much about life by being parents.

We are figuring out life as we go, appreciative of all it brings—from the wondrous joy of a new day to the rocky mountain that may stand in our path. Life is short, so enjoy every moment!

ACKNOWLEDGMENTS

WE WOULD LIKE TO acknowledge all of the people who have loved, encouraged, and supported us:

To Lisa Pulitzer, Martha Smith, Steve Ross, and the wonderful team at Simon & Schuster, without whom this book would not be possible.

Our wonderful children, William Ri Jin Klein and Zoey Nidhi Klein.

Our ever supportive, inspiring, and loving parents and stepparents, David and Judy Arnold, Bill and Debbie Klein, Barbara and Chuck Croner.

Our most awesome brothers, stepbrothers, and fantastic families, Thomas, Christine, Riley, and Reagan Klein; Joseph, Karen, Dorinda, and Joseph T. W. Klein; David and Lisa Arnold; Jonathan, Debra, and Maddie Richman; and James and Kayla Richman.

To our dogs, Rocky and Maggie, for being warm and fuzzy all of the time. To all our pets that have gone on to heaven.

Our extended family: Jack and Barbara Douglas; Pat, Dawn, Patrick, and Paige Diecidue; Diane Diecidue; John Klein; Al and Carol Cook; Eleanor Madigan; Lorraine Croner; Aunt Jean Carey; Dennis Jr., Cindy, Juliet, Grace, and Dennis III Carey; Donald and Pat Pappas; Joe Iuliucci; Sandee Caldwell Shuman; Tish Houts Russell; Wayne Shipman; Sybil Shipman; Cheryl Shipman; Linda Underwood; Michelle Jolly Martinez; Pam Arnold; James Arnold; Buddy; Debbie Charest; Donna Charest; Russell Charest; Erica Charest; and of course, Raymond Charest.

Our dearest of friends Nikhil Shirali and Lakshmi Reddy, David and Cindy Daubel, BJ and Andria Donohue, Tara Kaheny, Susan Raine, Dan and Susan Leong-Stine, Rick and Leigh Ann Cates, Amit and Chetna Bhattacharyya, Rajiv and Manju Kulkarni, Christopher DeLuccio, Mike and Andrea Sperduti, Joan Sperduti, Eileen and Sebastian Tongston, Danny and Jenn Hart, Paul Sirbaugh, and Rick and Cheryl Kuykendall.

To Julie Carson May and Roger Armstrong for your professional and personal guidance.

To my colleagues at Baylor College of Medicine and Texas Children's, especially Drs. Welty, Kline, Lorin, Giardino, and Schutze and Mr. Mark Wallace.

To Kate Apffel for everything you do for our family.

To Maria Smith for taking care of our home.

To Jessica, Tasha, and the Rocky & Maggie's team, past, present, and future!

To the simulation center team and leaders: Kelly Wallin, Claire Tallinger, Melissa Cashin, Dan Feux, Leisa Chancey, Courtney Washington, Mary Jo Andre, and Trudy Leidich.

To the newborn center faculty and staff at Texas Children's Hospital for your collaboration.

To my simulation mentors at UPMC, especially Drs. Mindy Fiedor Hamilton and Patrick Kochanek.

To my colleagues and mentors from Children's Hospital of Pittsburgh, especially Drs. Dena Hofkosh, Ellen Wald, Jennifer Kles, Andy Nowalk, Andy Urbach, and all my co-residents, especially Jodi and Eyal, Lara, Roy, Dina, and Melinda.

To my former bosses, Drs. Jan Larson, Ann Stark, and Gary Silverman.

To Gay Dunton and Adrienne Otto Frame for mentoring me as an RA.

To Tad Foote for believing in me at the U of M.

To Niki Kazaskos for getting us out there!

To Chloe Dao for getting Jen all dressed up.

To Dr. Robert Boostanfar, the staff at HRC, and the team at CSP.

To our LP friends, especially Bobby and Angela Van Etten, Martha Holland Stanley and Steve Stanley, Bazhena and Tony Barker, Jeff Weiser, Charla Baklayan Faddoul, Vincent and Nicole DePaul, Laura Stout, Barbara Spiegel, Matt and Amy Roloff, Patti Yoder, Doreen Lackner, Frank Shomilak, Mark Trombino, Clinton Brown III, Gary Arnold, Francisca Winston, Michelle Kraus, Anna Adelson, Melody Winn, and Michelle Struss.

To my friends from Johns Hopkins Class of 2000, especially Aimee Nielson, Michelle Nee, and my roomies Aruna, Carmen, Traci, and Asma.

To the countless physicians, nurses, therapists, technicians, and staff at Johns Hopkins Hospital and St. Joseph's Hospital in Townson, Maryland.

To Drs. Michael Bober and William MacKenzie for being such caring specialists for our children.

To everyone from LMNO, including Eric Schotz, Ed Horwitz,

Ruth Rivin, Melissa Rabinowitz, Lisa Bourgoujian, Jan Lonsdale, Jared Podos, Art Sarkisyan, Carol-Ann Merrill, Ricky Wiebe, Ben Hurvitz, and our editors Ryan Ely and Adrian Herrera.

To our local film crew that has followed us around the world, twice, including Anne Hill, Jimmy Wong, Jaime Cervantes, Pierre Meunier, Erica Olivarez, Ben Kenniston, Will Zilliox, Jeanene Wood, Lainie Jasko, Tiff Winton, Luke Neslage, JR Rodriguez, Trisha Boyd, and Raul Casares.

To Steve Neild, Zane Wilmans, and Michael Leal for watching our backs.

To my classmates at St. Charles, Bishop Moore, and my fellow pediatric residency friends.

To Asha Sadan and New Day for caring for our beautiful children until we found them.

To Children's Hope, especially Tina Qualls and Illien Adoptions and Anna Belle Illien and Michele Henry for helping us get our children.

To LPA Adoptions and Rainbow Kids for helping orphans with medical complexities find their forever families, including ours.

To Colleen Giofreida and Martha Osbourne for finding our beautiful children for us.

To all of the supportive folks at Discovery Communications, including David Zaslov, Joe Abruzzese, Eileen O'Neill, Marjorie Kaplan, Nancy Daniels, Jennifer Williams, Howard Lee, Wendy Douglas, Laurie Goldberg, Dustin Smith, Elizabeth Melcher, Michelle Theisen, Ed Sabin, Amy Winters, Meaghan Werner, and Shannon Llanes for documenting some of the most trying and triumphant moments in our lives.

To Victoria Calloway and Cinthia Moore for making us look good and feel good. To Grayson Jacobs and Kitsa Stefanidis for friendship and good-looking hair, even when Jen had none.

To my University of Miami foursome: Sonal Patel, Suketu Mansuria, and Walter Wilcox (aka Wally).

To my NYU gang: Albert and Jennifer Heffez, Sara Bowman, Karin Tracy, Michelle Blaustein, Kathy Reeves, Jordan Hoffman, Jorge Matos, AKB, Seth Margulies, Joanna Harp, and Sam Heffez.

Thank you to the brave men and women of the Terryville Fire Department for always looking out for us and our family.

To the teachers and staff of Comsewogue School District in Port Jefferson Station, Long Island, New York, for being great educators and supporters and for providing guidance when I needed it.

To our matchmaker, wedding singer, and right hand to Dr. Kopits for many, many years, Diane Hawes.

To Gloria Brannon and Lulu Santos for taking care of our family so many times.

To Cindy and James for trying to help us have a baby.

To our friends and nurses Donna Buscemi, Bill Goff, Mary Beth, Katie, Janine, Mary Anne, and Mary Joe.

To Dr. Conchi Diaz-Arrastia for saving my wife's life.

To Patti Frimmer, Gloria Daubel, Grace DeFabio, and Nancy Staudenraus for supporting me and my mom, and for watching out for my brothers when I couldn't.

We want to remember, acknowledge, honor, and celebrate those we've lost: Patrick and Desiree Diecidue, Isaac and Lorraine Shipman, Sally Charest, Sylvia Klein, Mo Croner, and Dr. Steven Kopits, whose contribution to the care of those with skeletal dysplasia cannot be underestimated. Especially grateful for the love and care we have received from Dr. Kopits, without which we may not be the people we are today.

And from Jen to Aunt Chrissy: I thank you so much for being my best friend. I pray each day that you are finally in peace.

Read on for a sneak peek at Jen and Bill's new book,

INTRODUCTION

I T WAS MONDAY, OCTOBER 21, 2013. That was the day my wife, Jennifer, taught me what bravery truly looks like.

It was about 1:30 p.m. My three-year-old son, Will, two-year-old daughter, Zoey, and I walked in the door after a twenty-four-hour journey home from New Delhi, India. Jen and I had gone to India to adopt Zoey, but Jen had had a medical emergency while we were there and had flown back a few days early, leaving me to bring Will and our brand-new daughter home.

Jen had undergone immediate testing, and we had just learned that Jen had a rare form of cancer, an aggressive choriocarcinoma. She was already being treated with intensive chemo. Her immune system was paying the price, and she could not be in the house with us, so she was staying with her parents nearby. I called Jen as we walked in the door to let her know we had arrived. We were all physically exhausted and mentally drained. A twenty-four-hour journey is difficult enough, but a twenty-four-hour journey with two toddlers was another experience altogether.

The camera crew for our TV show, *The Little Couple*, wanted to capture our arrival home. They had been with us on the journey to India and had been there when we met our daughter for the first time. Now they wanted to catch her first reaction to seeing her new home. Our exhaustion tempered any kind of initial reaction, though, and after documenting the otherwise anticlimactic arrival home, we said our goodbyes to the crew. Kate, our nanny, who'd stayed with me throughout the trip, helped us get settled, and then she too departed to get some rest.

After the cameras left, I barely had the strength to keep moving, struggling to get the kids settled, fed, and to bed. The house felt especially empty without Jen.

Once we were left alone, Will ran around a bit, excited to be reunited with his house, toys, and gadgets. Zoey, meanwhile, lay down, crying at the door. She was inconsolable. She was in a new, strange place, with people she didn't know. The little attachment she forged in India with Jennifer was waning, and her tendency to gravitate toward any female in the room made my role as her sole parent that much more difficult. I felt particularly helpless and alone as I had no real means of communicating with her. We were all deeply missing Jennifer.

Then there was a knock at the back door. I muttered under my breath, guessing someone from the camera crew had forgotten something in the house. I headed to the door, and much to my surprise, it was Jennifer! She had been staking out the house with her dad, hiding in his Jeep, waiting for us to arrive. She just wanted to make sure we got home safely and didn't intend to come in. Once everyone else had left, though, she knew it would be impossible to resist seeing us. She was wearing a surgical mask to avoid exposure to any viruses while immuno-compromised, but above it, her eyes smiled enough to make all of us incredibly happy. Zoey spotted Jennifer and stood up, stopped crying at once, and walked over to gently touch the glass that separated them!

Jen couldn't hug or kiss the kids, so we kept the door closed and talked through the glass. Will and Zoey were confused, but they kept their composure. As did their mom. I can't say their dad fared as well. Tears streamed down my face. I was a bit of a wreck—both happy to see my wife and disappointed that I couldn't give her a hug yet.

As I watched her interactions with her kids, smiling and laughing, it became clear to me just how brave she was. She was undergoing intensive treatment, fighting for her life, but she was standing there trying to make us feel better. Jennifer was upbeat, trying to stay positive, and I had never needed that more. In that moment I saw how she was going to fight cancer: on her own terms, in her own way. Showing up at doorways with a grin, even through exhaustion and despite all of the circumstances stacked against her. Cancer wasn't going to win. It was clear to me, even through the door, that this is what she believed.

And watching her, with all my strength gone, I began to believe it too. We were going to meet this challenge head-on, together. And we would win.

It wouldn't be the first time.

Both for Jen and for me, the first forty years of life have been filled with challenges. We were both born with a rare form of dwarfism, called spondyloepiphyseal dysplasia (SED). SED is characterized by short stature and a range of medical complications that have to do with the skeletal system. It affects approximately 1 in 100,000 births and is the product of a random genetic mutation, unless one of your parents has SED. And while having a disability of this nature is difficult to manage, painful to live with, and usually requires many adaptations to function "normally," it is possible to lead a happy and prosperous life. We are a case in point.

But people ask us all the time, how can we both have such a positive attitude despite all the challenges we've faced? These challenges could have led to emotional turmoil and negativity. We could have let our differences get the better of us, keeping us from being all we could be. So, people ask us, what happened? How did we end up with such positive attitudes?

That is what this book is about. What has touched us, forged our resilience, and more important, what we now turn to time and time again as new challenges continue to arise.

Unfortunately, there is no magic, no pill to take, to stay optimistic. But we have come up with something of a philosophy to live by, a way of approaching life. In this book, we would like to introduce to you our mantra: Think Big.

From everyday challenges to life-changing decisions, Think Big has gotten us through a lot. We imagine each letter in those words as a sort of tool in our toolbox.

THINK BIG

T is for Try
H is for Hope
I is for Initiate
N is for No
K is for Know

B is for Believe
I is for Improve
G is for Go For It

These are the words we live by. We try to explore every opportunity and complete every task using this approach. Remembering to Think Big helps us give an honest and complete effort to everything we do. When we Think Big, it becomes less important whether we succeed or fail, and more important how we approach any given situation. Think Big is a way of thinking that has radically changed our lives, and we hope that by sharing some of what we've learned, it will help you as well.

Jen and I believe that if you apply Think Big to your challenges, big and small, you'll find greater success. You'll also recognize greater satisfaction with your journey toward achievement and find joy in the things that matter most.

We have shared this Think Big message in some talks we've given, and we have found that people always respond well. Not everybody has spondyloepiphyseal blah blah blah, but everybody has something difficult they are facing. Everybody has challenges that feel too big to endure. And no matter what obstacles you face, we believe Think Big can help you approach them with optimism and courage. Our hope is that our words will help you feel like you, too, can face any challenge.

To illustrate the points we're making, we're going to use examples from our lives. From childhood experiences to some of the most serious adult situations a human being can face, you will see how Think Big has helped us in nearly everything we do and how it can help you to achieve your goals too.

Laugh with us, cry with us, and Think Big with us.

ABOUT THE AUTHORS

Jennifer Arnold, MD, completed her medical degree at Johns Hopkins School of Medicine in Baltimore, Maryland, and graduated in 2000. She is currently an attending neonatologist at Baylor College of Medicine and medical director of the Simulation Center at Texas Children's Hospital. Dr. Arnold is married to her best friend, Bill Klein. They live in Houston, Texas, and have adopted two special needs children. Jennifer and Bill are the stars of TLC's *The Little Couple*.

Bill Klein grew up on Long Island, New York. After earning a degree in biology from NYU, Bill became an entrepreneur. Today, he works with companies large and small, in the area of strategic direction, sales, and operational efficiency. He plays an active role in every business he owns, including Candu Enterprises, where he and his wife, Jennifer, provide a variety of media-related services, including making appearances at schools and other institutions to aid in the campaign to stop bullying. Most recently, Bill created Rocky & Maggie's, a pet supply business named after the family dogs. Bill Klein is married to his best friend, Jennifer Arnold. They live in Houston, Texas, and have adopted two special needs children. Bill and Jennifer are the stars of TLC's *The Little Couple*.